MOTHERS-IN-LAW AND DAUGHTERS-IN-LAW

MOTHERS-IN-LAW AND DAUGHTERS-IN-LAW

Understanding the Relationship and What Makes Them Friends or Foe

DEBORAH M. MERRILL

PRAEGER

Westport, Connecticut
London

Library of Congress Cataloging-in-Publication Data

Merrill, Deborah M., 1962–
   Mothers-in-law and daughters-in-law : understanding the relationship
and what makes them friends or foe / Deborah M. Merrill.
        p. cm.
   Includes bibliographical references and index.
   ISBN 978-0-313-34721-4 (alk. paper)
   1. Mothers-in-law. 2. Daughters-in-law. 3. Mothers and daughters—
Psychology. I. Title.
   HQ759.25.M47   2007
   306.87—dc22   2007028220

British Library Cataloguing in Publication Data is available.

Library of Congress Catalog Card Number: 2007028220
ISBN: 978-0-313-34721-4

First published in 2007

Praeger Publishers, 88 Post Road West, Westport, CT 06881
An imprint of Greenwood Publishing Group, Inc.
www.praeger.com

Printed in the United States of America

∞™

The paper used in this book complies with the
Permanent Paper Standard issued by the National
Information Standards Organization (Z39.48–1984).

10   9   8   7   6   5   4   3   2   1

To the memory of my maternal grandparents
Kenneth A. and Virginia Forbes Lane
for all that they did and all that they were

CONTENTS

ACKNOWLEDGMENTS

Let me begin my expressing my sincere gratitude to the mothers-in-law and daughters-in-law who participated in this study. Hearing their life stories and sharing their families with them has been one of the most rewarding experiences of my career. I am thankful to the women not only for their invaluable assistance, but also for the warmth, hospitality, and graciousness that they offered while providing it.

I would also like to acknowledge the role of my colleagues at Clark University in completing this book. Each and every one of the members of my department has provided assistance or advice in one way or another. Patty Ewick listened to my ideas and offered invaluable insight from the very beginning of the project. Shelly Tenenbaum chaired the department while I was on sabbatical and, as always, gave her unwavering support. Kay Jenkins, former department member but forever friend and colleague, also served as a sounding board and intellectual partner. Bob Ross, Eric Gordy, Parminder Bhachu, and Bruce London provided advice and were always generous with their time, and Diane Mercon Griffin and Sheila Hokanson provided help of all types "at the drop of a hat." My thanks also go to Nancy Budwig, Associate Provost and Dean of Graduate Studies and Research, for her support and encouragement. When I accepted my position at Clark fifteen years ago, I did so because I was convinced that I would have wonderful colleagues. I am fortunate in never having regretted that decision.

I would also like to thank my own in-laws for making my family life so rich. My grandparents-in-law, Mr. and Mrs. Paul and Margaret Basye, welcomed me into their family without hesitation and made me feel loved and accepted from the beginning with their unique graciousness. I will forever feel thankful for having known them for a short but important part of my life. I think of them often. My father-in-law and mother-in-law, Dr. Charles and Mrs. Lynda Basye, have always made me a part of their large and loving family, for which I am most grateful. I feel truly fortunate in having them for my in-laws. Dad, in particular, has graciously filled the void left by the absence of my own father. Thanks also to my brothers- and sisters-in-law in Arizona who always welcome us into their homes and families.

I would also like to thank my mother-in-law, Ms. Rosalie Smith, for her place in our lives and her thoughtfulness over the years. She and I have struggled over our own relationship, and I have benefited from the effort on both of our parts. Our experience certainly gave me much to think about. I also thank her for raising the wonderful son with whom I share my life. I would also like to acknowledge my brothers-in-law and sisters-in-law spread across the country. I wish them continued loving and fulfilling marriages and families. Special thanks go to my sister-in-law Aimee Basye for her encouragement in this project.

My own family has made my life a rich one from the start. I am grateful to my parents, Mr. and Mrs. Jay and Nancy Merrill, for their unconditional love and support while I was growing up and to my mother for always being there for me. I also thank her for being such a wonderful mother-in-law to my own husband and for her friendship. All four of my grandparents were an important part of my life while I was growing up, and I am grateful for their love and guidance. No family tribute would be complete though without acknowledging my brother, Larry Napoleone, his children, and now their families. Most importantly, I give thanks for my best friend and husband, Ken Basye, and our life together. Thanks also to Gracie for her constant companionship through the writing of this manuscript.

Finally, my thanks to my editor at Praeger Publishers, Debora Carvalko, for giving me this opportunity and providing the venue to share my ideas about a topic that is so important to me and, I believe, other women.

One

INTRODUCTION

Shortly after I started my research on relationships between mothers-in-law and daughters-in-law, I received an e-mail message from one of my two mothers-in-law, my husband's stepmother. It went as follows:

> Karen [another daughter-in-law] tells me that you are writing a book on mothers-in-law and daughters-in-law. I just want you to know that I do my best for you girls and that I think of you as my daughters. But if there is anything that you can tell me to improve, just let me know.[1]

Being an in-law can be difficult, and, as is illustrated by my mother-in-law's comment, women are anxious that they will be seen as a "bad" in-law. Mothers-in-law worry that they may be exhibiting those very same behaviors that we loathe in the stereotypical mother-in-law: that they are intrusive, domineering, or unkind to their daughters-in-law. Daughters-in-law worry, but to a lesser degree, that they may not include their husband's mother often enough or successfully overlook her faults. Even the topic itself is a hotbed of thorny issues. Friends and colleagues have said to me over and over again, "You're writing a book on in-laws? Wow, you're brave!" as if the topic itself is too controversial to address. Our true feelings about our in-laws are not something that most people feel comfortable talking about, except perhaps to our closest friends and family. To the extent that in-laws are family, or even our spouse or child's family, relationships with in-laws remain a private concern. The purpose of this book is to make those private matters public. The book begins by capturing the range of in-law relationships. It will address both the formidable and delicate issues of in-law relationships and systematically examine the nature of the bond. In so doing, this book will dispel many of the myths surrounding in-law relationships.

My interest in this topic began during the first year of my own engagement. It was weeks before my future father-in-law's birthday. I sat in my apartment in Santa Monica contemplating whether or not it was appropriate to buy a card that would be from my fiancé and myself, buy a separate card that would be from me only, or leave it up to my fiancé altogether. Although a seemingly minor matter, I knew that the card would send a message of my intentions. My first visit with my father-in-law and his wife went beautifully, and I wanted them to know that I wished to be a part of the family and that I cared for them. However, I did not want to overstep any boundaries, wherever they might be, and intrude on the relationship between father and son. It opened up an entire series of questions for me. Primarily, what is a daughter-in-law's role in the family? What are the expectations of a daughter-in-law? Are in-laws members of the family or involved only peripherally? Researchers have since described this as the difficulty of being both kinfolk and strangers simultaneously.[2,3] More recently I have begun to think of it as being both "in" and "out" of the family. I decided to follow my instincts, and in the case of my father-in-law and his wife, sharing in their relationship with their son was the right thing to do.

My relationship with my fiancé's mother was much more complicated. There was a pervasive feeling of being on the outside looking in, that is, of being more "out" of the family than "in" it. This experience too raised many questions. Primarily, why are mother-in-law and daughter-in-law relationships so difficult? I refused to believe that my mother-in-law and I were somehow "competing" for my husband. I thought that we were both above that. Nor was the problem one of individual incompatibilities. I believed that there was something deeper, in particular, a social structural explanation for why in-law relationships are so hard and why mother-in-law and daughter-in-law relationships are the hardest of all. I also wanted to know what other in-law relationships were like and how they changed with time. I was interested in the sources of conflict and how families resolved conflict. These questions and others are addressed in this book.

A number of researchers have examined in-law relationships in the twenty years since my introduction to my own in-laws. In a recent study of twenty-three daughters-in-law who had been married for five to ten years and who had at least one child, most of the daughters-in-law described their relationship as positive.[4] Others have found that the quality of mother-in-law and daughter-in-law relationships runs the gamut from extreme conflict and resentment to extreme devotion.[5,6] Fischer[7] found that while most of the daughters-in-law in her study got along well with their mothers-in-law, they were more likely to say negative things about and almost always expressed less emotional involvement in their relationship with their mother-in-law than with their mother. Arnstein[8] found that while 48 percent of the relationships were good and 52 percent were poor, the good relationships were better than expected.

This book also examines the range of in-law relationships. However, this study has the advantage both of including the perspective of the mother-in-law and having a (relatively) large sample; it is based on intensive interviews with fifty-three daughters-in-law and a subset of their mothers-in-law (see Appendix 1 for greater detail on the methodology). Mothers-in-law and daughters-in-law were examined since conflict seems to be greatest with parents-in-law of the same gender.[9] Unlike previous researchers though, I have gone further in my analysis by systematically categorizing the relationships along more than one dimension and instead taking into account several characteristics that are central to in-law relationships. Thus, in-law relationships are divided into six categories ("tight knit," "distant but positive," "obligatory," "estranged," "cordial," and "conflicted but affectionate") based on the following characteristics: presence of conflict, degree of affection, and frequency of interaction.

As stated earlier, in-law relationships run the gamut. Imagine the following two scenarios. Kristen is a middle-aged daughter-in-law with three children. She and her husband have been married for fourteen years. Kristen has a college degree and works full-time. She describes her relationship with her mother-in-law as follows:

> We are very close. We have an excellent relationship.... I invite her here and we do things [with my boys] like taking them to the movies and things. She is fun to be with. She is a goofy girl and I like that.... She is so appreciative of the things that I do for her, it makes me want to do more. She is always sending me cards to say how much she appreciates me.

Kristen's mother-in-law Dot confirmed Kristen's description of the relationship. She added:

> My relationship with Kristen has always been great. She is the best thing that happened to our son. She is just a love. We feel very comfortable. I can just pop in if I am in the neighborhood, although I don't do it very much.... I

know her so well. If I see something that I think she will love, I buy it for her.... I know that I am very lucky to have her for a daughter-in-law.

In contrast, consider the example of Maureen:

> My relationship with my mother-in-law is fine as long as I don't have to see her. I call her Mrs. ——— because I don't feel comfortable calling her any-thing else. She calls my younger son "Kyle" not "Caleb" and me either "Donna" or "Martha," not "Maureen." She sends gifts and boxes of clothes to my husband and my older son but not me or my younger son who looks like me. They are both her grandsons.... It is a very bad relationship.... I think it is because I married her son. He is still her little baby. She prefers my oldest son even because he favors my husband.

Unlike Kristen, Maureen did not want me to interview her mother-in-law. Maureen was also middle-aged, had been married for thirteen years, and had two children. What accounts for these two vastly different experiences for daughters-in-law?

Earlier research attributed the personal characteristics of the individuals involved as the cause of friction between in-laws.[10] Since then, Fischer[11] and Cotterill[12] have argued that the nature of the relationship and other structural factors account for the difficulties in the relationship. This includes the fact that in-laws are both kinfolk and strangers simultane-ously.[13] That is, they do not share a history with their in-laws and are estranged from the family culture. As such, they lack the intimacy and familiarity of a life-long investment. Likewise, there are no real rules for an appropriate relationship. That is, there is ambiguity in the roles.[14] In this book, I will go on to argue that there are other structural factors pertaining to families that account for the difficulty in in-law relationships and thus why many in-laws do not get along. This includes the fact that in-law rela-tionships are based on the creation of a separate and autonomous family for which the extended family (parents-in-law and siblings-in-law) may not be prepared. Boundaries around the extended family need to be permeable to incorporate daughters-in-law and to allow sons to leave. If they are not, the stage is set for long-term conflict and difficult relationships. In-law relation-ships are based on a life-course development that necessitates support in some families. In addition, in-laws are expected to treat one another like family even when they do not reap the benefits of family relationships.

Family relationships have changed over the past half century. My mother lived one mile from my paternal grandparents and saw my grandfather approximately three or four times a week and my grandmother at least once a week. I, on the other hand, live 2,250 miles from my father-in-law and one mother-in-law and 1,720 miles from my other mother-in-law. Likewise, I work outside of the home. All of these changes that characterize the postmodern family—women working, divorce, and geographic mobility—are likely to affect in-law relationships. The question is, how?

Picture a family with one or more generations that have experienced divorce. You would have the children, their divorced (and perhaps remarried) parents, and the third generation, the parents-in-law, who may or may not be divorced as well. Assume that the mother-in-law's grandchildren are from her son's first marriage and that her second daughter-in-law has also been previously married and has children from that marriage as well. Which of the two daughters-in-law does the mother-in-law feel closer to: the mother of her grandchildren or her son's current wife? Does she consider one or both women as her daughter(s)-in-law? Does the fact that the second daughter-in-law is still tied to her first mother-in-law through her own children make a difference in her relationship with her current husband's mother? If the mother-in-law is also divorced, what difference does that make in her relationship with her son and daughter-in-law? In other words, how has the divorce revolution affected the bonds between mothers-in-law and daughters-in-law? Some scholars have argued that the divorce revolution has deeply undermined the family.[15,16] Others have argued that the effects of divorce on the family are much more nuanced and dependent upon intervening variables.[17] More central to this study, researchers have found that in-law relationships deteriorate immediately following separation, although they are more likely to survive if they involve a custodial parent.[18–20] No one has examined though how a previous divorce, and whose divorce (the husband's, wife's, or parents-in-law's), affects current in-law relationships. This and the effect of other factors relevant to the postmodern family, that is, women's employment and geographic mobility, will be investigated in this book.

It has been twenty years since I sat in my apartment in Santa Monica wondering whether or not to buy my future father-in-law a birthday card. I now have friends and family members (of a similar age) who are becoming parents-in-law themselves. Recently, my friend Susan met her son Sean's new long-term girlfriend. Susan was quite excited that Sara's first visit to her home had gone smoothly. Susan felt that Sara would fit well into their family. She and her daughter had even knit a gift for Sara; she referred to it as "knitting her [Sara] into the family." All seemed to be going well in

Susan's initial experiences as a (future) mother-in-law. Then Sean called home to tell his mother that he and Sara were getting engaged; they had been looking at rings. Susan suggested to Sean that they wait to take such a big step because they had not known one another long enough. Sean told Sara who immediately worried that this meant that Susan did not like her. Susan had to make quick reparations to fix what we both knew could lead to long-term problems in their relationship. I felt for Susan. She really did like Sara; I could tell by the way that she talked about her. However, she was a mother first and foremost, and in trying to watch out for her son, she may have committed the ultimate sin of a mother-in-law by seeming to interfere. Mothers-in-law are in a tough situation. They are still mothers, but they are expected to step back and allow their sons to develop their own autonomous families. They know that they can easily step on their daughter-in-law's toes, so they must tread lightly and watch for signs of overstepping the boundaries. Based on interviews with a subset of the mothers-in-law (see Appendix 1 for more detail), this book addresses the mother-in-law's perspective as well as the daughter-in-law's and the implications of marriage and in-law relationships for the life course of later life families. This book also examines the role of the mother and son relationship on her relationship with her daughter-in-law and the son's involvement in maintaining the bond between his wife and mother.

Beyond looking at the nature of family relationships, *Mothers-in-Law and Daughters-in-Law: Understanding the Relationship and What Makes Them Friends or Foe* investigates a number of key issues in the field of sociology using in-laws as instructive cases. In particular, it examines how the role of the daughter-in-law is socially constructed and how daughters-in-law create an identity for themselves, that is, the "making" of a daughter-in-law. Unlike other family bonds in Western society, in-law relationships are ambiguous and without normative expectations. On what then are in-law roles and identities based? Do they vary from family to family, or is there some overlap suggesting at least some normative expectations? What is the role of popular culture and women's perceptions of mothers-in-law in creating that identity? Furthermore, how does popular culture represent mothers-in-law and daughters-in-law, and how close are those representations to reality? What do these findings overall tell us about the nature of creating identity and family roles in Western society? In addition, this book will examine the impact of other family relationships on the mother-in-law and daughter-in-law bond. In particular, it will examine the role of the daughter-in-law's relationship with her own mother and the mother-in-law's relationship with her own daughter. To the extent that in-law relationships mirror or replace other family bonds, understanding these effects will lead us to important insights on the nature of in-law ties. These findings will further our understanding of the complicated matrix of women's family relationships.

This research has taken place during a time in which the family has undergone extensive change and experienced significant turmoil. What does this book tell us then about the nature of family at such a critical time? Is extended family no longer important? Are marriage and family growing apart as some researchers have suggested? How have changes in women and work, gender role expectations (i.e., the sex role revolution), and marital expectations affected in-law relationships, and what does that tell us about the nature of the evolving family? What is the future of the family? As will be seen, I argue that in-law relationships are really a public issue and not just a set of private concerns as has always been assumed. They are about marriage and mother–son relationships, with important implications for both divorce and intergenerational support at a time in which divorce rates remain high and the population is aging rapidly. As such, what important policy implications can this book offer in the end?

THE PLAN OF THE BOOK

I begin the book in Chapter 2 by examining representations of mothers-in-law and daughters-in-law in popular culture. This includes a ten-month survey of letters in the popular "Dear Annie" column, a one-month survey of Web sites for and about in-laws, and an examination of in-laws in television series, films, self-help books, and popular magazines. The focus here is to assess representations of mothers-in-law and daughters-in-law in different avenues of popular culture and to examine what the different outlets offer to the two groups of women (such as sources to vent one's frustrations or to provide advice) and the nature of any advice that is offered (e.g., whether one is expected to improve one's self versus "manage" the other person). Later it will be argued that these representations become part of a cultural repertoire of images that women use in creating their identities as daughters-in-law. This initial chapter is also used as background to examine whether the nature of in-law relationships is, in fact, similar to the representations in popular culture.

In Chapter 3, I examine the quality of mother-in-law and daughter-in-law relationships and the range of relationships that exists. I create a typology of relationships similar to the rubrics used to designate parent–child relationships but instead based on characteristics more appropriate for in-law relationships. Relationships are categorized according to the frequency of interaction, presence of conflict, and degree of affection, resulting in six different categories. I illustrate cases from the two most extreme (and most popular) categories, the "tight-knit" relationships and "estranged" relationships, as well as cases from the more moderate category, the "cordial" relationships. This is done for both the daughters-in-law and mothers-in-law's descriptions of the relationships. In addition, I examine the level of emotional closeness that the women feel for one another, as well as the level and source of conflict that they experience. This is done for both groups of women and includes a comparison of the mother-in-law's responses with her daughter-in-law's responses. In situations where the mother-in-law had several daughters-in-law (including ex-daughters-in-law) or the daughters-in-law had more than one mother-in-law, I examine the differences in those relationships and why women feel closer to one in-law than another.

Chapter 4 examines the factors that determine the quality of those relationships. This includes sociocultural factors such as religion, ethnicity, class, and education. I also consider the effect of the in-laws' earlier history to see whether initial experiences have long-lasting implications for the relationship and the effect of each of the women's attitudes regarding in-law relationships. In-law bonds, however, do not occur in a vacuum. As such, I look to see how the daughter-in-law's relationship with her own mother affects the relationship, including whether she lost her own mother before early adulthood. I also examine how the mother-in-law's relationships with her own daughter, if she has one, and her own mother-in-law have impacted her relationship with her daughter-in-law. Chapter 5 looks at how the changes that characterize the postmodern family have also impacted in-law relationships. This includes the effects of divorce (the wife's, husband's, and parents-in-law's), women's employment and occupational mobility, and geographic distance. Visits with "distant" in-laws are described.

In Chapter 6, I investigate the development of the relationship between a mother-in-law and daughter-in-law and the creation of the daughter-in-law role. This involves recognizing and learning one's obligations in the role and learning to resolve any conflict. The "making of a daughter-in-law" also includes the development of an identity as a daughter-in-law. I examine the process by which women create an identity for themselves as daughters-in-law and discuss the array of identities. I also analyze the sources for those identities, including the repertoire of cultural images that women hold. I show how women create identities as daughters-in-law that are consistent with other identities in their lives.

Chapter 7 highlights the mother-in-law's perspective on her relationship with her daughter-in-law. This chapter also looks at the nature of the mother and son relationship and how it changes after marriage. Here I also examine the effect of that tie on the in-law bond and the son's involvement in nurturing the relationship and resolving conflict between his wife and mother. Finally, this chapter includes an examination of the impact of the mother-in-law and daughter-in-law relationship on the marriage. I discuss the implications of this in Chapter 9.

In Chapter 8, I discuss why in-law relationships are so hard. I examine eight sources of difficulty in the relationship including the incongruous nature of the relationship, that is, the fact that in-laws are expected to treat one another like family without the benefits of a shared history and unconditional love that characterize other family relationships. I also discuss how the son's marriage and the creation of a separate and autonomous family affect in-law relationships and how differences in the women's expectations of how close the couple should be to his family (or how involved the mother-in-law should be) also impact the relationships. Finally, I consider the effect of negative images in popular culture, the "generational divide" between mothers-in-law and daughters-in-law, and the ambivalent and ambiguous nature of in-law ties. This chapter also describes the situations in which in-law relationships appear to work best and includes the advice that mothers-in-law and daughters-in-law offered to one another.

Chapter 9 summarizes the main findings and discusses what it means to be an "in-law" in American society. Here I discuss what it means to be both "in" and "out" of the family and how being an in-law differs from biological family. The implications of the findings for family relationships are highlighted. I discuss what mothers-in-law and daughters-in-law want of each other and the "bargain" that in-laws implicitly make with one another. I also discuss the "making of a daughter-in-law," that is, the social construction of the role and identity of daughter-in-law. I show how this is a social phenomenon and how the roles are constituted by the interplay of the mother-in-law and daughter-in-law and, to a lesser extent, the son/husband. I argue that in-law relationships are actually a public matter since they affect marriage and may likely affect support of the elderly in the future. Policy implications are offered. I end by discussing what our findings tell us about families during a time of significant change and turmoil.

TWO

MOTHERS-IN-LAW AND DAUGHTERS-IN-LAW IN POPULAR CULTURE

Representations of mothers-in-law and daughters-in-law appear throughout popular culture. We could all sketch in our minds what we think of as the prototypical mother-in-law or daughter-in-law. How accurate are those images though, and where do they come from? As important, how do those images affect the kind of in-laws that we become? This chapter will examine advice columns, the Internet, media (i.e., films and television series), and books and magazines to capture the array and frequency of popular images of mothers-in-law and daughters-in-law. We will also examine depictions of in-law problems and the advice that is given by popular "experts," where appropriate. Finally, we will look to see what, if any, resources are offered in popular culture for the two groups of women and how these resources then reinforce our images. In Chapter 3, we will examine to what extent popular images reflect the actual quality of mother-in-law and daughter-in-law relationships in American society. That is, are in-law relationships as "bad" as is represented? In Chapter 6, we then consider how in-laws use these images in creating roles and identities for themselves.

"DEAR ANNIE"

Letters from and about in-laws were collected from the popular advice column "Dear Annie" for a period of ten months.[1] Thirty-four letters were published in total. Women wrote twenty-five of these letters, and men wrote nine. An additional three letters commented on in-law relationships in general or were written in regard to earlier letters. The most common categories of letters included the following: wives with problems or concerns with their in-laws overall (five letters), wives writing about their sisters-in-law (four letters), wives writing about their mothers-in-law only (three letters), and mothers writing about their daughters-in-law (including a divorced daughter-in-law) (three letters). However, wives and mothers were not the only women to send in letters. Sisters also had concerns about their siblings' spouses (two letters), and widows and future wives sought advice about past and future in-laws. Among the men, the most common categories of letters included: husbands writing about their mothers-in-laws (two letters), their fathers-in-law (including a step-father-in-law) (two letters), and their in-laws overall (two letters).

The types of concerns addressed in the letters ran the gamut. Five of the family members wrote that they did not like or loathed their in-laws and/or their behaviors. It was difficult for them to be around their in-laws, but they felt obligated because of their spouses. For example, one woman wrote that her husband's family constantly made racist and "dirty" remarks that she found offensive. In four of the letters, family members expressed concern that they were left out of the family or not invited to particular events. One mother-in-law wrote that her daughter-in-law had asked her to eat in the kitchen during a family meal because there was not enough room at the dining room table, only to find later that, in fact, there had been an empty seat at the table. These letters were written not only by mothers-in-law and daughters-in-law, but by sons-in-law as well.

Family members wrote of other in-law problems as well. Nine of the letters (26 percent) were concerns that we typically associate with in-laws. These letters described situations in which in-laws were intrusive, outspoken, disrespectful of the couple's decisions, likely to overstay their welcome, or unwilling to take "no" for an answer. One mother was angry that her daughter's mother-in-law tried to make the couple's decisions for them. Two of the mothers wrote about concerns with their divorced daughters-in-law. For example one grandmother was upset that her former daughter-in-law told her son (i.e., the grandson) to put his stepfather's last name on his baseball jersey. Another mother-in-law wanted to invite her first daughter-in-law (who was the mother of her grandchildren) to family events, but her son and second daughter-in-law were upset that she did so. Interestingly, three of the authors were actually more concerned, or as concerned, with their own spouses as with their in-laws. For example, one of the wives felt that her husband was inappropriate in his physical demonstrations to his mother. Only one of the letters mentioned any sort of cross-cultural or class difference. This mother was uncomfortable with the idea that her future daughter-in-law's family (who were Kenyan) insisted upon a dowry. The mother said, "Giving money for a bride rubs us the wrong way."[2]

Family members wrote about their in-laws not speaking to them in three of the letters. One wife was upset that her brother-in-law had ceased communicating with her and her husband ever since her husband had refused to cosign a loan to buy their parents a new home. Another wife wrote that her sister-in-law had stopped speaking to her and her husband ever since she and her sister-in-law had an argument six years ago. Because of this, the author now wanted to end the tradition of holiday gift giving. Other family members wrote about general concerns. One husband was troubled that his in-laws never asked how he and his wife were. A wife was bothered that her brother-in-law and his wife did not exchange Christmas gifts since her daughter looked forward to receiving a package from her uncle. Finally, a sister was agitated that her brother-in-law had not buried her dead sister's ashes, which was her sister's wish. Only one mother-in-law wrote about her ambiguous role as a step-grandparent. Two of the authors felt that their in-laws blamed them for various issues. For example, one widow wrote that her husband's family blamed her for her husband's suicide and said unkind things about her in front of her children. Only one man wrote in to praise his partner's mother.

THE INTERNET

Portrayals of mothers-in-law took on a much more negative tone on the Internet. One popular Web site exaggerated the worst popular images of mothers-in-law.[3] For example, this Web page included links to sites with jokes about mothers-in-law, as well as a mother-in-law "mall" that sold mugs, hats, t-shirts, and so on with offensive logos such as "Top Ten Thing I Like About My Mother-in-Law" with ten empty spaces. This comprehensive site also included a chat room, celebrity in-law quiz and word search, a message board, poll site, and a site with advice from Dr. Terri Apter, the Webmaster. However, the most frequently used link was devoted to women's stories about their mothers-in-law and the worst gifts that they had received from their in-laws. There were no links, however, for mothers-in-law to complain about their daughters-in-law or to offer daughter-in-law stories.

This link was monitored for four weeks. In a typical week, there were eighteen mother-in-law stories and three worst gift stories, with some slight variation on other weeks. The postings all appeared to be written by women;

none were clearly written by a man. Unlike the "Dear Annie" letters, these postings were much more bitter and angry. Here, daughters-in-law were more likely to gripe or complain about their in-laws rather than to present a problem in search of a solution. For example, one woman wrote,

> My MIL and her flying monkeys harassed me and almost caused me to have a miscarriage. Even though I was high-risk and having contractions early, they still would not leave me alone. When people would congratulate her on becoming a GM [grandmother], she would say, "Oh, that's NOT MY GRANDCHILD. He is NOT a "(last name)." She told DH [dear husband], "I don't know why you're so HAPPY. That kid's gonna wake you up every night!!" I thought GM's were supposed to give kisses and cookies and stuff. Well, NOT my MIL. She only cares what DH can do for her.[4]

A second Web site focused on funny stories about mothers-in-law's aberrant behavior.[5] Twenty stories were submitted over the course of a month. These included stories about a mother-in-law who faked being sick in order to stay with her son and daughter-in-law until the daughter-in-law found her at home and clearly not sick, a mother-in-law who told her nurse that her daughter-in-law tried to put soapy water in her tea, and a daughter-in-law who wrote in praise of her mother-in-law for accepting her into the family and treating her like a daughter. These stories were less venomous than the ones on the former Web site and were intended more to be humorous rather than a source for venting one's frustrations.

There were fewer references to daughters-in-law than to mothers-in-law on the Internet. Among these were links to research on daughters-in-law as caregivers and to books and novels about in-law relationships overall. There was also a link to one cartoon about daughters-in-law, although that same directory included twenty-two jokes about men and their mothers-in-law.[6] The most vivid portrait on the Internet of daughters-in-law though was depicted in the poem "Daughters-in-Law Are Our Grandchildren's Mothers" by Turlough O'Carolan.[7] According to the poet, the older generation should be grateful for and are lucky to have their daughters-in-law because they are the caregivers for grandchildren. Here we see daughters-in-law as venerated by the family because of their role as grandchildren's nurturer and the generativity that they represent.

Finally, the Internet included a reference to one daughter-in-law in particular, Ruth, who was the daughter-in-law of Naomi in the Bible.[8] According to the story, after Naomi's sons had been killed, she offered that each of her daughters-in-law could return to their own families. Ruth, out of loyalty to her mother-in-law and her husband's people, however, chose to stay. Consider the following passages of the Bible:

Ruth 1:8: Naomi said to her two daughters-in-law,
"Go, return each of you to her mother's house."

Ruth 1:16: Ruth said, "Don't entreat me to leave you ...
For where you go, I will go; and where you lodge,
I will lodge; your people shall be my people, and
Your God my God."

Although a biblical source, this was also an Internet reference for daughters-in-law. Here we see the daughter-in-law depicted as a loyal member of her husband's family. In fact, it is her husband's family whom she considers to be her primary family.

In contrast to multiple sites on the Internet for daughters-in-law to air their anger or to share humorous situations about their mothers-in-law, there were no equivalent sites for mothers-in-law. The daughter-in-law is not targeted as unreasonable or a source for humor. Instead, references to the daughter-in-law tend to focus on popular representations of the loyalty of a daughter-in-law to her new family and the appreciation those families have towards her.

TELEVISION AND FILM

Relationships between mothers-in-law and daughters-in-law are frequently depicted in popular entertainment. The Internet Movie Database (IMDb) includes references to thirty-two movies and series that feature in-law relationships.[9] The majority of the films are about male characters and their mothers-in-law. These include titles such as *A Cowboy's Mother-in-Law* (1910), *Getting Rid of His Mother-in-Law* (1914), and *He Fell in Love with His Mother-in-Law* (1913, 1915). Most of the references are comedies (including short films), as well as a few movie and television dramas. Since the films and series go back as far as 1901, they also include silent and black and white films. While most of the films were made in the United States, there were also Australian, Malaysian, European, South Korean, Egyptian, and Swedish films. Combined they suggest a universal interest in in-law relationships, particularly mother-in-law relationships.

Current films tend to depict mothers-in-law as controlling and manipulative while their daughters-in-law are at their mercy to be accepted. In the comedy *Monster-in-Law*, wealthy and widowed Viola does not want her only son to marry fiancé Charlie.[10] Not only is Charlie, a dog-walker and temp worker, "not good enough for her son the surgeon," but Viola is also worried about being left alone. Viola then tries to sabotage their relationship by making herself unbearable as a future mother-in-law. She takes over their wedding plans and feigns illness to move into their home until Charlie realizes what is happening. The conflict is resolved when the two women reach a compromise. Viola agrees that she will call her son a maximum of twice a day, while Charlie reassures Viola that she will be in the front and center of their lives as well as their children's lives.

In this film as in television sitcoms like *Everybody Loves Raymond*, the mother-in-law is seen as being fully responsible for the conflict.[11] Mothers-in-law are portrayed as being fearful of losing their sons and as interfering at a level that is beyond acceptable to the daughter-in-law. They barge in without being invited, criticize their daughters-in-law as wives and mothers (e.g., their cooking, housekeeping, and childrearing skills), and visit or call far too often. Fathers and sons are reluctant to intervene and may not even be aware of the conflict. Likewise, as in the case of *Monster-in-Law,* the conflict is passed from generation to generation, and in the case of *Everybody Loves Raymond*, the conflict is never fully resolved.

This depiction of mothers-in-law has been a constant in American society for decades. In the 1960s sitcom *The Mothers-in-Law*, two neighboring families whose children marry feud over the smallest of issues, all in the name of what is best for their children.[12] However, it is the mothers-in-law who are cast as the most meddlesome and from whom most of the comedy is derived.

Television dramas also feature mothers-in-law, although they are usually more peripheral characters. In the popular 1970s family series *The Waltons*, Grandma Walton played a loving but sharp-tongued mother-in-law. Although she and her daughter-in-law worked side by side in the kitchen for the good of the extended family, there was also some tension in the relationship as the two women shared the role of the primary homemaker. For example, in the series pilot, "The Homecoming," Grandpa Walton praises how it would not be Christmas without daughter-in-law Olivia's applesauce cake, to which Grandma coolly replies, "It has too much nutmeg for my taste."[13]

Finally, talk shows are a popular television source for our common understanding of in-law relationships. However, they tend to depict the relationships as rife with conflict and misery. For example, the *Dr. Phil* show featured an episode on future mothers-in-law; the message given was that the mothers are going to be meddlesome in-laws causing problems for *both* their children and children-in-law. Part of the advertisement for the episode read, "Could a mom's good intentions ruin a relationship?"[14] Likewise, a caption for one of the guests read, "Mom in the Middle: Donny says that his mom is forcing him to choose between her and his girlfriend. His mom, Christine, claims that she is being forced out of her son's life."

POPULAR MAGAZINES AND SELF-HELP BOOKS

Articles in popular magazines depict a more balanced view of mother-in-law and daughter-in-law relationships. Out of four articles found in a search of popular magazines, all focused on daughters-in-law rather than sons-in-law, and three focused on positive mother-in-law and daughter-in-law relationships. For example, in one of the articles, a mother-in-law, after just hearing that her son and daughter-in-law were divorcing, wrote, "I don't want to divorce my daughter-in-law.... No, I don't want to divorce Elisabeth—daughter-in-law, adult friend and daughter I never had."[15] Similarly, another article described the in-law relationships of six women who "genuinely like(d) the "other woman" in their men's lives."[16] In contrast to other sources, these articles then depict loving and caring in-laws, or, at the very least, ones in which the in-laws like one another.

Books on in-law relationships are almost always either novels or self-help books. One search of in-law books on a popular Web site uncovered thirty-seven books written in English. This included fifteen novels. Most of the book titles suggested that the relationships are riddled with competition, such as *The Mother-in-Law Dance: Can Two Women Love the Same Man and Still Get Along*,[17] as well as ambiguity, such as *Mothers-in-Law and Daughters-in-Law: Love, Hate, Rivalry, and Reconciliation*.[18] Six of the books were written for mothers-in-law and primarily focused on how to become a better mother-in-law. Consider such titles as *How to Be the Perfect Mother-in-Law*[19] and *Just Call Me Mom: Practical Steps to Becoming a Better Mother-in-Law*.[20] There is also a collection of essays written by mothers of the groom[21] and a book titled *What Every Mother-In-Law Wishes Her Daughter-In-Law Knew but Was Afraid to Tell Her*.[22] While most of these books written for the mother-in-law focus on what *she* can do to be a better mother-in-law, books for the daughter-in-law focus more on recognizing the erroneous behaviors of mothers-in-law and coping with them. Consider, for example, the titles *Mothers-in-Law Do Everything Wrong: M. I. L. D. E. W.*[23] and *The Daughter-in-Law's Survival Guide: Everything You Need to Know*

About Relating to Your Mother-in-Law.[24] Four of the books, however, focused on either of the women understanding or improving the relationship. The book *Between Mothers-In-Law and Daughters-In-Law: Achieving a Successful and Caring Relationship* was a typical example.[25] Overall, all of the books depicted in-law relationships as problematic and in need of improvement, often portraying the mother-in-law as the source of the problem (written for the daughter-in-law) or as the one who can and should improve the relationship (written for the mother-in-law). Likewise, the books emphasized the rivalry between the two women and the potential for ambivalence.

POPULAR VERNACULAR AND EVERYDAY LIFE

Jokes about mothers-in-law are fairly common. Interestingly though, the jokes are usually about men and their mothers-in-law, while books, Web sites, and advice columns are more often for women. While a son-in-law's interaction with his mother-in-law is often seen as a source of humor, a daughter-in-law's relationship is a cauldron of problems needy of self-help and advice. We can easily image women talking with their friends about their mothers-in-law but have greater difficulty imagining men doing the same thing. Furthermore, we use the popular perceptions of mothers-in-law detailed above as metaphors or adjectives for other articles in our daily lives. Consider for example the plant "mother-in-law's tongue" (also referred to as "snake plant" or "devil's tongue"). The popular image of a mother-in-law's harping and verbal interference serve as a metaphor for the tall, sharp, elongated leaves of this plant.

In-law relationships also make their way into other areas of our everyday lives. For example, improving relationships with mothers-in-law is a common topic on Christian Web sites and in Christian periodicals. In an article on a Web site for *Today's Christian Woman*, readers described valuable life lessons that they have learned from their mothers-in-law.[26] Thus, while the mainstream popular culture depicts the relationship as very negative, the Christian culture, with its emphasis on improving family relationships, seeks to promote the positive in in-law relationships.

SUMMARY AND IMPLICATIONS

Cultural representations of mothers-in-law differ considerably from those of daughters-in-law. In self-help books and on Internet Web sites, daughters-in-law are depicted as sympathetic players that need to handle their mothers-in-law. Mothers-in-law are depicted as the source of any and all problems and in need of change. In films and television, daughters-in-law are portrayed as reasonable but at the mercy of their mothers-in-law in trying to gain their approval and acceptance. They are sweet and kind. Mothers-in-law, on the other hand, are cast as manipulative, interfering, and unable to let go of their sons. They make their daughters-in-law's lives difficult. Only infrequently do we see them as helpful or a role model. Other popular representations also portray the daughter-in-law as loyal to the husband's family and deserving of their appreciation for their role in the family. Finally, mother-in-law and daughter-in-law relationships are seen as competitive and fraught with rivalry for the woman's place in the home and for the son/husband's time and love.

Daughters-in-law have access to numerous resources in popular culture. They have Web sites where they can vent their frustrations and read about other people's in-law problems. They have self-help books to better manage their relationships with their mothers-in-law and, if they choose, to improve those relationships. They have access to advice columns and comedies to laugh at other mothers-in-law who may or may not be like their own. In contrast, mothers-in-law have fewer resources in popular culture, perhaps because they are less likely to be thought of as the victim. For example, they do not have comparable Web sites to vent their frustrations or to poke fun at their daughters-in-law. While they too have self-help books, the emphasis is on what *they* can do to improve the relationships. There are few, if any, books that poke fun at daughters-in-law or berate them. While they too have access to advice columns, the comedies that they watch are making fun of them, or at least the role that they occupy.

The problems that in-laws write about tell us much about the nature of in-law relationships. For many family members, in-laws are not easy to be around because of their seemingly foreign behaviors and values. However, people feel obligated to be with them and to be a part of their family despite these differences. Family members also believe that they cannot say what they would like to their in-laws; they must carefully edit their speech to family who are not biological kin. Thus, despite feeling that they should be close, family members recognize that there are significant differences between in-laws and biological family. Likewise, in-law relationships are often thought to be fragile, and as such, people have to tiptoe around their in-laws. Finally, we should note that sometimes in-laws problems are actually problems with one's spouse.

Popular representations reflect our understanding both of other people's experiences as well as our own experiences. How close though are these representations to reality? This will be answered in the following chapters as we explore the range of in-law relationships. Popular representations not only reflect the world though, they also inform our expectations of the world, in particular family roles and the behaviors of people in them. Is it possible then that they create the reality of in-law roles by changing behavior? Cotterill argues that the negative representations of mothers-in-law in popular culture and humor act as a control that regulates the mother-in-law's behavior.[27] That is, mothers-in-law alter their behavior so as to not appear like the images in the media. Later I will argue that daughters-in-law also develop an identity that is a response to these cultural representations. In particular, Chapter 6 examines the process by which women anticipate problems as daughters-in-law and mothers-in-law based on popular images and how that then affects their experiences as in-laws. Let us first turn though to the reality of in-law relationships in American society today.

Three

THE QUALITY OF MOTHER-IN-LAW AND DAUGHTER-IN-LAW RELATIONSHIPS

Honestly, there have been times when I wondered if it was worth this. It is. In the past, she has definitely put a huge strain on us. I would say that she was our biggest obstacle in the first few years of marriage.

—Suzanne (daughter-in-law)

I would have to say that my mother-in-law is my best friend. There is nothing that I cannot tell her, and that goes both ways. She has always been there for me, and I will always be there for her too.

—Pat (daughter-in-law)

As the two descriptions above suggest, there is a great deal of variation in mother-in-law and daughter-in-law relationships. The quality of the relationships runs the gamut from extreme conflict and resentment to extreme devotion.[1-3] Most daughters-in-law get along well with their mothers-in-law although some do feel significant hostility towards them. However, there is almost always less emotional involvement than with one's own (biological) family. In a recent study of twenty-three daughters-in-law who had been married for five to ten years and who had at least one child, most of the daughters-in-law described their relationship as positive.[4]

Fischer found three types of in-law relationships.[5] These included friendships (20 percent), minimally involved relationships (41 percent), and quasi mother–daughter relationships (38 percent). In-laws who were friends usually shared personal or professional interests. Those who were minimally involved saw one another infrequently and had little emotional involvement. They were also more likely to be geographically distant. In quasi mother–daughter relationships, the mother usually had no daughter of her own living nearby. However, daughters-in-law resisted being substitute daughters. Daughters-in-law overall tended to report more conflict in the relationship than their mothers-in-law did. Fischer argues that this is because mothers-in-law have more at stake in making the relationship work. In addition, Cotterill[6] argues that formal boundaries in the relationship are one way that in-laws minimize conflict.

Other researchers have also found that a high proportion of in-law relationships are positive, although they also point out that there are a high proportion of in-laws who do not get along. One author found that 48 percent of the relationships were good, whereas 52 percent were poor.[7] However, those that were good were better than expected. These relationships were characterized by love, emotional support, and loyalty. Likewise, the poor relationships were worse than expected. They were described as non-communicative and fraught with raw pain, hurt, and anger.

A more recent study of twenty-three daughters-in-law and nineteen unrelated mothers-in-law found that most of the daughters-in-law hoped to have a warm and loving relationship with their mother-in-law.[8] They expected the in-law experience to be similar to their experiences as a daughter or to replace the family that they never had. The reality, however, did not meet their expectations. Daughters-in-law often felt that their in-laws did not accept them. They had assumed that the bridge linking them to their in-laws would be automatic at marriage. Mothers-in-law took more of a "wait and see" attitude toward the relationship and, as such, they were defined as distant and uninvolved by their daughters-in-law. Likewise, mothers-in-law wanted their daughters-in-law to acknowledge them as important in their lives but often felt that they were not. The authors argue that these very painful experiences are often the result of misunderstandings and different ways of perceiving the same event. Cotterill[9] also found that daughters-in-law expected an in-law relationship to be similar to a friendship or a quasi mother–daughter bond but found that the reality was that they were often neither.

This book provides a systematic analysis of the quality of in-law relationships using a typology created to understand multiple differences in mother-in-law and daughter-in-law relationships (described later in this chapter). This analysis also improves upon those described above because it is based upon a comparatively large number of daughters-in-law (fifty-three) and, where possible, a subset of *their own* mothers-in-law. (See Appendix 1 for a further description of the data.) This not only allows for the perspective of the mother-in-law, but it also permits a comparison of the mother-in-law and daughter-in-law perspective. These features combined provide a more complete understanding of in-law relationships.

A TYPOLOGY OF IN-LAW RELATIONSHIPS

In her examination of parents and adult children, Ingrid Arnet Connidis[10] developed a rubric to categorize the relationships along a number of key characteristics. By substituting characteristics more appropriate for in-law relationships, I have developed a similar rubric, or typology, to categorize the range of in-law relationships (see Table 3.1). In particular, I use the frequency of interaction, the presence of conflict, and the presence of affection to differentiate the relationships into six separate categories.[11]

Before examining the distribution of in-laws in each category, let me first describe the categories themselves. "Tight-knit" relationships are ones in which the women interact frequently, feel little conflict, but feel affection for the other person. This then includes women who perceive their in-law to be a friend as well as those who deem her to be just like a daughter or just like a mother. In the second category, "distant but positive," the women also have low conflict and high affection. However, they do not see their in-laws very frequently. This includes in-laws who live far from one another. However, not all who live far from one another experience no conflict or feel affection for their mother-in-law. The third category, "obligatory," includes women who interact frequently but who feel high conflict and no affection for their in-law. This includes women who get together

TABLE 3.1 A Typology of Mother-in-Law and Daughter-in-Law Relationships

	Frequency of interaction	Presence of conflict	Presence of affection	% of daughters-in-law	% of mothers-in-law
Tight knit	High	Low	High	30	65
Distant but positive	Low	Low	High	8	6
Obligatory	High	High	Low	17	0
Estranged	Low	High	Low	23	0
Cordial	High or Low	Low	Low	15	24
Conflicted but affectionate	High or Low	High	High	8	6

Source: Adapted for use with in-law relationships from Ingrid Arnet Connidis, *Family Ties and Aging* (Thousand Oaks, CA: Sage Publications, 2001).

with their in-laws for the sake of their spouse and children. It also sub-sumes in-laws who live with one another for financial reasons or daughters-in-law who provide care despite their negative feelings for their in-laws.

There are three more categories. "Estranged" in-laws are those with the worst relationships. The presence of conflict is so high that the in-laws have little interaction. Those who live far away do not make the effort to see one another more frequently. Those who live nearby choose to stay away. Those in-laws who have a "cordial" relationship feel a low level of conflict but they also have little or no affection for their in-law. They describe the relationship as being "okay" but not close. Finally, the last category includes those who often feel conflict with their in-laws but who also feel affection for them. This category is referred to as "conflicted but affection-ate." These relationships are marked by a high degree of ambivalence.

PERCEPTIONS BY THE DAUGHTERS-IN-LAW

Daughters-in-law most commonly described their relationships with their mothers-in-law as being either "tight knit" (30 percent) or "estranged" (23 percent). In other words, they most often saw their relationships as being one extreme or the other. Few daughters-in-law (8 percent) described their relationships as "distant but positive." This suggests that daughters-in-law who have little conflict and who like their in-laws will choose to see them frequently if it is geographically feasible. The result may also be due to the fact that most of the women that I interviewed lived relatively close to their in-laws (only 17 percent lived more than three hours away, and 70 percent lived less than one hour away). Likewise, few daughters-in-law (8 percent) felt "conflicted but affectionate." This implies that those who feel conflict at present tend not to feel affection as a result. There are some women though who recognize that the relationship is at times difficult and who feel some conflict, but they care for the other person anyway.

A high percentage (17 percent) of the daughters-in-law described an "obligatory" relationship. They felt a high level of conflict and little or no affection for their mother-in-law, but they saw her frequently. Contact with their in-laws was out of an obligation to their husbands or children, but secondarily out of an obligation to their in-laws as well. As stated earlier, this also includes women who live with their mothers-in-law for financial reasons (for either person) or who provide care for her. This last type suggests that obligations as a daughter-in-law can be quite high, high enough to overcome both conflict and the difficulties of care giving. Last are those daughters-in-law (15 percent) who described their relationships as "cordial." These women felt little conflict but little affection for their mothers-in-law.

These findings are similar to those of earlier researchers who noted a high proportion of daughters-in-law describing their relationships as being very poor or very good.[12] In contrast, others found that the proportion of positive relationships was somewhat higher.[13,14] Yet, Fischer[15] too found that some of the women felt extreme hostility towards their mothers-in-law. All of the research, however, suggests a broad range of relationships and that a high percentage (38 percent or more) of daughters-in-law have a very good relationship with their mothers-in-law.

PERCEPTIONS BY THE MOTHERS-IN-LAW

Because the mothers-in-law were identified through the daughters-in-law, a high percentage (65 percent) described their relationship with their daughters-in-law in terms that were defined as "tight knit." The second most common response (24 percent) was to describe the relationship as being "cordial." Interestingly, while none of the mothers-in-law described their relationships as "obligatory" or "estranged," a small percentage (6 percent) did describe them as being "conflicted but affectionate." Similar to the mothers-in-law, only 8 percent of daughters-in-law felt "conflicted but affectionate," but 17 percent described the relationship as "obligatory" and 23 percent as "estranged." These differences suggest that even when mothers-in-law experience some conflict with the other in-law, they are more likely than daughters-in-law to feel affection also.

We can also compare the responses of the mothers-in-law with their matched daughters-in-law. Of the seventeen matches, twelve (71 percent) of the mothers-in-law described the relationships similarly to their daughters-in-law, but five (29 percent) did not. In situations where there was a discrepancy, mothers-in-law always described the relationships more positively. In three of the cases, mothers-in-law described the relationships as "tight knit," while daughters-in-law described them as "cordial." In addition, two of the mothers-in-law described the relationship as "cordial," while their daughters-in-law described them as "estranged" or "obligatory." Why this difference? In some situations, the mother-in-law may feel affection while the daughter-in-law does not. The mother-in-law may not be as bothered by the things that the daughter-in-law does as the daughter-in-law is by what her mother-in-law does. Their experience may truly be a more positive one, or they may be more motivated to put a positive spin on the relationship since they have more at stake in getting along with their daughters-in-law. Fischer[16] also found that daughters-in-law report more conflict in the relationship than mothers-in-law. Other researchers have also found that parents tend to report the quality of their relationships with their adult children more positively than their children do.[17–20] In this regard then, daughters-in-law behave like children and mothers-in-law like mothers.

In order to best portray the range of in-law relationships, the following two sections will describe the experience of daughters-in-law at either end of the spectrum (i.e., "tight-knit" and "estranged" relationships) followed by a description of relationships in the middle (i.e., "cordial" relationships).

"TIGHT-KNIT" RELATIONSHIPS

Cindy is a middle-aged professional woman. Although from a large, Italian family, she and her own mother were not very close. She stated,

> My relationship with my family is very strained.... I think that they feel threatened because I "left the family." You were expected to live on the same street with your family for the rest of your life.... My mother wasn't educated, and she didn't understand that I wanted to be independent. I call her "Mother" or [first name] which I think says a lot.

Cindy felt that she was much closer to her mother-in-law than to her own mother. Although she saw her mother-in-law only a couple of times a month, they spoke on the phone regularly and spent holidays and vacations together. She visited her mother-in-law alone as well as with her husband. Cindy described their visits as warm and welcoming. The two women brought one another little gifts that they knew the other person would appreciate, such as favorite foods.

Although Cindy's mother-in-law, Grace, had her own daughter whom she visited regularly, she and Cindy described their relationship as being like a mother and daughter. In fact, whenever Cindy mentioned her mother-in-law, her eyes would well up and she would start to cry. She was clearly very moved by Grace's feelings for her and the depth and quality of their bond. She shared with me,

> It is a very loving relationship. I can call her at any moment for anything. I was able to confide in her during a difficult time with my husband. I told

her, "I know he is your son...." She understood, and I knew that she would keep everything in confidence.... On her 80th birthday, my sister-in-law said that her mother feels that she has two daughters. I think of her as a second mother too [crying].

Although Cindy met her mother-in-law only once or twice while she and her husband were dating, she noticed an immediate change when she and her husband became engaged. Her mother-in-law and sister-in-law went out and swiftly bought her a beautiful engagement gift and planned a wonderful dinner for the couple. She stated, "I felt very welcomed and embraced into the heart of the family." Earlier researchers also found that early acceptance into the family often led later on to more positive relationships.[21]

Although Cindy and Grace were very close, Cindy recognized that Grace was closer to her own daughter. Cindy did not take this personally though. Instead she said, "I know that she doesn't love me any less [because of the sister-in-law]." Cindy felt that if her mother-in-law ever needed anything, she would be there in a heartbeat.

Susan also felt closer to her mother-in-law than to her mother. She, however, spent a great deal more time with her mother-in-law than did Cindy. For years, Susan spent the weekend with her mother-in-law, Rose, who lived fifteen minutes away. It was in part because she helped Rose with the housecleaning and laundry. Susan said that the main reason though was to spend "quality time" together. She would drive over to Rose's apartment (and then later on, her house) on Friday night and would stay until Sunday. The two women played cards, talked, went shopping, or "did whatever we felt like doing," according to Susan. She believed that the time together "doing the little things" had been crucial to their feeling so close.

Susan and her husband had moved in with Rose to help her financially two months prior to the interview. Susan continued to do all of the housekeeping, grocery shopping, and laundry. She said that it was hard though because both of the women were used to having their own home. Rose had been living on her own since her husband passed away twenty years ago, and Susan and her husband had lived by themselves for the eighteen years that they were together. Susan then had to compromise on privacy to help Rose. When I asked Susan about any conflict, she shared with me:

It is just over small things. Kyle is her son. The things that she does for him though, I think that I should be doing to take care of him. I bite my tongue though because he is her son. It is getting better though. She now gives us some privacy when he gets home so that he can tell me how his day went.... I don't think it needs to be confronted. It just takes compromising. I don't want to put gas on the fire.

Although Susan's dedication to her mother-in-law was remarkable under any circumstances, it was particularly telling because Rose had two daughters and three other daughters-in-law who lived in the area. Susan, however, chose to take care of Rose by herself. When I asked Susan if she minded helping Rose as much as she did, she said, "Oh, no. I love doing it." Later when I asked her about her relative feelings of obligation to her mother versus her mother-in-law, she said, "Well, first of all, I think Rose is more of a mother than a mother-in-law to me.... I feel like I have more obligations to Rose than to my own mother." When I asked her why she felt that way, she replied, "her being there for me and not being judgmental and all of the quality time that we have shared together."

Susan and Rose were more than a typical mother and daughter though. Susan confided in Rose like a best friend and described her as a combination of a best friend and mother. In fact, Susan told me of a secret that she had shared with Rose many years ago, and it was indeed the sort of thing that you would share only with your best friend. At one point, Susan started to cry when she said, "I don't know what I will do if she passes on.... I worry about her, about her health." Susan shared with me that it was Rose who had helped her to get over her "insecurities" as an example of just how close they were. While asking Susan about her husband's previous wife and the other daughters-in-law in the family, Susan shared the following:

> I was afraid that Kyle would go back to his first wife because they had children together. I cannot have children. [Rose] made me realize that Kyle chooses to be with me and that if he wanted to be with someone else, he would have. I was crying one day, and she made me look in the mirror; she made me realize that I am a good person.

Susan and Rose were not always as close as they were at the time of the interview. Susan pointed out that the kind of relationship that they had takes time and does not happen overnight. Susan felt welcomed though, both in Rose's home and in the family, from the beginning. When they first met, Rose looked askance at Susan because of the tattoos on her arm. Susan said that Rose now gets upset when people make assumptions about Susan because of those same tattoos.

Susan believed that she was closer to Rose than the other four daughters-in-law (plus ex-daughters-in-law) were. She felt that it was because they had not spent as much time with Rose due to having their own children. She did say though that none of the children or children-in-law had ever said anything negative about Rose and that they all loved her. I interviewed one of the other daughters-in-law as well. She too got along well with Rose, although they did not have a "tight-knit" relationship. She also felt that Rose was closest to Susan. When I asked Rose whether she was closer to one daughter-in-law than any of the others, she diplomatically said that they were all the same and that she invited the ex-daughters-in-law to family events as well. When I asked her whether she was as close to her daughters-in-law as her daughters, she did note some difference by explaining:

> Of course, my daughters are my daughters. They have been in my life their entire lives. It is a different relationship. My daughters-in-law have come into my family whereas my daughters were my family. They are all equal in the family though. I treat them all equally. The only difference that I can see is that my daughters-in-law might hesitate to ask me to do something more than my daughters would.

"ESTRANGED" RELATIONSHIPS

At the other end of the spectrum are the "estranged" relationships. Diane's association with her mother-in-law is a typical example. Diane saw her mother-in-law Cynthia only on holidays, even though Cynthia lived only twenty minutes away and Diane and her husband had two of Cynthia's grandchildren. Diane felt that she worked at making it pleasant and tried not to react to Cynthia's insults but that Cynthia would "dig [Diane] every chance that she had."

Diane felt that the underlying problem was Cynthia's belief that Diane was not "good enough" for her son. Diane shared with me,

> It bothered her that I was uneducated. Everyone else went to good colleges, and I was a nobody. My father-in-law was [a prominent businessman], and my brother-in-law is [a politician]. The other daughter-in-law is a teacher, and I came from nothing. She would make comments. They were very class prejudiced. She had a big house and a lot of money. She thought that I went after my husband for his money, but we lived in an apartment.

At times Cynthia treated Diane like an outsider while at other times she treated her like the "black sheep of the family." This was particularly hard because Diane's own mother had died when she was a child, and she had hoped that her mother-in-law would be a substitute mother. As an example, Diane told me of an incident when her in-laws had a surprise party for her husband's birthday. There was an entire table of presents set up for him, lots of food, and a cake with his name on it. Despite the fact that Diane's birthday was only one week away, not one person in the family even mentioned her birthday or brought her a gift then or later.

Diane and Cynthia's relationship was a poor one from the beginning. Diane and her husband were both in their mid to late thirties when they met. Cynthia had expected that her son would always stay home and take care of her instead of marrying. At the very beginning of their relationship, Cynthia made the comment to Diane that she should not "go out and get herself pregnant." When Diane grew her hair out for her wedding, Cynthia said to her, "I've got scissors in my car. Let me go out and get them." Diane said that Cynthia was always like that with her, "blunt and mean."

Cynthia did get along fairly well with her other two daughters-in-law, at least according to Diane. Diane felt that her other two sisters-in-law "doted on" Cynthia, which Diane was not willing to do. The other two women called Cynthia "Mrs. ———," but Diane did not think that family should have to do this. Although Diane always encouraged her husband and sons to visit their mother/grandmother without her, Diane's two sons stopped visiting when they were old enough to realize that their grandmother did not like their mother. Her husband would call his mother approximately once a month, but no more often. Diane said that her mother-in-law was not close to her sons because she wanted granddaughters not grandsons. Despite the fact that Diane and her husband had been married for over twenty-two years, things with Cynthia had never improved.

"CORDIAL" RELATIONSHIPS

In the middle of the range of relationships are the "cordial" relationships. In this category, the in-law feels little conflict but also has little affection for the other woman. They may or may not see one another frequently. Rebecca lived only five minutes away from her mother-in-law, Delores, but she did not see her mother-in-law often. When I asked Rebecca what a visit with Delores was like, she explained,

> It is not tense, but it is not affectionate. I am comfortable with how she is by now. She is abrupt and talks about herself. We don't stay long.... She

likes her space. She comes to our house or my parents' house for holiday meals. It is enough for her.

Rebecca attributed their relationship to her mother-in-law's personality. She used to be an alcoholic but had both quit drinking and divorced during the time that Rebecca had known her. While Rebecca thought that both events had been good for Delores, they had hardened her and made her abrupt with people. Delores tended to be very negative about family members.

When I asked Rebecca to describe her relationship with Delores, she said, "It is comfortable because we have known each other for so long. It is not negative, but there is something missing. I wouldn't call her if I was upset. We don't do things together." Rebecca felt much closer to her own mother. Delores saw her own daughter who lived in Vermont frequently, but they were not emotionally close either. There was a second daughter-in-law living in the South that Delores saw only a few times.

EMOTIONAL CLOSENESS AND CONFIDENCE

Over one-third (38 percent) of the daughters-in-law felt that there was affection and little conflict with their mothers-in-law. Similarly, 40 percent felt emotionally close to their mothers-in-law, and 47 percent felt that they could confide in their mothers-in-law. Interestingly though, some of the daughters-in-law expressed affection for their mothers-in-law, but did not feel emotionally close nor could they confide in their mother-in-law and vice versa. Clearly, these are different dimensions of in-law relationships. Some of the women felt close because they had spent so much time together and shared loved ones, but they had not made an emotional connection as individuals. For example, one of the women said, "I feel [emotionally] close to the extent that she is my mother-in-law, but I would never call her if I was upset or needed support." In contrast, a few women had been able to forge an emotional bond even though there was conflict in the relationship. I will argue later that often the conflict is the result of social structural barriers and is not due to individual incompatibilities. As such, the women do become close to one another despite the conflict. A few of the women pointed out that they could confide in their mothers-in-law, but they did not share personal things with them, only their concerns about the family. In other words, the connection to one's mother-in-law remained defined by their family.

Another indicator of the closeness that a daughter-in-law feels for her mother-in-law is the name that she uses for her. According to family theorists, the language that family members use gives meaning to and reflects upon those relationships in vital ways.[22] The vast majority of the daughters-in-law (74 percent) called their mothers-in-law by their first names. This suggests a more peer-like and potentially friendly relationship between the two women. These daughters-in-law may have also chosen to reserve the name "Mom" for the unique relationship that they had with their own biological mother. Ten (19 percent) of the women, however, did call their mothers-in-law "Mom." All except for one of these women had a "tight-knit" relationship with their mothers-in-law. The one exception was a woman whose relationship was "conflicted but affectionate." Two of the women said that their mothers-in-law had specifically asked to be called "Mom." One of these women said that she sometimes reverted to using a first name despite her mother-in-law's request. All of the other women though said that their mother-in-law felt like a second mother. They had clearly created a primary familial bond. That is, they felt more like another one of the adult children in the family rather than being just the spouse of one of the children.

In contrast, three of the women called their mothers-in-law "Mrs. [last name]." All three had "estranged" relationships with their mothers-in-law and a high degree of conflict. Susannah, for example, told me that her mother-in-law, Mrs. Cooper, made it clear that she did not want Susannah to be part of the family. Mrs. Cooper was from a family of old wealth and had tried to "buy off" Susannah with a significant amount of money. She had also told her son that he would no longer be able to receive any income from the family or live in the family-owned home if he stayed with his wife. She had gone so far as to throw some of Susannah's personal items from the family home out onto the street. One can certainly understand why Susannah had not progressed beyond calling her mother-in-law "Mrs. Cooper" in establishing a closer relationship. Finally, one of the women had managed to avoid calling her mother-in-law by any name after twenty-one years of marriage. Instead, she waited until she made eye contact with her mother-in-law if she had something to say. Sophie wanted to call her mother-in-law by her first name but was not certain if that would be acceptable. Her mother-in-law had never said anything about it.

CONFLICT

Nearly half of the daughters-in-law (42 percent) reported no conflict with their mothers-in-law during their marriages. This is certainly a higher percentage than one might expect given popular conceptions that in-law relationships are fraught with conflict (See Chapter 2). In situations where the daughter-in-law did not report conflict, the mother-in-law also noted no conflict. It is possible then, and even highly likely, for women from two different families to "get along" in what are socially constructed in-law relationships over the long run.

Slightly over half of the daughters-in-law (58 percent) did report at least some conflict with their mother-in-law during their marriage though. Appendix 2 lists the source of conflict according to the daughters-in-law. (For those mothers-in-law who were also interviewed, their perspective on the source of the conflict is reported underneath in bold letters.) Similar to Fischer's findings, daughters-in-law were more likely to report conflict than mothers-in-law.[23]

The sources of conflict, according to the daughters-in-law, were as varied as the relationships themselves. The conflict ranged from isolated incidents early on in marriage, and even before marriage, to much more serious situations that continued over time. Extreme examples of conflict included one daughter-in-law who said that her in-laws tried to "buy [her] off" and another who fantasized about killing her mother-in-law. The most common source of conflict though, according to the daughters-in-law, was that the mother-in-law was controlling of people and situations or was "territorial" of her son (eight daughters-in-law). While this is certainly not how many mothers-in-law wish to see themselves, it does coincide with the difficulty of "letting a son go" referred to by others.[24] Six other daughters-in-law felt that differences in personality and the fact that the husband's family was not as close to the couple as the wife's family caused the conflict with in-laws. The husband's family may pull back though if the couple spends more time with the wife's family, a finding that was documented by previous researchers.[25] Three of the daughters-in-law felt that the conflict with their in-laws stemmed from the way that the in-laws ignored their grandchildren or mistreated them with verbal insults.

Conflict also resulted when in-laws did not offer approval early on in the marriage. In one isolated incident, a mother-in-law disapproved of the fact that her son and daughter-in-law were living together before marriage. This, however, was resolved in a letter that the daughter-in-law sent to her mother-in-law encouraging her to trust in her son's decisions. In three other instances the disapproval continued throughout the marriage however. The mother-in-law did not like the fact that her new family member was of a different class or religion or was divorced. It was also common for daughters-in-law to feel conflict because their mothers-in-law stepped on their toes or intruded on their role as wife. Another daughter-in-law felt that she was fighting with her mother-in-law for her husband's time and that her mother-in-law was too dependent on her son. Finally, one daughter-in-law felt that her mother-in-law was negative about marriage in general and, therefore, did not respect her marriage.

Five of the daughters-in-law reported some conflict from the seventeen mother-in-law and daughter-in-law pairs. Of those five, three of the mothers-in-law said that there was no conflict or that they always worked it out. That is, they did not see the conflict that their daughters-in-law saw. In the other two instances, the mothers-in-law noted a different source of the conflict than their daughters-in-law. For example, one of the daughters-in-law thought that the conflict was due to her mother-in-law's personality and that she was "just too cold," while the mother-in-law thought that it was due to her daughter-in-law's feelings of insecurity. The mother-in-law felt that her daughter-in-law feared that her husband loved his mother more than her. These findings suggest not only that in-laws experience different relationships (hers and hers) or have different perspectives on the relationship, but also that daughters-in-law are more likely to experience (or at least report) conflict and problems in the relationship. This is consistent with earlier findings that daughters-in-law report more conflict than mothers-in-law[26] and that children report more problems than parents in their relationships with one another.[27] Fischer[28] argues that mothers-in-law report less conflict because they have more at stake in getting along and that they do not notice the conflict because daughters-in-law tend to "hold things in." Cotterill[29] also argues that daughters-in-law hold the balance of power in the relationship. These findings also highlight the indeterminacy or varied interpretations that family members might have of a relationship.[30]

Although many of the problems that the daughters-in-law mentioned clearly would create conflict for any daughter-in-law, some of the concerns eventually led to conflict because of the daughters-in-law's personal reactions. For example, having your mother-in-law try to "buy you off" or ignore your children would create conflict for most daughters-in-law. However, the fact that some of the daughters-in-law felt that their in-laws stepped on their toes or were vying for their husband's time is certainly open for interpretation and might not bother all daughters-in-law. The subjective experience and the stock of knowledge about in-law relationships that women take with them into their marriages is therefore very important in determining the kind of relationship that they have with their mother-in-law. People's life world, or experiential world, and their interpretation of their mother-in-law's actions thus matter in determining family dynamics.

AMBIVALENCE

Previous researchers have applied the concept of intergenerational ambivalence to explain the coexistence of both positive and negative sentiments (referred to as solidarity and conflict) that parents and adult children may feel for one another.[31,32] They argue that intergenerational relations are inherently structured to create this ambivalence as a result of contradictions in the roles and norms for the relationship. For example, adult children and their parents are expected to be both mutually dependent upon one another as well as autonomous of one another.[33]

Such ambivalence is fairly frequent. In fact, the closer the family relationship, the greater the ambivalence.[34] Pillemer and Suitor[35] found in their study of 189 mothers sixty years of age and older that approximately 54 percent of mothers agreed or strongly agreed with one or more statement of ambivalence.[36] Characteristics that determined ambivalence, however, were distinct from those that predicted the quality of the relationship, confirming that this is in fact another dimension of intergenerational relations. Mothers were more likely to express ambivalence if their children had failed to achieve normal adult statuses (i.e., completing college and being married) or to be financially independent. Older mothers were also more likely to express ambivalence. Spitze and Gallant[37] found such ambivalence to be common in older women as well, particularly when it came to the issue of receiving assistance from their adult children. They wanted to be independent, but hoped that their children would help them when needed. In addition, they felt that their children were overly protective, but they appreciated their concern.

Adult children, however, express greater ambivalence than their mothers.[38] Ambivalence increases for children when parents are dependent or in poor health, when they had poor relations with their parent in childhood, if they are care giving, and if they are part of a mother/daughter dyad. Thus, ambivalence intensifies when adult children feel that there are responsibilities that they must now meet in the relationship.

Yet, adult children feel even greater ambivalence towards their in-laws than towards their own parents.[39] The fact that they want to be part of the overall in-law family while also wanting to isolate and protect their own nuclear family is one indicator of this. I will argue that ambivalence results

from the obligations that women feel as daughters-in-law and the expectation that they should treat their in-laws like family when, in fact, they feel
less close. Although both men and women report higher affective closeness
to their own parents than their parents-in-law, the difference is greater for
women than for men.[40] This suggests the possibility that daughters-in-law
will experience greater ambivalence than sons-in-law.

Author Pamela Cotterill[41] also notes the ambiguity that daughters-in-law
experience. It is not clear how daughters-in-law are to act because there are
no real rules for appropriate relationships or norms for social behavior. Such
ambiguity adds to feelings of ambivalence.[42] Ambivalence is also often
manifested during status transitions in the family.[43] This might include the
introduction of a daughter-in-law into the family.

Surprisingly, only half of the daughters-in-law in this study expressed
ambivalence in their relationships with their mothers-in-law. This may have
been due to the fact that respondents were not asked directly about ambivalence but instead were asked to describe their relationships with their
mothers-in-law overall, leaving the opportunity to explain in their own
words any number of ways that there might be opposing feelings or uncertainty in their relationships. Ambivalence tended to stem from any of three
sources: (a) an ambiguous role and thus uncertainty as a daughter-in-law,
(b) contradictory emotions towards the mother-in-law, and (c) feeling both
attached to and detached from the family.

Sally felt a great sense of ambiguity in her role as a daughter-in-law. In
fact, she was one of only a few daughters-in-law who questioned whether
or not her partner's parents were her family too. Maintaining boundaries
was particularly important to her, in part, because of what she saw as her
in-laws' intrusiveness and, in part, because of the unclear nature of their
relationship. Still, in many ways Sally acted like family, joining in on family
get-togethers and so on, even though she would have preferred not to do
so. Sally stated, "There is an awkwardness in our relationship that is not
comfortable. The sad thing is that she feels that we are close though. A lot
of the time, it [the relationship] just doesn't work for me." The ambiguity
in Sophie's relationship with her mother-in-law was so great that she had
still not chosen a name by which to call her mother-in-law even after
twenty-one years of marriage. She added,

> It is hard to put your finger on. I have spent a ton of time with her, but it is
> not a warm relationship. We have good laughs, but it is no deeper. She
> doesn't treat her in-laws like family. For example, she doesn't remember our

birthdays. So it is hard to know how I should then treat her. To her, in-laws are just there to take care of her kids, but they are not her family. She doesn't realize that there is something missing, but I feel it.

The most common source of ambivalence was the presence of contradictory emotions. Many of the daughters-in-law felt both conflict and closeness. For example, Pat made the point many times that her mother-in-law was like a second mother to her. Her own mother died while she was in her twenties, and she felt that she and her mother-in-law had a very warm and loving relationship. However, she also made the point several times that her mother-in-law could be very intrusive and pushy and that it took her a long time to learn how to deal with it. A few of the daughters-in-law pointed out that the contradictions led to a feeling of "nothingness." One woman summed it up by saying, "It is not hostile, but it is not cordial either. It is somewhere in between. There is really nothing there.… We are nice to each other, but I wouldn't shed a tear if she died."

Feeling both attached to and detached from their in-laws, or "in" and "out" of the family simultaneously, also contributed to ambivalence. Maria, for example, said that she felt obligated to do the kinds of task for her mother-in-law that she did for her mother and to join in on family activities for her mother-in-law's sake. Yet, her in-laws made it clear that it was her husband that they wanted to spend time with and that their relationship, as far as they were concerned, was primarily with him. As a result, she did not feel the same level of affection for her in-laws that she did for her own family.

Mothers-in-law also expressed ambivalence about their daughters-in-law, but it was not as common. Only 24 percent of the mothers-in-law (compared with approximately half of the daughters-in-law) described an ambivalent relationship. In all cases, they had mixed emotions about their daughters-in-law or felt that their daughter-in-law had mixed emotions about them. Two of the mothers-in-law described how they kept their distance from their daughters-in-law, in one case because the daughter-in-law seemed so strained around her and in another because the daughter-in-law had had a bad experience with her first mother-in-law. In both cases then, the mothers-in-law deliberately maintained some distance despite being family. Another mother-in-law explained that she felt close to her daughter-in-law and saw her regularly without any friction, but she was put off that her son and daughter-in-law lived above their means and were constantly in debt. She attributed this to the fact that her daughter-in-law was raised "differently" than her own children but made no mention of why her son might have also been a part of this. The last mother-in-law also loved her son's wife very much but was angry that her son and daughter-in-law spent so much more time with her family than with his family. She said, "I love her, but she ruined my family too."

MULTIPLE IN-LAWS

Relationships with *different* in-laws vary considerably, suggesting that it is often the interplay of the two individuals and not any one individual that makes a difference in the relationship. Of the ten mothers-in-law who had more than one daughter-in-law, all stated that they were closest to one daughter-in-law over the others (although it was not always the daughter-in-law that I had interviewed). In two of the cases, the mother-in-law was much closer to one daughter-in-law because the others lived a considerable distance and the mother-in-law rarely saw them. What was most common (50 percent of cases) though was for the mother-in-law to feel closer to one of the women over the others because of her personality. In particular, mothers-in-law referred to how one daughter-in-law was much more out-going than the others or that she reached out to their family more. Like-wise, three other mothers-in-law felt closest to one daughter-in-law because she was more thoughtful of them or called more frequently. Again, it had to do with what the daughter-in-law did for her mother-in-law and her family or her tendency to reach out. For example, one of the mothers-in-law stated,

> I have gotten closest to Debbie. It could be that she is more mindful of my needs. Patty, I just didn't understand. She never did things for the family... family barbeques and things. I don't think she appreciated having family.

Another added,

> I don't love any of the others [i.e., other daughters-in-law] any less, but Kyle's wife comes over more. She helped me move in and comes over to stay every week. It is not because of anything that I do, but it is because of who she is and what she wants to do.

Which of the daughters-in-law was the parent of grandchildren did not make a difference, however. Finally, mothers-in-law discounted daughters-in-law for aberrant behavior such as alcoholism and mental illness.

All of the daughters-in-law were also asked to identify which of the daughters-in-law their mothers-in-law felt closest to (including themselves) and why. Although a few of the women said that their mother-in-law had similar relationships with each daughter-in-law (whether good or bad), the majority felt that she was closest to one over the others. Again, the difference was usually due to her living closer to one or spending more time with one as well as being due to one daughter-in-law reaching out more. However, one of the daughters-in-law felt that her mother-in-law was closer to her than her other three daughters-in-law because she lived the *furthest* away (an entire continent away) rather than being in the same city. She felt that living in the same city produced *more* conflict with her mother-in-law for the other three sisters-in-law because it provided greater opportunity for her mother-in-law to try to dominate the families. Other daughters-in-law said that their mother-in-law did not feel as welcome in their sisters-in-law's homes or that one daughter-in-law was more likely to be a loner than the others in explaining why others were less close to their mother-in-law.

Daughters-in-law mentioned additional factors as well in determining favoritism. Two women felt that their mother-in-law was closest to one daughter-in-law over the others because that daughter-in-law had the grandchildren. This was contrary to what I found with the mothers-in-law that I interviewed. Another daughter-in-law felt that her mother-in-law was closest to her because she married her favorite son. Three said that their mother-in-law was closest to the "newest" daughter-in-law, and they were thus in a "honeymoon phase." They predicted that these in-law relationships would worsen with time. Finally, two of the women felt that their mothers-in-law were more critical of their sisters-in-law than themselves, one because she was more outspoken and the other because she was an alcoholic. Overall, daughters-in-law's perceptions were very similar to their mothers-in-law's when both were interviewed.

Among the eleven daughters-in-law who had been married more than once, eight had experienced more than one set of in-laws.[44] All except for two daughters-in-law had very different relationships with the different in-laws. Among these two, one of the women had very estranged relationships with both sets of in-laws, while the other was very close to both sets of in-laws. In fact, this latter daughter-in-law had remained quite close to her former in-laws, and both sets of in-laws (as well as her mother) got together for holidays and weekend events regularly. She still referred to her first set of in-laws as her mother-in-law and father-in-law and saw them both for the benefit of her children as well as for her own close relationship with them.

Daughters-in-law were no more likely to have worse or better relationships with their second set of in-laws than their first. One factor that determined the difference in relationships though was the length of time that they were married to each husband. For example, one of the daughters-in-law felt much closer to her second mother-in-law than her first because she has been married to her second husband for eight years while she was married to her first husband for only two years. However, it was not just a matter of the amount of time that they spent together. Allison also mentioned that she did not respect her first mother-in-law because "she let her [adult] children walk all over her."

The second factor that made a difference in the relationships was the contrasting ways that the mothers-in-law treated their daughters-in-law. Nina had three different mothers-in-law. She was quite close to her first mother-in-law whom she said was like a second mother (which her mother-in-law confirmed). Her relationship with her second mother-in-law was not as good although there was no hostility. Both Nina and her second mother-in-law tried to be a close family for the benefit of the husband/son and the children/grandchildren. However, Nina's mother-in-law favored her biological grandchild over her adopted grandchild, and Nina found this intolerable. Her relationship with her third mother-in-law was the worst. Her mother-in-law did not even allow her into her home for the first three years of her marriage. Nina had inadvertently offended her brother-in-law in front of her mother-in-law. More importantly, her mother-in-law thought that she was a "gold digger" looking for someone to take care of her and her two children despite Nina's steady employment and her own supportive family. Nina's relationship with her third mother-in-law did improve with time. She believed that this was because she found things that she, her husband, and in-laws could all do together, such as going to the theater.

SUMMARY AND IMPLICATIONS

Results of this research suggest a broad range of in-law relationships as described by daughters-in-law. The majority of relationships, however, fell at either end of a distribution; over half were either "tight knit" or "estranged." Many of these were very good relationships; 38 percent of the daughters-in-law described relationships with high affection and little or no conflict. This suggests then that in situations that are devoid of conflict, the tendency is for the in-laws to develop a close and caring relationship rather than remaining on middle ground. However, mothers-in-law tended to describe the relationship more positively than their daughters-in-law. This implies both the indeterminacy of the roles and the fact that each of the women experiences the relationship differently. Mothers-in-law express less conflict because they have more at stake in making the relationship a positive one. In particular, it is their daughters-in-law who invite them for dinners and holidays and who maintain kin ties. Without their good will, they would see less of their sons and grandchildren.

I will also argue that there are additional factors that determine the difference in perceptions. The social structural conditions that lead to conflict are different for the two women. The mother-in-law experiences fewer of the outcomes from these conditions, leading to less conflict from her standpoint. As will be discussed later, daughters-in-law experience conflict as the result of starting a new family and being both insiders and outsiders in their husband's family. They are the ones who have to integrate themselves into the larger family pattern. Mothers-in-law experience conflict as a result of their sons becoming more peripheral in their family and possibly from having to integrate this new daughter-in-law into the family as well (see Chapter 7). These differences then lead to daughters-in-law feeling greater conflict.

Other indicators suggested positive relationships, although most were neither friendships nor quasi mother–daughter bonds. Nearly half of the daughters-in-law felt emotionally close to their mothers-in-law and could confide in them. Some pointed out though that they would only confide about family matters and not personal things, emphasizing that their connection was primarily about shared family. A few pointed out that they felt close because they had shared so much time together, but that they did not feel "emotionally" close or have a personal connection with their mother-in-law. Feeling close to their mother-in-law and feeling affection for her were not synonymous. Approximately one-fifth of the daughters-in-law called their mother-in-law "Mom." It was these daughters-in-law who had created a primary family bond with their mother-in-law as if they were another one of the adult children in the family.

Over half of the daughters-in-law had at least some conflict with their mothers-in-law while they were married. What is surprising though is that nearly half did not. This is in direct contrast to popular images of in-law relationships as being conflict-ridden. The most common sources of conflict according to the daughters-in-law were their mothers-in-law being controlling or territorial of their sons (while they were trying to create a separate family), differences in personality, unhappiness with the way grandchildren were treated, disapproval by their mother-in-law early on, and feeling like their mother-in-law stepped on their toes. Finally, children-in-law felt ambivalence towards the older generation as do adult children. However, the causes differ for children-in-law versus children. Common sources of ambivalence for daughters-in-law included the ambiguous nature of the role, feeling contradictory emotions, and feeling both in and out of the family simultaneously.

Overall then, good relationships between mothers-in-law and daughters-in-law are possible and even likely. The nature of the relationship though does have a tendency to lead to both conflict and ambivalence. It results in daughters-in-law feeling simultaneously "in" and "out" of the family. As such, in-law relationships need to be cultivated and nurtured. As will be discussed in Chapter 9, family life specialists can benefit families by providing educational opportunities at the community level. This would lessen the likelihood of misunderstandings and the tendency to attribute the cause of difficulties to the other person.

I will argue that ambivalence is more destructive to in-law relationships than parent–child relationships because in-laws feel fewer "pulls" into the family or benefits from being part of the family. That is, there is less to counteract the negative effect of the ambivalence. A daughter-in-law's ambivalence is also destructive to the parent–son relationship and other relationships within the husband's family because of the daughter-in-law's role as kin keeper. Mothers-in-law, particularly early on in the relationship, may undermine the importance of their daughter-in-law's role in maintaining their relationship with their son. Likewise, daughters-in-law may undermine the extent to which problems with their mother-in-law can affect their marriage, as well as their long-term relationship with her. It is to everyone's benefit across the later life family then for in-laws to learn to communicate effectively early on in the relationship to create a mutually comfortable situation. This and other interventions will be discussed in greater detail in Chapter 9.

Certain factors increase the likelihood of the mother-in-law and daughter-in-law having a positive relationship. What makes in-laws friends versus foe is the focus of the next two chapters.

Four

DETERMINING THE QUALITY
OF THE RELATIONSHIPS

*My own mother-in-law tried every trick in the book to destroy my relation-
ship. I found my own way to survive.... I vowed never to do anything like
that to my own children.... I think I am a better mother-in-law for
having such a negative example of what not to do.*

—Kim (mother-in-law)

Earlier researchers have examined a few of the factors that can improve or
worsen relationships between mothers-in-law and daughters-in-law. One
study found that having clear relational boundaries, a level of involvement
in the family by the mother-in-law that was acceptable to the daughter-in-
law, open communication, and the daughter-in-law's early acceptance into
the family all improved the relationship from the perspective of the
daughter-in-law.[1] Most of the daughters-in-law entered marriage with an
expectation of how their relationships would be with their mothers-in-
law.[2-4] Relationships, however, were often not what they expected.[5,6]
Those daughters-in-law who were able to adjust their expectations once
they were married perceived the relationship more positively than those
who held on to their earlier assumptions. Finally, in-law relationships
appeared to improve over time[7] and with the age of the daughter-in-law.[8]

Author Britta Limary[9] looked at the concerns that both mothers-in-law
and daughters-in-law voiced. In her interviews with twenty mothers-in-law
and twenty-one daughters-in-law, she found that the daughters-in-law's
chief concerns were that their mothers-in-law were intrusive and that they
felt like strangers to them. In contrast, the mothers-in-law's chief concerns

were that their loved ones were not taken care of properly by their daughters-in-law, their daughters-in-law were different from them, and they felt cut out of their sons' families. Living in close proximity, however, did not appear to increase the stress level of either mothers-in-law or daughters-in-law in farming families.[10]

This chapter examines several other factors that may influence the quality of the relationship between the mother-in-law and daughter-in-law. These include sociocultural variables, the history of the relationship, both women's attitudes about in-law ties, the daughter-in-law's relationship with her own mother, and the mother-in-law's relationship with her own daughter(s) and her own mother-in-law. It is believed that a daughter-in-law's relationship with her mother-in-law does not occur in a vacuum. Instead, it will be affected by other relationships within the family, particularly those that mirror the relationship, such as the mother–daughter bond, and those that affect the mother-in-law's own experiences as a daughter-in-law. In-law relationships are also affected by the sociocultural context in which they occur. This includes class, religion, and ethnicity, all of which affect family life. Likewise, later relationships will be strongly impacted by the daughter's feeling of acceptance early on in the relationship. The role of the son/husband and the nature of his relationship with his mother and how it affects the in-law relationship will be discussed in Chapter 7.

THE SOCIOCULTURAL CONTEXT

The effects of religion, ethnicity, class, and education, for both the mother-in-law and daughter-in-law, were examined. Unexpectedly, religion plays only a minor role in determining the quality of a daughter-in-law's relationship with her mother-in-law. Catholic daughters-in-law were somewhat more likely to have a very positive relationship with their mother-in-law, although the difference was slight. Of those daughters-in-law with a "tight-knit" or "distant but positive" relationship, 62 percent were Catholic compared with 55 percent of the daughters-in-law with an "estranged" or "obligatory" relationship who were Catholic. This may be due to the emphasis that is placed on family and respect for one's elders in the Catholic religion. Jewish daughters-in-law were more likely to have a "cordial" or "conflicted but affectionate" relationship. Seventy-five percent of the Jewish daughters-in-law fell into one of the two categories that were defined by their contradictions (low conflict but low affection or high conflict but high affection). These then are the women who are able to see beyond the conflict and care about their mothers-in-law *or* for whom the relationship offers very little (both little conflict and little affection). This is surprising given the Jewish faith's emphasis on family. Such an emphasis does explain though why the relationships are less likely to be estranged.

Ethnicity does play an important role in the relationship though. Among the Italian daughters-in-law, two-thirds had positive relationships compared with one-third who had poorer relationships.[11,12] Likewise, all of the French daughters-in-law had positive relationships with their mothers-in-law. Why would there be this ethnic difference? In other parts of the book, I point out that it was important to the mothers-in-law that daughters-in-law reached out and included them. Relationships are likely to be better for Italian and French daughters-in-law if they are able to include their mothers-in-law in the extended family. They may be more accustomed to getting along with (and including) extended family and have the security of their own family when in-law relationships feel problematic.

The ethnicity of the mother-in-law and father-in-law seem to matter less though, at least for some ethnic groups. Daughters-in-law were as likely to have a very positive relationship as a negative one with French, Italian, or Greek in-laws. Daughters-in-law felt that they had a very good relationship with all of the Irish mothers-in-law though. Why would Irish mothers-in-law be able to get along better with their daughters-in-law? One of the daughters-in-law whose in-laws were both Irish explained that the family placed greater emphasis on the couple and their children (i.e., the nuclear family) rather than the extended family. So her mother-in-law tended to be "hands off" and not give advice. All of the Irish respondents, both mothers-in-law and daughters-in-law, talked about children having their own families and wanting their children to settle down with their own families.

The daughter-in-law's class made little difference in her perception of the relationship. What did make a difference though was whether there were substantial class differences between the in-laws. Two of the women described very estranged relationships because of class disparities. As was mentioned in the previous chapter, Diane's mother-in-law, Cynthia, felt that Diane was "not good enough" for her son. Whereas Diane had been raised in an orphanage since her mother's death and had only a GED, Cynthia and her children were well educated and prosperous. Diane believed very strongly that the cause of their estranged relationship was her mother-in-law's class bias. Class differences may affect the relationship in a number of ways. The two in-laws have few shared cultural references, and as Diane said, very different lifestyles. Diane pointed out that all of her in-laws lived in a wealthy suburb and that none of the women worked outside of the home. She said that she and her husband, in contrast, lived in an apartment and then a small house "in the 'hood.'" Likewise, Diane's mannerisms were not polished like those of upper-class women, and that likely caused a rift as well. Because of financial constraints, Diane and her husband did not have large family parties like her in-laws did. In fact, because of being raised in an orphanage, Diane may not have known how to reach out to extended family.

Susannah also had a very estranged relationship with her mother-in-law, Mrs. Cooper, due to their class differences. The elder Mrs. Cooper had thrown all of her daughter-in-law's clothes out of the house that Susannah and her husband shared (although it was owned by her in-laws). Mrs. Cooper was from a long-standing well-to-do family and felt that her daughter-in-law was a "gold digger" according to her daughter-in-law. She wanted her son to go back to his ex-wife, who was also from a "blue blood" family. Mrs. Cooper had even gone so far as to bribe Susannah to leave her husband and had threatened her son with cutting off his financial support if he did not divorce his wife. Susannah felt that she was disliked only because she embarrassed the family with her lack of social standing.

Similarly, two other daughters-in-law had "obligatory" relationships, but no better, because they too were "from the wrong side of the tracks." In both situations, the problems were due to perceived differences in morality. One of the women felt that her mother-in-law never approved of her because she was pregnant when she and her husband married. A second woman said that her mother-in-law would not talk to her for the first three years that she and her husband were married because she had been dating her husband while he was still married to another woman.

Finally, the daughter-in-law's education made an important difference in the quality of her relationship with her mother-in-law. Among those daughters-in-law who had a very positive relationship with their mother-in-law, 71 percent had an associate's degree, college degree, or postgraduate degree, whereas only 29 percent had a high school diploma or some high school education. Among those with a poorer relationship, 60 percent had an advanced degree, whereas 40 percent had, at best, a high school diploma. A college education provides one with important problem-solving skills and self-confidence. Having a degree may also improve the daughters-in-law's standing with their mothers-in-law whose generation was less likely to be well educated.

Since the vast majority of the mothers-in-law tended to view their relationships with their daughters-in-law in a positive light, it was not feasible or instructive to examine the effect of sociocultural factors on their perception of the relationship. That is, there was not enough variation for such an analysis.

THE IN-LAWS' HISTORY

The mother-in-law and daughter-in-law's earlier history also impacted their current relationship. All of the daughters-in-law who described "tight-knit" or "distant but positive" relationships had started out feeling very welcomed and accepted by their mothers-in-law. Only one of the women said that her mother-in-law was "a bit taken aback" by her tattoos, but she felt welcomed into the family anyway. These daughters-in-law made comments like, "She liked me from the start" and "She was happy for us." One said, "We had a very good relationship from the beginning. She was happy that we were dating. My husband even took her with him to pick out my diamond. She said that I brought things to him, that I was good for him. She said that I made him happy." A few of the women had spent little time with their in-laws while they were dating, but then grew much closer after the engagement. As an aside, one of the daughters-in-law pointed out that she did not get along with her *father*-in-law at the very beginning because her father-in-law felt that she was interfering with his son's commitment to sports. In doing so, she may have also lessened the time that the son spent with his father. This daughter-in-law felt as though she has never had a good relationship with her father-in-law.

Some of the daughters-in-law told funny anecdotes about their earlier relationships with their mothers-in-law, although the experiences did not affect their feelings of acceptance. Elizabeth, for example, lived with her boyfriend for a while on the second floor of the family's double-decker home (her in-laws-to-be lived on the first floor). She said that she was very uncomfortable, but they were warm and embracing and did not mention the situation. Ginny's mother-in-law was upset, however, with both Ginny and her son when they moved in together, but their warm and accepting relationship continued soon thereafter. Ginny's first meeting with her in-laws though was a family party of "*fifty* Italians and French Canadians." She laughingly said,

> It was frightening! I could tell that I was being surveyed and studied all over. I could hear people talking about me, and they didn't stop talking about me when I got closer! I felt welcomed though. Everyone was welcoming me even though we were just dating. Now I know my husband's family better than he does.

Libby described how her mother-in-law had liked her from the start. Libby felt that her mother-in-law appreciated and always remembered how Libby had sent a bouquet of flowers to her mother-in-law after an operation when she and her husband, John, were first dating. Libby felt that no one else would have thought of it, and it meant a lot to her future mother-in-law. Libby said, "Later that year I knit some doll clothes for John's little sister, and she thought that was just so wonderful that I would do something like that for this little girl. She thought I could do no wrong and that is how it stayed."

Daughters-in-law remember early positive experiences indefinitely. For example, Ginny, who thinks of her in-laws as substitute parents, gave the following anecdote:

> When we first bought our house, my mother-in-law used to give me things. It helped a lot.... My father-in-law made furniture. His company was having a sale for employees, only it was on a weekday from 6:30–8:30. I wasn't going to pick out furniture without my husband, but Mom and Dad said I had to [get the sale]. I went, but I didn't want to buy anything without my husband's input. When I got home, he didn't know why I didn't buy what I liked. So we called his Dad to see if we could get the things that I liked, but he said that it was too late. The next week I was at their house, and he said that he had a surprise for me. In the back of his truck was all of the furniture that I wanted! I thought it was just so nice of him to get it for me and then to surprise me. Plus he saved us a lot of money.

The fact that Ginny remembered this so many years later suggests the lasting impact of early tokens of acceptance and love.

In contrast to the situations described above, less than half (45 percent) of the daughters-in-law with "estranged" or "obligatory" relationships felt welcomed and accepted from the start of their relationships with their mothers-in-law. For example, Sally stated, "Did I feel welcomed? Absolutely. I would say very much so. She was never anything but, 'Oh, we love Sally!'" Naomi explained that her mother-in-law, Sylvie, would frequently have her over for dinner and would cook some of Naomi's favorite foods. Sylvie would even go so far as to pick up some of Naomi's favorite chocolate frosted donuts for her from downtown whenever she knew that Naomi would be visiting. It was more likely though that daughters-in-law with poor relationships did not feel accepted by their in-laws from the beginning. One of the daughters-in-law pointed out that her mother-in-law was pleasant at the start of the relationship because she did not think that her son's relationship with this woman would ever "go anywhere." When they announced their engagement, her mother-in-law's attitude changed drastically. For some daughters-in-law then, problems start later on in the relationship.

Most of the women whose current relationships with their mothers-in-law were "estranged" or "obligatory," that is, the worst of the relationships, had difficulties from the start. Some of the offenses were relatively minor. For example, Stacey stated, "No, they never made me feel welcome. They didn't even say 'hi' to me. I was just Jesse's girlfriend." The mother-in-law's references to (and continued affection for) former girlfriends were a frequent cause of anxiety for daughters-in-law. For example, Mira stated, "She used to bring up all of his old girlfriends even five or six years after we were married. She was trying to make me jealous. It worked because I was still a little insecure." Two other daughters-in-law also stated that their mothers-in-law would bring up their son's old girlfriends, women that the mothers-in-law had liked. Nicole's mother-in-law kept a picture of her son's ex-girlfriend with photos of the other family members even after Nicole and Scott were married, while Sophie's mother-in-law kept a vase from her "almost daughter-in-law." (This was the mother-in-law's expression.) Sophie said, "You don't forget things like that, but you take it from where it is coming.... After he proposed, we were at his family's camp. My husband went to tell his mother that we were engaged. She came over a little while later and said, 'I suppose I have to look at this [the ring].' I just brushed it off." Another daughter-in-law added,

> It was horrible. I felt like it was a power struggle. She was critical of me before she even met me! I had sent [Scott] some homemade cookies, and she made a nasty comment about how could anyone eat those cookies with the smell of perfume on the box. I had deliberately put a little perfume on the box because Scott liked it. I thought that was mean [of her].

The early tensions between the mother-in-law and daughter-in-law did have repercussions for the couple. Patti and her husband, Sam, postponed their wedding by several years because of his mother's objections to Patti. Patti explained that her in-laws would send hostile letters about her to Sam. They told him that she was marrying him for a meal ticket and that she would quit her job when they got married to "live off him, along with her kids." This, coupled with Sam's lack of response to his mother, created tension between Patti and Sam.

Among the more horrific examples though was Cynthia's experience.
Consider the following:

> You forgive but you don't forget. My mother-in-law didn't talk to me for
> three years when I started dating my husband. She started rumors about me
> at work, sent me a dead bird and an empty box of chocolates. My husband
> was married, but we were attracted to each other. She called me a "slut." My
> family is wealthy ... no one had ever called me a slut.... Other relatives
> arranged for her to meet with us before the wedding to help her to accept it.
> She came [but] wanted to change things (my hair, the menu etc.) even
> though my father was paying for it. I went along with it; I am always the
> peacekeeper. I look at the pictures from my wedding, and it still irks me
> about my hair!

Throughout the discussion of the early years of dating and engagement,
the daughters-in-law said over and over again that they "did not forget"
what happened early on in the relationship. Early experiences not only
color the daughter-in-law's later interpretations of her mother-in-law's
behaviors, but as importantly they define the relationship from the beginning as problematic. While those daughters-in-law who feel accepted at the
beginning of the relationship may still develop problems later with their
mothers-in-law, the early feeling of acceptance increases the likelihood of
overcoming those problems by defining the relationship as a good one.

THE WOMEN'S PERCEPTIONS OF IN-LAW ROLES

Both the daughter-in-law and the mother-in-law were asked what they
thought made a good mother-in-law and a good daughter-in-law, whether
in-laws are family, and whether the obligations to in-laws and biological relatives are the same. These questions were asked to ascertain the women's
perspective on the nature of in-law ties. The majority of all of the daughters-
in-law stated that in-laws are family and that the obligations are the same to
both in-laws and biological kin. One daughter-in-law pointed out though
that while the obligations may be the same, the ease of doing them might
not be the same. She explained that she used to change her father's
colostomy bag when he was very ill, but she did not think that she would
have been able to do the same for her mother-in-law because "the bond was
different."

Daughters-in-law were also asked what makes a good daughter-in-law.
The following was a typical response, "To be part of a new family that you

marry into…. You should try to have a healthy relationship with the new family. They should bring you in and welcome you." In other words, a good daughter-in-law is someone who will become part of the family. Being a good daughter-in-law had nothing to do with one's role as a wife or mother or one's individual relationship with her mother-in-law, but instead focused on her ability to blend into the overall family. One insightful daughter-in-law said, "I used to think it meant you loved your in-laws like your parents, but it is harder than you think. My situation is probably extreme though."

Daughters-in-law, including those who were mothers-in-law themselves, were asked what makes a good mother-in-law. A typical response was as follows: "The mother-in-law should say to herself, 'Now I have another daughter' and treat her accordingly." Similarly, one daughter-in-law said, "A mother-in-law should love her children's spouses because her children love them, in spite of everything else." Good mothers-in-law were also described as people who kept their opinions to themselves and who did not interfere. One daughter-in-law articulately stated,

> You have to walk the line between being supportive and being unobtrusive. Knowing when to butt out and knowing when to provide support and what that support should be. That would take asking from time to time which suggests good communication. A good mother-in-law should also suspend judgment.

Thus, a good mother-in-law should treat her children-in-law just like her children, which may at times require suspending judgment, and keep her opinions to herself. Daughters-in-law were much more likely to have "tight-knit" relationships with mothers-in-law who met this description and were more likely to have "obligated" or "estranged" relationships with those who, according to them, did not meet this definition.

A minority of the daughters-in-law felt either that in-laws were not family or that they did not warrant the same obligations as biological kin. These daughters-in-law were more likely to have "estranged" or "obligated" relationships with their mothers-in-law. While only two of these daughters-in-law said that in-laws were not family, more felt that the obligations were not quite the same. They made comments like, "no, it is a level removed" or " [the obligations are the same] to a point, but not totally." One of the daughters-in-law said, "No, they are different. Your real family is what you put emphasis into." Two of the daughters-in-law, one with an "estranged" and one with an "obligated" relationship, saw even a *good* daughter-in-law as having fewer obligations to her in-laws. Sally, for example, said,

> A good daughter-in-law should say as best as she can what is meaningful for her and what will work best for her. She should say, "Here is what works for me. There is this other person and how can I do that without shutting myself off in some uncomfortable way." A lot of the time it means getting support from other people. You should try not to hurt people overtly.

Thus, for Sally, a good daughter-in-law was able to meet her own needs foremost while trying to "work with" her mother-in-law as well. Likewise, Nicole said that a good mother-in-law is "one who is respectful and who gives you the boundaries to be your own family. She should treat her daughters-in-law like her own kids and not personalize the boundaries that they establish." When I asked her what made a good daughter-in-law though, she said, "I don't know. I am not a very good daughter-in-law. Be sympathetic, I guess." This daughter-in-law then had clear expectations of her mother-in-law's obligations but had less of a sense that she too had responsibilities. Daughters-in-law who felt fewer obligations to their in-laws and or who had atypical expectations of what makes a good daughter were more likely to have a negative relationship with their own mothers-in-law.

Those daughters-in-law who wanted more from their role as a daughter-in-law, but who had a difficult relationship, were often disappointed. Consider Sydney's example,

> A good daughter-in-law should be a friend. I wish that we could have been friends. I would like to learn what my husband was like when he was little. I could never sit down with her though. We should have been friends. I see these plaques in the stores that say "A daughter-in-law is like a daughter." It was never like that though. She should have realized that this is the person who is going to take care of her son. It is too late now though. It is probably too late for her too.

Earlier research also noted a similar sense of disappointment in many in-law relationships.[13,14]

THE EFFECT OF THE DAUGHTER-IN-LAW'S OWN MOTHER

A daughter-in-law's relationship with her own mother has an important impact on her relationship with her mother-in-law. Not surprisingly, the absence of a mother in a daughter's life also impacts her relationship with her mother-in-law. What was surprising though was the high percentage of respondents (17 percent), all of whom had volunteered for a study of mother-in-law relationships, who had lost their own mothers. These women may spend more time thinking about their mother-in-law and their relationship to her. The role may also be more important to them. As such, they may have been more likely to volunteer for the study than other women. The effects of mother loss and the effects of the daughter-in-law's relationship with her mother on her relationship with her mother-in-law are discussed separately below.

Instances of Mother Loss and Its Effect on Mother-in-Law and Daughter-in-Law Relationships

Of the fifty-three daughters-in-law, 17 percent (or nine) had lost their mothers either as children or very young adults (up to age twenty-five).[15] One of the women had had two mothers-in-law though, making for a total of ten relationships for examination. Five out of ten (or 50 percent) of the relationships were poor in comparison to 40 percent of the overall population. This would suggest that not having a mother is somewhat more likely to harm one's relationship with a mother-in-law.

Only one of the women from the five poor relationships ("estranged" or "obligatory") truly tried to have a better relationship with her mother-in-law and was disappointed that her mother-in-law did not think she was "good enough" for her son. The other women seemed ambivalent to their relationships. One of these daughters-in-law had a poor relationship with her mother-in-law from the start because she was dating her current husband when he was still married to another woman. She did not seem disappointed with the "obligatory" relationship that she continued to have with her mother-in-law. Likewise, the daughter-in-law who had had two mothers-in-law stated:

> I always wanted someone to substitute as a mother. My mother was an intelligent, loving person. Neither of my mothers-in-law has been in the same league, either as people or relationships.... Maybe I held them off because they could not come close.

This is consistent with Hope Edelman's[16] findings that motherless daughters have difficulty creating close relationships with other women. Motherless daughters may also have idealistic expectations of mother-daughter relationships and thus be more dissatisfied by their relationships with their mothers-in-law.[17]

Not all was negative though. Two of the women did point out that they enjoyed their mothers-in-law *more* because they did not have their own mothers. Ellen stated,

> She really feels like a substitute mother. I treasure her more because my own mom has been sick for as long as I can remember. Like, we go out to lunch or go shopping. I never had someone call me and say, "Ellen, I will treat you to lunch. Let's go." She handed down all of the family recipes when we got married. I don't have any heirlooms like that from my own mother.

Likewise, Stephanie stated,

> My relationship with my mother-in-law is very good. My mother died when I was 23, and she has become a second mother. She is a very nice person, very thoughtful. She has even become a grandmother to my niece (my brother's daughter). She makes her beautiful mittens and comes to her recitals and brings her presents.

Thus, while not all women form substitute relationships with a mother-in-law as a result of mother loss, it is possible. It was more likely though that mother loss hindered relationships with mothers-in-law.

When Mothers Are Present in Adulthood

The remaining forty-four daughters-in-law all had mothers present during a significant part of their adulthood. Of these, only eight (or 15 percent of the total) described their relationships with their own mothers as poor or very poor. Interestingly, none of these eight had poor relationships with their mothers-in-law. In fact, half of them described very good or excellent relationships with their mothers-in-law.

Janet said that her own relationship with her mother was always poor. She added, "She was not warm, friendly or social. I would be in plays and things at school, and my parents never came. I called her Mother or Margaret. That says a lot." In contrast, when I asked about her mother-in-law, she became more lively and stated,

> She is like a first mother. I am closer to her than my own mother. She considers me like a daughter too. She treats everyone equally. She treats her children-in-law just like her children.

In contrast to her mother, she described her mother-in-law as being present at all of her children's events and an integral part of her own life. With her in-laws, she could be part of a large and loving family. In fact, she referred to her in-laws as "Mom" and "Dad." When I asked her to describe the difference in her relationships with her mother-in-law versus her mother, she stated, "I am friendly to my mother-in-law but not my mother. She is more affectionate. I feel closer to my mother-in-law."

Cindy offered a similar story. When I asked her to describe her relationship with her mother, she stated, "There has been family discord for a long time. We were never close. It is very strained. I think they feel threatened because I 'left the family.' You were expected to live on the same street with your family for the rest of your life, and I did not do that." In contrast, Cindy developed tears and began to cry whenever she described her relationship with her mother-in-law. She stated,

> It is a very loving relationship. I can call her at any moment for anything. I was able to confide in her during a difficult time with my husband.... On her 80th birthday, my sister-in-law said that her mother feels that she has two daughters. I think of her as a second mother too. I am much closer to my mother-in-law than my mother.

The remaining thirty-six daughters-in-law described their relationships with their mothers positively. Twelve of these women used glowing terms in their descriptions. For example, they described their mothers as their best friends. Among these, four had "tight-knit" or "distant but positive" relationships with their mothers-in-law, four had "cordial" or "conflicted but affectionate" relationships, and four had "obligatory" or "estranged" relationships with their mothers-in-law. That is, women with excellent relationships with their own moms are equally as likely to have poor, moderate, or very good relationships with their mothers-in-law. However, they comprise a smaller overall percentage of the women with "tight-knit" relationships with their mothers-in-law (43 percent versus 57 percent). That is, those with the closest relationships with their mothers-in-law are slightly less likely to have had very close relationships with their own mothers.

Not having a mother present in an adult woman's life hinders her relationship with her mother-in-law. This is consistent with Edelman's finding that mother loss impedes women's relationships with other women.[18] This does not negate, however, those few daughters-in-law who had mothers-in-law that substituted as mothers. However, when the relationship with one's mother is poor, daughters-in-law are more likely to have positive relationships with their mothers-in-law. Likewise, those with the closest relationships with their mothers-in-law are slightly less likely to have had very close relationships with their own mothers. Overall, these findings suggest that to some extent a very good relationship with a mother-in-law is a reflection of unmet needs and that in-law relationships can substitute for poor or

missing mother–daughter relationships. This implies some mirroring of biological and in-law relationships.

HAVING SOMETHING IN COMMON

Having something in common with one's mother-in-law was related to
whether the daughter-in-law had a good versus a poor relationship with her.
In particular, shared interests made a good relationship even better. Many of
the daughters-in-law with very good relationships described having a common regard for gardening, cooking, movies, antiquing, or reading, or they
jointly attended church, the theater and art exhibits, or Weight Watchers
and the gym. Half of the daughters-in-law with "tight-knit" or "distant but
close" relationships also felt like they had a similar outlook or personality as
their mothers-in-law. For example, several of the daughters-in-law explained
how they thought alike, had the same high level of energy, or had the same
way of raising their children (which could be important to a grandparent) as
their mother-in-law. Kristen said, "My mother-in-law is a goofy girl.... She
likes to have fun and to be around my kids; those things are important to
me too." Other daughters-in-law said that they and their mothers-in-law had
similar personalities. This was certainly true of Valerie and her mother-in-
law, Rosemary, who seemed like twins. These two women even finished one
another's sentences. They also had a similar lifestyle and outlook. For example, both of the women smoked frequently, something another in-law might
not have been comfortable around. Other daughters-in-law described how
their mothers-in-law took an interest in what was important to *them*. Jamie
explained how her mother-in-law would ask about the mundane things in
their lives, remember what Jamie had said, and then inquire again. Kristen's
mother-in-law went to Kristen's church with her even though religion was
not as important to her as it was to Kristen. Kristen said, "She makes a point
of coming with me because she knows that it is a big part of my life."

Those daughters-in-law with "estranged" or "obligatory" relationships
with their mothers-in-law had much less in common with them. Three of
the women said that they shared a common religion but nothing more.
One of the women said that she and her mother-in-law both liked being
with family. Another four pointed out that they shared their husband/son
and children/grandchildren, but that was all.

The likelihood that women develop a negative relationship with their
mothers-in-law if they have nothing in common is small, but possible.
However, not having something in common may make it harder to improve

a difficult relationship. Also, individuals in problematic relationships may not see when they have something in common, while those who are close may look for something to share or support one another's interests. As such, those with better relationships tended to have more in common or at least showed an interest in what was important to the other person. However, it is unlikely that the worst relationships would improve even if the women had a great deal in common. If women from two different families are to come together as one family, they need more than a tangential connection.

THE MOTHER-IN-LAW'S DAUGHTER(S)

None of the daughters-in-law mentioned their sisters-in-law as coming between them and their mothers-in-law or causing problems in their in-law relationships. However, several daughters-in-law mentioned that their mothers-in-law and sisters-in-law were much closer to one another than they were to them. This was not related to the quality of the relationship with their mother-in-law though. In other words, their perception of their mother-in-law's relationship with her daughters(s) did not affect how daughters-in-law got along with their mothers-in-law. However, two of the daughters-in-law mentioned having the same problems with their husbands' sister(s) as they had with their husbands' mother. In both situations, the daughter-in-law felt that the women interfered and were too opinionated. Relationships with sisters-in-law did not seem as central or important to the women's lives as relationships with mothers-in-law.

Not surprisingly, the majority of the mothers-in-law felt that they were closer to their own daughters than to their daughters-in-law. However, they were very careful to seem impartial. As one of the mothers-in-law stated, "I try to treat my daughters-in-law like my daughters because they are family as well." Kristen's mother-in-law diplomatically explained that she had a "special bond" with her daughter both because she could see herself in her daughter and because she had been through all of her daughter's trials and tribulations with her, neither of which she shared with her daughter-in-law.

Not all of the mothers ranked their daughters as closer though. Eighteen percent of the mothers-in-law interviewed said that they felt closer to their *daughter-in-law* than to their daughter(s). Two of these women were estranged from their daughters. Another explained the difference in her feelings by saying, "My own daughter is not as sensitive. She is more independent. Valerie [the daughter-in-law] is more lovable." These women were very clear though that their relationships with their daughters-in-law were not a substitute for their poor relationships with their daughters. For example, one of the women said,

> My daughter-in-law respects me while my daughter didn't. She would always argue and was very offensive with me. I feel closer to my daughter-in-law at this point. I am just angry with my daughter.... I don't think of her [my daughter-in-law] as a second daughter [though]. I think of her as being close to my family.

Many of the mothers-in-law mentioned that they had to be more careful of what they said to their daughters-in-law than to their own daughters (or sons) no matter how close they were. For example, one of the mothers-in-law said that if she disapproved of how one of her grandchildren was being raised, she would feel comfortable telling her son or daughter, but not his or her spouse. Grace said, "You have to be discreet. You don't want to seem like you are interfering." The converse was also true. Kim mentioned that her daughter-in-law was more cautious with her than her daughters were. She said, "My own daughters would tell me off, but Ellen has never done that. Ellen would swallow something."

Based on the daughters-in-law's descriptions, women with only sons, that is, no daughters, were more than twice as likely to have a negative relationship with their daughters-in-law than a positive one. This supports the finding that daughters-in-law are not necessarily substitutes for daughters. Only one of the daughters-in-law, with a "distant but positive" relationship, said that she and her mother-in-law's other daughters-in-law were particularly important to her mother-in-law because she did not have her own daughters. According to Lindy, "She sees herself as having daughters-in-law *replace* [emphasis my own] the daughters that she never had." This finding also raises the possibility that mothers may be closer to their sons when there are no daughters (and thus have a harder time accepting their wives). They may also be less knowledgeable of how to relate to a daughter-in-law when there is no daughter available.

THE RELATIONSHIP WITH THE MOTHER-IN-LAW'S OWN MOTHER-IN-LAW

A little over half of the mothers-in-law believed that they had a good to very good relationship with their own mother-in-law. One of the women had a poor relationship with one of her mothers-in-law but a very good relationship with the other one. All of the others had a poor to very poor relationship with their mother(s)-in-law.

The vast majority of the women felt that their own relationship with their mother-in-law affected the kind of mother-in-law that they became and hence their relationship with their daughter-in-law. Only two of the women said that it did not. One of them explained, "No, it had no effect. I am who I am." Those with good mothers-in-law believe that they have patterned themselves on their role models. One of the women said, "I appreciated her for not butting in. I am sure that I do the same thing." Another woman added,

> I could see the difference between the way that my mother-in-law treated people and the way that my mother treated people. I loved her [my mother-in-law] as much as my own mother. I didn't want to be one of those horror story mothers-in-law. I try to be like her—accepting of my sons-in-law and daughters-in-law.

Those with poor relationships with their own mothers-in-law believed that they were different with *their* daughters-in-law. In other words, they tried to be unlike their role models. One of the mothers-in-law said, "I would never yell at them or call them a bad name like my mother-in-law did. She would call me a bitch!" Another woman said, "I try hard to never be an interference because of my own experience. My mother-in-law tried every trick in the book to destroy our relationship! I vowed never to do that to my own children. In a way, I am glad that she was so difficult. It helped me to be a better mother-in-law." A more typical response though was the following: "Yes, it did affect the kind of mother-in-law that I am. My first mother-in-law tried to direct us too much. My second mother-in-law ... I didn't want to be as cold as she was. So I try to be different from both of them."

THE MOTHER-IN-LAW'S HEALTH AND CORESIDENCE

The mother-in-law's health needs were independent of her relationship with her daughter-in-law. That is, daughters-in-law were as likely to have a good relationship with their mothers-in-law as a poor relationship if the mother-in-law's health was poor. Likewise, many of those women with "obligatory" relationships provided care for their mothers-in-law despite their negative feelings.

What did make a difference in the in-law relationship though was whether or not the mother-in-law moved in with her son and daughter-in-law for financial or health reasons. Relationships, whether good or bad to begin with, worsened under these conditions. For example, Naomi's mother-in-law, Sylvie, moved in with her and her family after Sylvie's husband died. Naomi and her husband had been running all of Sylvie's errands for her and taking care of her. They invited Sylvie to move in because she had no social interaction. Naomi shared,

> It went from great to horrible! Things definitely changed when she moved in with us. We used to get along fine. But now it is like having company all the time—the guest who stayed too long. My husband does everything for her and waits on her. She is the queen of the house! You lose all of your privacy. When my husband comes home and has only a few hours in the evening, he has two people who want his attention. So I don't have much time alone with him. We are fighting for the same time slot.... We lost that sense of friendship. Last year I told her that the three of us need to talk. I said, "You are telling my husband things...that I left you only a sandwich for dinner." Now she goes to Florida for a few months in the winter. It is like Felix and Oscar trying to be roommates. She is so messy, and now I have to clean up after her. She tells my husband and son that I hurt her feelings, so I end up the bad guy. We just can't get along anymore.

A second daughter-in-law whose mother-in-law came to live with her experienced a similar decline in the relationship. Only one of the mother-in-law and daughter-in-law pairs continued to be "close knit" even after the daughter-in-law and son moved in with their mother (in-law) to help her out financially.

SUMMARY AND IMPLICATIONS

Results suggest that many factors affect the quality of the relationship between a daughter-in-law and her mother-in-law. These include several sociocultural variables, such as the daughter-in-law's ethnicity and education. Well-educated daughters-in-law and those with French or Italian backgrounds tended to have more "close-knit" relationships with their mothers-in-law. Well-educated daughters-in-law may be better at problem solving, while those from French and Italian backgrounds may be more accustomed to including extended family. Likewise, mothers-in-law may have more respect for well-educated daughters-in-law. In-law relationships are also affected by relationships between other family members such as the daughter-in-law's relationship with her own mother. Daughters-in-law whose mothers died or became unavailable due to mental illness while the daughters were children or still young adults tended to have poorer relationships with their mothers-in-law.

This is consistent with Edelman's finding that mother loss inhibits a daughter's relationship with other adult women.[19] Motherless daughters may have also had unrealistic expectations of what a relationship with a mother (and hence, a mother-in-law) would be like. However, daughters-in-law who had a poor relationship with their own mother were more likely to have a better relationship with their mother-in-law. These women may be more likely to turn to their mothers-in-law or to see the good in them when there are difficulties with their own mothers. Likewise, women with no daughters tended to have poorer relationships with their daughters-in-law. These women may have been closer to their sons than mothers with daughters and thus more resentful of their daughters-in-law. Another important factor in the quality of the relationship is the effect of the in-law's earlier history, and in particular, the daughter-in-law's perception of being accepted and welcomed early on into the family.

Together, these findings suggest that daughters-in-law do not necessarily substitute for daughters and mothers-in-law do not always substitute for mothers. In fact, the inability of either woman to model her expected in-law behavior by having biological kin in that same position makes it harder for the women to relate to one another as in-laws. That is, motherless women have a difficult time incorporating mothers-in-law into their lives, and daughterless mothers have a difficult time incorporating daughters-in-law. Some women though do find a second daughter in their daughters-in-law or a second mother in their mothers-in-law, particularly when mother–daughter relationships are not going well. Thus, there is some substitution when there is unmet need. This is certainly not the rule, however, and in-laws may be disappointed if their expectations are too high.

It is important though for mothers-in-law to make their daughters-in-law feel accepted and welcomed early on in the relationship. It is also important for daughters-in-law to bridge the gap between themselves and their mothers-in-law and to include them in the extended family. This may be second nature to women in some ethnic groups, but it is something that all daughters-in-law can do.

In-laws who are not getting along need to consider the importance of structural factors and their effect on the relationship. Class differences and the lack of a mother for the daughter-in-law or the lack of a daughter for the mother-in-law may impede the relationship. Often, however, women assume that the difficulties in the relationship are personal and are not able to see the importance of the structural context within which the relationship takes place. The next chapter will look at the effect of characteristics of the postmodern family on mother-in-law and daughter-in-law relationships.

Five

THE EFFECTS OF POSTMODERN FAMILY LIFE ON IN-LAW RELATIONSHIPS

I think that I have two mothers-in-law, but I would say that my first one is more of my mother-in-law. She has been in my life for thirty years. People ask me why I keep in touch with them.... Why wouldn't I?
—Becky (daughter-in-law)

This chapter looks at how various aspects of the postmodern family affect in-law relationships. The three factors to be considered include: divorce, geographic distance, and work and occupational mobility. With 43 percent of first marriages ending in separation or divorce within fifteen years of marriage,[1] generations often living far from one another, and more women working outside of the home than in previous generations, relationships between mothers-in-law and daughters-in-law are likely to be impacted. In-law relationships are complicated, but how and to what extent do various aspects of postmodern family life complicate them even more? This chapter also examines the format and nature of visits that take place when in-laws do live far from one another. These are referred to as "distant in-laws."

DIVORCE

The impact of divorce on in-law relationships can provide important insights into the meanings of those relationships. For example, if the relationship were mainly instrumental and the indirect result of the primary relationships between parent and son and grandparent and grandchild, then one would expect the in-law relationship to end or wane with divorce. If, instead, in-laws become family and form their own primary bonds, one would expect those relationships to continue in some form even after divorce. What earlier researchers have found though is an interesting mix of effects highlighting the complexity of the relationship. Whether in-law relationships continue after divorce depends on two things: how they were perceived during the marriage[2] and whether or not there are children involved.[3–5] Maintaining access to grandchildren following divorce is of greatest importance to parents-in-laws. Johnson argues that ex-in-laws redefine their relationships and initiate strategies to navigate (what becomes) a much more complicated web of relationships when there are children involved.[6] Divorced women, in particular, work to maintain these mutually supportive relationships, while men are less likely to continue contact with their in-laws.[7,8] This is likely due to the fact that mothers are usually the custodial parents and, therefore, their assistance is more necessary in maintaining ties to paternal grandparents. These findings and the fact that ex-affinal relationships begin to deteriorate immediately following separation[9] suggest that the relationships are mainly instrumental and based on primary relationships between other family members.

Interestingly, however, former in-laws are more likely to be included as primary kin following the loss of a spouse through death than through divorce.[10] Former in-laws may move toward a primary role to compensate for the loss of a loved one, either spouse or son, but do not create direct ties when the indirect ones are severed through divorce. One could predict that this would be even more likely if the divorce were a bitter one or if in-law relationships were poor prior to the divorce.

It is expected that divorce will affect intergenerational relationships in a number of ways depending in part on whose divorce it is. To begin with, we know that a *parent's* divorce differentially affects his or her relationship with an adult child, depending on the gender of both the parent and the child. Overall, divorced parents have less contact than married parents with their adult children.[11–13] Ties between the generations are more voluntary and less obligatory, and the typical exchanges between generations are absent. Divorced mothers, however, report receiving more advice, financial help, emotional support, and services from their children than do divorced fathers.[14] Almost half of mothers but less than one-fifth of fathers found their children to be their most helpful source of support following divorce.[15] However, children of divorce view relationships with both parents more negatively than do children of still married parents,[16] and the relationship is less likely to rebound between opposite sex ties (e.g., mothers and sons).[17,18] How then might a possible increase in the son's assistance to his divorced mother or a son's negative view of his mother affect the relationship that a daughter-in-law has with her mother-in-law?

A mother-in-law's divorce is not the only one that will likely impact the relationship. A *daughter-in-law's* earlier divorce or her *husband's* earlier divorce is also expected to affect the relationship between a mother-in-law and daughter-in-law. If a son has been divorced and has children with a previous wife, his mother may feel greater allegiance toward, or at least the need to keep in touch with, the other wife. If she and the second daughter-in-law do not share grandchildren/children, the bond between them may not be as strong. However, if the daughter-in-law role is based primarily on the shared connection to the husband/son, the lack of grandchildren should make little difference. A son's earlier divorce will also result in having fewer shared life events that bring the women together. Likewise, a daughter-in-law's earlier divorce may mean that her children's grandmother is not her mother-in-law. Without this shared bond, the two women may not be as close or have as great a sense of being family. By looking at which of her two mothers-in-law a woman feels closest to (her children's grandmother or her current husband's mother), we will learn more about the nature of in-law bonds.

The Influence of a Daughter-in-Law's Earlier Marriage

Nearly one-quarter, or 21 percent, of the daughters-in-law in this study had previously been married. The majority of these, 55 percent, had a negative, that is, an "estranged" or "obligatory," relationship with their current mother-in-law. This is in comparison to 40 percent of the overall sample of daughters-in-law. In contrast, 18 percent had a "tight-knit" or "distant but positive" relationship (versus 38 percent of the overall sample), and 27 percent had a "cordial" or "conflicted but affectionate" relationship (versus 23 percent). Why would women who have been divorced be so much more likely to have a negative relationship with their mothers-in-law? An important key to understanding this is that those women who had a *positive* relationship were the only ones who stated that their mothers-in-law treated their children from their former marriage like the other biological grandchildren. All of the other women with children from a former marriage felt that their mothers-in-law treated those children differently, with it being much more noticeable to those women with an "estranged" relationship with their mothers-in-law. Interestingly though, one of the mothers-in-law made a point of mentioning that it was her daughter-in-law's little girl who drew her to the daughter-in-law when she was first dating her son and that she had had to "back off" when she became too attached to the child. Overall though, treating a daughter-in-law's children from a former marriage like one's own biological grandchildren enhances in-law relationships. Because this often does not happen though, divorced women are more likely to have poor relationships with their mothers-in-law.

Only one of the daughters-in-law felt that she had a good relationship with both of her mothers-in-law. A second daughter-in-law was very close to her first mother-in-law but did not get along well with either her second or third mother-in-law. All of the other daughters-in-law with a current "estranged" relationship had a poor relationship with both mothers-in-law. Why would this be the case? It may be that those women who divorce are less likely to get along with in-laws overall or that those women whose first in-law relationships were bad were less likely to invest in a relationship with their second mother-in-law. Only one of the women had a poor relationship with her first mother-in-law and a better relationship with her second mother-in-law.

Unexpectedly, one of the daughters-in-law said that she considered her first mother-in-law to be more of a mother-in-law to her than her current mother-in-law. Becky said that it was because she had known her first mother-in-law for over thirty years (since she was twelve years old), whereas she has known her second mother-in-law for only three years (although she had known *of her* throughout her adulthood). For Becky then, the mother-in-law relationship is based more on her own individual connection to someone rather than it being defined by her marriage and husband. Her first mother-in-law was also the grandmother of her children, and she took Becky and her children into her home when Becky separated from her abusive husband, their son. Becky then has experience with being able to count on these in-laws when necessary.

Patti did not consider her first husband's mother to be her mother-in-law once she and her husband split up. However, she did not consider her second husband's mother to be a mother-in-law either because she had never played any sort of mother-in-law role (she had been opposed to her son marrying Patti). Patti rarely saw her second husband's mother and did not talk to her on the phone. For Patti then, a mother-in-law at least has to be her husband's mother, but she also has to have some sort of personal relationship as well.

It was most common for women to define their mother-in-law as their current husband's mother. Nina knew her first mother-in-law while she was a teenager and shared a child/grandchild with this first mother-in-law. Yet, she considered her current husband's mother to be her mother-in-law even though she has had a much poorer relationship with this woman and did not share a child/grandchild with her. Nina did say though that she still considered her first mother-in-law to be family and that she would do anything for her. Other women also felt that their former husband's mother was no longer their mother-in-law.

Most of the women had little contact with their former in-laws. Becky was by far the exception. As stated earlier, she still considered her ex-husband's parents to be her in-laws. In addition to their formal relationship based on the children, Becky enjoyed spending time with them. They went to the movies together, played cards, or went blueberry picking with one another. In fact, Becky's mother and both sets of in-laws went on day trips together, and all four families gathered together for the holidays.

The other women had much more limited contact with their former mothers-in-law. Allison felt that she and her former in-laws were pleasant around one another, but they did not go out of their way to see one another. Karen saw her former mother-in-law at events for her sons and used to see her when she visited while Karen's sons were still living at home. Other than that, they had very little contact. Karen explained, "I just try to fend her off, keep her from being intrusive in my life." Nina and her mother-in-law were exceptional in that they sometimes went out together for dinner, as well as seeing one another at parties for their son/grandson.

The remaining daughters-in-law had almost no contact with their former mothers-in-law. They did not invite former in-laws to their children's birthday parties nor did they exchange pleasantries when their former in-laws called their children. Those women without (grand)children at home had no reason even to call one another. There was one exception to this. Toni kept in touch with her mother-in-law years after her divorce even without children/grandchildren. The two women made a special point of getting together once or twice a year (they lived approximately two hours from one another) and exchanged letters. Toni was very pleased that her mother-in-law still referred to her as her daughter-in-law.

Former mothers-in-law were more positive about the relationship. Patti's mother-in-law Sandy still considered Patti to be a daughter-in-law even though Patti did not think this. Sandy stated, "Oh, yes, Patti is still my daughter-in-law. We have an extended family from all kinds of places. We reach out. We are that kind of a family." Although she got along better with her son's second wife, she felt that she and Patti had become closer since the divorce and that Patti appreciated their family more than she had in the past (Patti did not share this opinion). Claire said that her relationship with her daughter-in-law was strained when she was first divorced due to the acrimony surrounding the break-up. She felt that her first daughter-in-law was still a daughter-in-law although she had shared grandchildren more with her second daughter-in-law. For Claire then, being a mother-in-law could be based equally on a personal connection or shared family members.

The Effect of the Son's Prior Divorce

Whether or not the son/husband had been divorced significantly impacted the current daughter-in-law's relationship with her mother-in-law. Fifteen percent of the daughters-in-law were married to divorced men. Of these, 62 percent of the women had a positive relationship ("tight knit" or "distant but positive") compared with 38 percent of the overall sample, while 38 percent had a negative relationship ("obligatory" or "estranged") compared with 40 percent of the overall sample. Women with divorced husbands did not have "cordial" or "conflicted but affectionate" relationships though. Mothers-in-law may be very appreciative of their current daughters-in-law having seen their sons go through an earlier divorce. What also makes a difference in how well a mother-in-law gets along with her second daughter-in-law though is how well she got along with her first daughter-in-law, but the effect is in the unexpected direction. That is, all of the second daughters-in-law who had a positive relationship with their mothers-in-law stated that their mothers-in-law did *not* get along with their sons' first wives. In addition, those women with "estranged" or "obligatory" relationships believed that their mothers-in-law preferred their first daughters-in-law to them. Whether this is true or not, the daughter-in-law's perception of the earlier relationship is important in determining her own relationship with her mother-in-law.

Those daughters-in-law with "tight-knit" or "distant but positive" relationships with their mothers-in-law believed that their mothers-in-law were either currently or previously unhappy with their first daughters-in-law. Debbie stated, "I think on some level, Sheila [the mother-in-law] has some anger with Patti now because the divorce came out of the blue. [Husband's name] wasn't expecting it or prepared. Other than that, she treats us both the same." Sheila did not mention being angry with Patti, but she did say that she had maintained her distance from Patti during their marriage because she thought it was best for the marriage. Patti had had a difficult relationship with her first mother-in-law, and Sheila was afraid that she would "open old wounds." Sheila did not have these problems with Debbie. She felt that Debbie "gave 110 percent" and was "more mindful of [Sheila's] needs." Debbie had a "distant but positive" relationship with Sheila.

There were others in this same situation. Millie felt that her mother-in-law, with whom she had a "tight-knit" relationship, had little regard for her son's first wife. Millie explained, "She [the first wife] was a flake. She left the children alone when they were little. Lynn would go look in on them and stay with them. My mother-in-law did not like the things she saw. I know she was concerned. There might have even been conflict." Two other daughters-in-law who were very close to their mothers-in-law said that their husbands' first wives had bipolar disorder and that this had made the relationships with their mothers-in-law very strained.

Unexpectedly, mothers-in-law did not necessarily prefer their first daughters-in-law when they were the mothers of their grandchildren. In fact, all of the mothers-in-law with positive relationships with their second daughters-in-law had grandchildren from the son's first marriage and not his second. For these mothers-in-law then, in-law bonds were not based on sharing grandchildren. One of the daughters-in-law did say though that her mother-in-law was angry with her son for not spending more time with his children from his first marriage, especially because their mother had bipolar disorder. Toni felt that this anger did not extend to her as their stepmother though.

All of those women who felt that their mother-in-law preferred her first daughter-in-law had either an "estranged" or "obligatory" relationship with her. Alexa, for example, stated,

> She treated my husband's first wife more like a daughter. She [the first wife] was a big drinker, and they drink too. She had the only grandkids for a while. They lived close too. Mary [the first wife] depended on them a lot. My step-kids would be at my mother-in-law's house all the time.

However, Alexa too had children with the son. Alexa felt that her mother-in-law did not think her son should have had a "second family" though, and so she ignored Alexa and the grandsons.

Nearly one-quarter (23 percent) of the mothers-in-law who were interviewed had sons who had been married two or more times. All four of these mothers-in-law had grandchildren from theirs sons' first marriages, and two had grandchildren from the sons' second marriages as well. They all stated that they kept in touch with their first daughters-in-law, in part to be close to their grandchildren. In addition, they all felt that *both* of the women were still daughters-in-law. Claire pointed out though that if she had to pick one as her daughter-in-law, it would be her son's current wife "no matter who that was."

The Effect of the Mother-in-Law's Divorce

Fifteen percent of the daughters-in-law had mothers-in-law who were divorced. However, they were spread equally across the categories of relationship types. That is, having a mother-in-law who is divorced does not affect the type of relationship that one has with her.

Most of the daughters-in-law felt that their mother-in-law's divorce had no impact on them. Two of the daughters-in-law stated that their husbands did not help their mothers anymore because they were divorced. Two other daughters-in-law said that they and their husbands did provide more help, but they did not mind doing so. While they did not provide financial assistance, they ran errands for the husband's mother and helped with heavy lifting and home repairs. Rebecca was just grateful that she lived close to her mother-in-law so that she did not have to travel far to help her. Her mother-in-law had actually become more *in*dependent following her divorce and would not ask for help. Like the others, Rebecca and her husband volunteered to help his mother. In contrast, Sydney did mind her husband spending time helping his mother. She stated, "I get aggravated because she makes it a big long session." Sydney did not feel that that was the source of their "estranged" relationship though. Sydney believed that her mother-in-law's mental illness, brought on by years of abuse, was the real culprit. Furthermore, she was very bitter that her mother-in-law had not removed herself and her children from her abusive husband until her children were adults. Only one of the daughters-in-law felt that her relationship with her mother-in-law improved following a divorce because she did not get along well with her father-in-law.

Only two of the daughters-in-law felt that their mother-in-law's divorce had any sort of negative effect on them. Suzanne felt that her mother-in-law was very unhappy following her divorce and that this had created some tension between her mother-in-law and her and her husband. In addition, Nicole felt that her mother-in-law, Fiona, had become very possessive of her sons since her divorce. Nicole saw Fiona's divorce and her subsequent insecurity as the culprit for their "estranged" relationship. When I asked Nicole what might improve her relationship with Fiona, she said, "If she got her own man." Nicole felt that Fiona tried to rely heavily on her sons for both emotional and instrumental assistance, but that it was difficult because of the geographic distance. Nicole believed that she would have a better relationship with her mother-in-law if she was still married and depended less on her sons. Nicole also pointed out that her mother-in-law did not have a good opinion of marriage, including Nicole and Scott's marriage, due to her own divorce.

THE EFFECT OF EMPLOYMENT AND OCCUPATIONAL MOBILITY

There have been significant changes in the number of women working and the types of jobs that they have had between the decades in which contemporary mothers-in-law were working and raising a family and today. In the 1950s, when today's older mothers-in-law were in their thirties, only 12.6 percent of married mothers with children under the age of seventeen worked outside of the home. By 1994, when today's youngest daughters-in-law were entering the job market, 69 percent of the comparable group of mothers and 58.8 percent of wives with children one year of age and younger worked outside of the home. In addition, fewer of these jobs were part-time in comparison to fifty years ago. More is also expected of today's workers. Over the past two decades, the average worker has added an extra 164 hours (or the equivalent of one month of work) of work per year.[19]

It was expected that working outside of the home would impact a daughter-in-law's relationship with her mother-in-law. Daughters-in-law who work outside of the home will have a very different lifestyle and experience from their mothers-in-law who were and are home full-time. Employed daughters-in-law will also have less time to visit with their mothers-in-law versus previous generations of women.

It was also expected that differences in the types of jobs that women have would also make a difference in their relationship. Today's daughters-in-law, with higher levels of education, have more opportunities for professional and higher level jobs. This again raises the possibility of differences in lifestyle that can affect in-law relationships.

Surprisingly, only 43 percent of the daughters-in-law had mothers-in-law who were primarily housewives throughout their lives. The other 57 percent of daughters-in-law had mothers-in-law who had worked, if even part-time, at some point during their marriage. This is much higher than the overall estimates for the 1950s, although the women certainly could have worked later in life when their children were adults. In contrast, 72 percent of the daughters-in-law themselves were primarily working outside of the home during their marriages. Only 28 percent had primarily been house-wives. Most of the mothers-in-law worked in sales, bookkeeping, social work, or clerical/administrative positions. The daughters-in-law, however, included engineers, hospital administrators, editors, nurses, public adminis-trators, business executives, and professors.

As stated earlier, 28 percent of the daughters-in-law were housewives. Of these, a somewhat higher percentage had negative relationships with their mothers-in-law compared with the overall sample (53 percent versus 40 percent). Likewise, 27 percent of the housewives had a positive relationship compared with 38 percent of the overall sample. Why would housewives be more likely to have an "estranged" or "obligatory" relationship with their mothers-in-law? This may be the result of education. Women who were housewives had lower levels of education, and education is positively related to having a good relationship with one's mother-in-law.

What did impact in-law relationships was whether or not professional daughters-in-law believed that their mothers-in-law appreciated the fact that they worked and what that work meant to them. Lindy, for example, was a professional wife and mother whose mother-in-law had not worked outside of the home. Lindy believed that her mother-in-law took much of her iden-tity from her husband, an upper level executive, and her four sons. When I asked Lindy if there was anything that she would want to say to her mother-in-law, she replied,

> I would tell her how much I love her son and that it is also important for her to recognize that I am a separate person with my own identity.... It is a lack of recognition [on my mother-in-law's part] that many women have identities separate from being mothers and spouses and that that identity for many women, such as myself, matters a lot. Like my identity with my work is important to me. My mother-in-law doesn't really realize that I work full-time and that that is important to me.

Like Lindy, Sally was the only daughter-in-law (or daughter) in her hus-band's extended family who worked outside of the home. Sally felt that this was one of the sources of tension in her relationship with her mother-in-law. For example, the other women in the family were flexible in scheduling family visits, while Sally had to shorten them due to her work. Sally felt that her mother-in-law could not understand why Sally continued to work after her son was born. When I interviewed her mother-in-law though, June mentioned how much she enjoyed observing her daughter-in-law at work and that she liked to read some of the books that were important to Sally's work. She seemed very proud of Sally's work even if she might not have fully understood how it impacted Sally's availability for family gatherings. Both of these are examples of the generational differences that can come between mothers-in-law and daughters-in-law.

THE EFFECT OF GEOGRAPHIC DISTANCE

Contrary to the alarmist cries of the press, most older people are not isolated from their children. Instead, the majority of older parents have at least one child living close by. Among those who do not *live with* a child, about three-quarters live within a 35-minute drive of the nearest child, and one-quarter have a child less than one mile away.[20] However, not all children live close by, and distant living is at least common for elderly parents and adult children. One-quarter of all elders have no living child closer than 100 to 200 miles, and 50 percent have at least one distant-living child.[21] Factors positively associated with parents and children living further from one another include the parent's health status and socioeconomic status, child's age, parent's marital status (being divorced or separated), and younger age of parents.[22] While distance limits personal contact, it does not affect the quality of parent–child relationships.[23,24] Distant children keep in touch with parents through infrequent overnight visits, telephone conversations, and letters.[25] Older persons do prefer living in their own homes as opposed to living with their children, referred to as "intimacy at a distance."[26,27] This, however, does not mean that they prefer distant living.

Author Jacob Climo[28] argues that distant living creates ambivalence in intergenerational relationships. In his study of adult children living at least 200 miles from their parents, he found that children experienced a gnawing sense that key elements of family protection, support, and security were missing even among children who were well adapted to the distance. According to his findings, distance precludes the continuity that is necessary to maintain relationships as they undergo change and to resolve earlier conflict. Communications and contacts are too infrequent and less meaningful.[29] Children want to be solicitous of their parents' health and well-being but also do not want to be burdened by problems that they cannot fix. Children sometimes feel conflict when they cannot provide services that they feel they should.

If relationships between parents and adult children are affected by distant living, relationships between in-laws may also be impacted. Mothers-in-law and daughters-in-law will have less opportunity to get to know one another and to create a shared history. While there may be less opportunity for conflict to develop, there will also be less opportunity to resolve it. Time spent together will include infrequent but intense visits, with extended contact hours.

The vast majority of the daughters-in-law in this study (70 percent) lived near (i.e., less than one hour away from) their in-laws. Thirteen percent lived between one and three hours away, while 17 percent lived further away. This latter group included those who had to fly to visit their in-laws.

Distant living does indeed have some effect on in-law relationships. Among those daughters-in-law who lived one hour or more from their in-laws, 31 percent had a positive relationship compared with 38 percent of the overall sample. In addition, 38 percent of the distant in-laws had a "cordial" or "conflicted but affectionate" relationship compared with 23 percent of the overall sample, and another 31 percent of the distant in-laws had an "estranged" or "obligatory" relationship compared with 40 percent of the overall sample. Why would those daughters-in-law who lived far from their in-laws be so much more likely to have a "cordial" relationship in particular? These daughters-in-law are able to "afford" a cordial relationship precisely because they are so far away. Because they see one another less frequently, they are able to maintain a genial veneer that might not be possible if they saw one another regularly. In these latter circumstances, there would be much more conflict. Those who lived closer would either have to work through their differences or live with greater conflict, possibly becoming estranged from one another. In addition, distant in-laws are less likely to have an "obligatory" relationship because there are fewer obligations when you live far from one another. Nor are distant relationships likely to be "estranged." They can be "cordial" because in-laws see one another less frequently.

The majority of the daughters-in-law with "distant but positive" relationships felt that the distance did not affect their relationship. However, several wished that they lived closer. Libby, for example, stated, "I wish that we were nearer. Paul's parents never, ever came to visit us because his father traveled for work and did not think that traveling was a vacation. After his father died and the kids were born, his mother started to visit but not often enough to make a difference [in their relationship with her]." Another daughter-in-law helped her mother-in-law to move closer to her and her husband. She explained,

> She is closer now [seventy-five minutes versus four hours]. I have more opportunity to include her now which I like to do. She is ninety. They are not as close as they should be though. They [her husband and sister-in-law] pay no respect to her. I tell him to be nicer to her. She appreciates the fact that I try to be nice to her.

Other daughters-in-law felt that the distance did not make a difference and that they would be emotionally close to their mother-in-law whether she lived near or not. Toni, who lives a little over an hour from her mother-in-law, shared the following: "It doesn't make a difference either way. She would never come unannounced. She is not one to interfere." To Toni then, living closer would not be a problem but neither is the distance difficult.

Only a minority of the daughters-in-law with positive relationships felt that the distance was actually good. Lindy felt that the 3,000 miles separating her from her mother-in-law kept her controlling mother-in-law "at arm's length," which aided their relationship. She explained, "It probably makes relations easier that we don't see one another frequently. We have our own lives separate from her life and therefore less chance for interference. Otherwise, it would be stressful because she wants to be the matriarch."

Daughters-in-law with "cordial" or "conflicted but affectionate" relationships saw the distance as positive but recognized that there were some limitations. Stephanie was pleased when her in-laws moved from New York to Florida because it gave them more interests and hobbies and diverted their obsessive attention away from Stephanie and her family. However, the drawback was that it was difficult to manage her mother-in-law's care from a distance now that she was disabled by a stroke. All of the responsibility for her mother-in-law's care fell to Stephanie's husband, the only child living in the United States.

Other daughters-in-law with "cordial" or "conflicted but affectionate" relationships saw the distance as nonproblematic. For example, one of the daughters-in-law who lived three hours from her mother-in-law said, "It is perfect. I actually consider [her mother-in-law's location] to be close. We can get there if we need to. But at the same time, she is not on top of us. She has her own life and likes it that way. She would never consider living here." Another daughter-in-law believed that being able to make phone calls made up for the distance. She said, "I feel close to her anyway. By talking to her on the phone, you feel like she is right there anyway. I talk to her quite a bit."

Kathleen, however, admitted that she and her husband deliberately moved away from their parents although she equivocated on whether that was optimal. Consider her statement:

> My husband wanted to move away so that we could get away from family issues... on both sides. It is good that we are far enough away to do our own thing but close enough that they can come for a picnic.... Sometimes I think that we miss out by not being closer. We might be closer if we lived closer. We would probably spend more time with them.

All of the distant daughters-in-law with an "estranged" or "obligatory" relationship saw the geographic distance as a good thing. Nicole's statement is an example of a typical response. She said, "It is better that she is 1,000 miles away. We had to set boundaries with her. Distance means that we don't have to fight battles on a regular basis." Stacey's in-laws, who are 2,500 miles away, lived in the same town as Stacey when she and her husband were dating. According to her, "If they lived nearby, we wouldn't be married. When they are around, they put a strain on the relationship. It [the distance] makes it better. We don't have to see their stupidity daily.... We don't have to worry who to visit on holidays."

Interestingly, all of the distant daughters-in-law with an "estranged" or "obligatory" relationship lived more than three hours away from their in-laws. Extensive distance may increase the likelihood of a relationship becoming "estranged" because the in-laws do not have the opportunity to work out their differences and conflict remains. Although it cannot be tested in this study, distance may also prevent "estranged" relationships from resulting in divorce.

VISITS

Approximately 30 percent of the daughters-in-law lived one hour or more from their in-laws. Visits between these in-laws were much less likely to be spontaneous and occurred less frequently compared with the visits of those who lived nearby. Still, among those with distant in-laws, 31 percent saw them relatively frequently (every other week to every three months). It was also common for in-laws to see one another once or twice a year (38 percent). In-laws who saw one another only once a year (13 percent) or less than once a year (19 percent) were in the minority. All of the daughters-in-law in these last two categories lived more than three hours away. In-laws who lived a distance from one another though spent intensive periods of time together when they did visit. Kathleen, who saw her in-laws most frequently with bi-monthly visits, still spent three hours with them every other weekend. Those who lived three or more hours from one another spent a minimum of two or three days together and up to two weeks together. This drastically changes the nature of the visit when in-laws spend so much time together, as will be discussed below.

Mothers-in-law were most likely to visit their son and daughter-in-law's home than vice versa (38 percent versus 25 percent). According to the daughters-in-law, it was easier for their in-laws to visit them because of their children's school schedules and the extra expense of flying with children. As important though, many of the mothers-in-law visited their sons' homes because the daughters-in-law refused to stay in their mothers-in-law's homes. Those daughters-in-law had the worst relationships with their mothers-in-law. In contrast, 31 percent of the distant in-laws visited one another; that is, both generations made visits. These were among the best relationships, according to the daughters-in-law. Only one of the daughters-in-law (7 percent) visited her mother-in-law in a separate town. Janette and her husband met her mother-in-law at her brother-in-law's house. Janette's mother-in-law always stayed with this son, who had more room in his home. Those daughters-in-law who visited their in-laws exclusively did so because one of the parents was incapacitated or their in-law insisted on it. For example, Libby and her husband visited her in-laws exclusively when her father-in-law traveled for work.

Visits with distant in-laws usually took the format of an overnight, long-term stay. The vast majority of these necessitated staying in one another's homes. Sally though insisted that her in-laws stay in a nearby hotel, in part because their home was small but also because she felt the need to set boundaries with her mother-in-law. She required that her in-laws spend a portion of each day away from their home so that Sally and her family could have some time alone during the visit. Two other daughters-in-law stayed at an alternative location while visiting their in-laws. Lindy and her family usually stayed at her brother-in-law's home rather than her mother-in-law's house so that they were not "under the same roof" and she was not on her mother-in-law's "turf." In earlier years, Lindy and her husband had actually lived with her in-laws though. Stephanie and her family stayed in a hotel when they visited because her mother-in-law was in a nursing home. Prior to that, they too had stayed in their in-law's home. Stephanie pointed out though that staying in the hotel made the visit seem more like a vacation.

Those in-laws who saw one another more than once a year tended to get together for holidays and the children/grandchildren's birthdays and activities. For example, Jane's mother-in-law visited during the high holy days and on the children's birthdays. In addition, Jane and her family visited her mother-in-law during long weekends. Her mother-in-law lived in a major city that allowed Jane and the family opportunities for sightseeing. The entire family (including Jane's sister-in-law and her family) got together once every year or two as well. Ginny's relatives also visited to participate in the children's activities and to share holidays. Ginny and her family also spent long weekends and vacations with their in-laws, who lived in a vacation community. Ginny had to convince her mother-in-law though that she and her family visited to spend time with them and not just to vacation.

A few of the daughters-in-law had difficulty finding things for their in-laws to do when they visited. This was particularly the case if there were no children/grandchildren or the children were too old to want to spend time with grandparents. Debbie's mother-in-law would tell her that she was bored and would then leave after a few days. Patti's in-laws would help with house projects as a way to pass the time together. It was Jane, however, who was most concerned about her mother-in-law's unoccupied time during visits. She shared the following:

> Visits have gotten harder as the kids have gotten older and I work at home. She has nothing to do; she just hangs around. It is stressful for me because she is in my space. It would be better if she came for a long weekend, not a week.... I feel like maybe I shouldn't work, but then I feel resentful about that.

In-law visits changed over time. For example, Stephanie and her husband started out their marriage twenty years ago with visiting her in-laws every few months for the weekend. They stopped going though because her in-laws controlled their stays. For example, Stephanie and her husband would tell his parents that they planned on spending Saturday with friends. When they would arrive, Stephanie's in-laws would inform them that they had made an appointment for Saturday on the other side of the city and thus needed to be driven there. As a result of this and because of the arrival of their children, Stephanie and Robert started visiting only twice a year. Once Stephanie's mother-in-law was in a nursing home and her father-in-law was deceased, they visited only once a year and stayed in a hotel. They spent anywhere from twenty minutes to two hours each day with Robert's mother. Most of their time was spent with their young children though on the beach.

The tenor of the visits varied considerably. Ginny described her time with her in-laws as being a great deal of fun. She explained, "They feed us constantly. It is noisy, boisterous, and active. It is typical Italian ... always fun and enjoyable." In contrast, Stacy refused to visit her in-laws after her initial visit of two weeks, and she refused to allow her in-laws to stay with them when they visited the area. She described their visit to her home as follows:

> They stayed with us a couple of times at the beginning, but never again. Woo, no! Slob city. They left garbage everywhere. They brought their bags in and just dropped them in the entryway. I had to move them to their room little by little. They don't do anything ... just watch TV.... By the time that they left, my husband and I were at each other's throats.

Sally spent her time with her in-laws making sure that they respected the boundaries that she and Steve established. She also tried to spend as much time as she could alone when she visited them. Among those with distant in-laws, nearly half (44 percent) described their visits as being tense or uncomfortable.

Friction during visits wasn't always between the in-laws though. Debbie said that there was endless tension between her husband and his mother when she visited. She stated, "My husband is constantly shouting at her when she visits. That is how their family is ... always shouting. [My husband] tells her the minute that she comes through the door not to move things, not to rearrange things. She tells him what to do, not me though."

The quality of the visits depended, in part, on where they took place. Lindy explained that her visits to her husband's family were relatively easy because they did not stay at her parents-in-law's home. They would get together with Todd's parents for dinner and with the entire family for a barbeque during their visits. The family barbeques were somewhat stressful though because of her mother-in-law's need to "play the family matriarch." Lindy, her husband, and his parents took a trip to France once that was even more enjoyable because "no one was on anybody's territory." In contrast, Lindy felt that her in-laws' visits to her home were stressful. She explained,

> Stressful in me working full-time and having a toddler and being pregnant and feeling that I have to accommodate [them]. It is frustrating that she and my father-in-law want things done for them immediately and not realizing that there is give and take and things cannot be priority number one for them all of the time.

These problems would not have surfaced though if Lindy's in-laws were not staying in her home where they were guests. Those in-laws who wish to improve their visits with one another might consider the effect of the location.

SUMMARY AND IMPLICATIONS

Various aspects of postmodern family life do affect relationships between mothers-in-law and daughters-in-law. According to the results of this study, they both improve and hinder the relationship. Unexpectedly, a daughter-in-law's employment has very little effect. There was no significant difference by employment status, even among those employed women whose mothers-in-law had primarily been housewives during their years of marriage. In contrast, a daughter-in-law's level of *education* was associated with higher quality relationships, as was reported in the last chapter. There was some generational lag, however. Several of the professional women felt that their in-laws did not fully appreciate what their work meant to them, which hindered their relationship. Geographic distance had an effect. Those daughters-in-law who lived some distance from their in-laws were more likely to have a "cordial" relationship and were less likely to have an "estranged" relationship compared with the overall sample. It is easier to get along with someone, if even superficially, if the person lives further away. Those distant daughters-in-law with an "estranged" relationship saw the distance as good though. This group of daughters-in-law lived more than three hours away from their mothers-in-law. Extensive distance may decrease the need to work out differences but also prevent divorce from occurring.

Visits with distant in-laws ran the gamut from being fun to being highly stressful. Nearly half of the daughters-in-law with distant mothers-in-law described their visits as tense or uncomfortable. These visits had the added challenge of occurring over a long time (up to two weeks) with near constant interaction. Like the relationships themselves, visits changed over time. In particular, visits tended to become shorter and more infrequent over time. This was, in part, the result of having less time as children/ grandchildren's activities increased, as well as a desire to spend less time together in difficult relationships. The tenor of visits also varied somewhat by where they took place.

The prior divorce of the daughter-in-law or son also made a difference, although whether or not the mother-in-law was divorced did not matter. Divorced women were more likely to have a negative relationship with their mothers-in-law. However, this was, in part, dependent on the mother-in-law's attitude towards the woman's children from her first marriage. In contrast, daughters-in-law were more likely to have a *positive* relationship with their mothers-in-law if their husbands had been divorced. This too was dependent, but it was dependent on how well the mother-in-law got along with her first daughter-in-law. That is, daughters-in-law were more likely to have a positive relationship with their mother-in-law if she had not been close to her first daughter-in-law.

Asking respondents which of their in-laws, current or divorced, was their actual in-law provided insight into the nature of in-law ties. Mothers-in-law identified their daughter-in-law as their son's wife, although who was the mother of their grandchildren did not make a difference. Likewise, the majority of daughters-in-law identified their husband's mother over their children's grandmother as their mother-in-law. Sharing children/ grandchildren and spending time together did deepen the relationship though. In a society in which the divorce rate is so high, what does this then do for the stability of the relationship? All except for one of the daughters-in-law expected her relationship to continue with her mother-in-law indefinitely, although several pointed out that it would end if something happened to their husband. What is important though is that all but one thought that the relationship would continue because they thought that their marriage would continue. Thus, while divorce may be happening around them, they do not expect it to affect their family and thus their tie to their mother-in-law.

What do these findings then mean for the future of in-law relationships in the postmodern age? Although divorce has leveled off and even slightly decreased since the early 1980s,[30-32] it is still quite high with a 43 percent likelihood of new marriages ending in divorce.[33] Divorce will continue to complicate family relationships of all types, including in-law relationships. It is good to know though that it does not mean the demise of these relationships. If anything, prior divorce can improve in-law relationships when mothers-in-law treat children from a previous marriage like the other grandchildren and when divorce results in a greater appreciation of the in-law. Likewise, some in-laws do maintain close relationships even after divorce, although they are in the minority. As cohorts move through the life cycle, we should see more parents-in-law who are also divorced. Results of this study suggest that this will not make a difference though in a mother-in-law's relationship with her daughter-in-law.

Geographic mobility is also likely to continue, in part due to the information age as well as globalization. For the women in this sample, that distance did not prove to be problematic for their relationships with their mothers-in-law. As one of the daughters-in-law pointed out though, it becomes more problematic when in-laws (and parents) begin to require care. Many in-laws may choose to move closer to their in-laws. However, as we saw in the previous chapter, coresidence does significantly harm the relationship. Today's daughters-in-law will also have fewer sisters-in-law to turn to for care giving due to the decline in the fertility rate following the middle 1960s.[33]

Other changes in the postmodern family will introduce new in-law relationships. Same-sex marriages in Massachusetts and civil unions in other states will legally formalize what have been informal relationships to date and thus normalize relationships between in-laws. How this changes those relationships and whether (and how) in-laws from same-sex marriages are similar to other in-laws remains to be seen. The possibility of moving from civil marriages to civil unions for all couples, advocated by philosopher Mary Lyndon Shanley,[34] would result in even greater transformation of in-law relationships, likely making in-law relationships more informal bonds that exist outside of the boundaries of the extended family. This and other possibilities loom in the distance as the postmodern American family continues to undergo a period of significant transformation.

Six

THE MAKING OF A
DAUGHTER-IN-LAW:
THE DEVELOPMENT OF
THE IN-LAW ROLE AND
THE CREATION OF IDENTITY

We were still babies when we were dating. She still had kids at home. She disapproved of our living together, but it was the seventies.... Something changed [when we got married]. I really became part of the family. I felt different. Now it was complete.... It has slowly evolved into me loving her.

—Sue (daughter-in-law)

Theorist Zygmunt Bauman argues that modernity's emphasis on the individual has resulted in the destruction of the norms and infrastructure by which people live and measure their lives. Individuals are on their own then to construct themselves and to develop an identity without institutional support. It becomes the right of the individual to be different from or similar to others and to pick and choose his or her own models of happiness and a fitting life style.[1,2] Thus, all individuals create their own identity for various statuses.

Certainly, not all norms have been destroyed for the postmodern family, however. There are still highly engrained expectations that guide our behaviors and experiences as family members. For example, while there is some fluidity in women's identity and behavior as mothers, there are certainly shared norms of motherhood across all races and classes within Western society.

Much less clear, however, is the role of a daughter-in-law. While many women have experienced seeing their own mothers and female family members as daughters-in-law, changes in marriage, the sex role revolution, and the family-specific nature of the bond leave women with few socially agreed upon expectations or role models for being a daughter-in-law. For example, daughters-in-law may not know whether to share in their husband's relationship with his family or to forge a separate relationship with their husband's parents, stepparents, grandparents, and siblings. Just how integral a member of the family the daughter-in-law is will differ by family as will her role in uniting her in-laws to their son and grandchildren. The obligations of the role are also unclear as women's roles as wives undergo change in the postmodern family. In contrast, in certain other societies such as Korea and China, the obligations and expectations are more embedded in the culture, although even there they are changing.[3,4] While this offers women a solid understanding of what is expected of them, being a daughter-in-law in these countries also carries with it institutionalized, seemingly onerous, expectations. In the West though, one can argue that being a daughter-in-law is one of the most fluid and ambiguous family roles.

How then do women decide what is expected of them and piece together their role and identity as daughters-in-law? This chapter will examine what women see as the expectations of their role (and how they learned them), as well as how they learn to resolve conflict in their relationship. I argue that learning to resolve conflict and to recognize expectations are an important part of the development of the role. Based on their experiences as daughters-in-law and what they see as the expectations of their roles, how then do women identify themselves as daughters-in-law? This chapter will examine the identities that they develop, the process by which they piece together an identity, and the cultural resources that they use to do so. We will begin by discussing the overall development of in-law relationships.

THE DEVELOPMENT OF IN-LAW RELATIONSHIPS

The development of an in-law relationship is quite unlike that of many other family ties, beginning with the onset of the relationship. While a parent may love a newborn child at birth, one cannot expect a loving relationship or friendship with a mother-in-law or daughter-in-law right away.[5] First meetings do set the tone, however, and may affect how well the women get along for some time and possibly indefinitely.[6,7] Among those mothers-in-law and daughters-in-law who felt initial friction or mutual dislike, 60 percent got along well only later, 10 percent never got along, and 30 percent got along well relatively early on in the relationship. Nuner and Chenoweth[8] also found that early acceptance into the family improved the relationship as much as five to ten years later.

Early on in the relationship, each of the women may have her own habits and ways of doing things that clash. Daughters-in-law enter the relationship with expectations that often result in disappointment. Those daughters-in-law who are able to adjust their expectations tend to have better relationships later on in time.[9] Likewise, mothers-in-law may have difficulty in relinquishing control over their grown children's lives, particularly if they have derived all of their self-esteem from being a mother.[10] The kitchen, in particular, can be a central source of a power struggle as feeding the family marks an important aspect of women's roles as mother and the central female figure in the family,[11] especially among more traditional women.

Interestingly, daughters-in-law do not necessarily model their relationship with their mother-in-law after their relationship with their own mother.[12] This suggests that whether they expect or intend their relationship with their mother-in-law to be a quasi mother–daughter relationship or not, they also recognize that there is a qualitative difference between the two relationships. Fischer[13] refers to this as an asymmetry in the relationships. It also reinforces the idea that this is a developmental process as daughters-in-law actively seek out models for their relationships with their mothers-in-law.

Relationships tend to improve as they develop.[14,15] In a national poll of 1,000 adults, people in their twenties and thirties tended to prefer their own mothers, whereas those in their forties and older tended to get along equally well with both mother and mother-in-law.[16] This suggests the possibility both that in-laws may eventually learn to work out their differences and to appreciate one another and that with maturity they are able to accept those differences that continue to exist. Daughters-in-law may also grow closer as they spend more time together and develop a shared history.

Results of research examining the impact that the birth of a child/grandchild has on the relationship are mixed. Nuner and Chenoweth[17] found that the mother-in-law becoming a grandmother had a positive impact on in-law relationships according to daughters-in-law. In contrast, Fischer[18] found that the birth of a grandchild brought greater relational *strain* to the in-law relationship, while it lessened that between a mother and daughter. While sharing a child/grandchild increases interactive involvement between the two women, it also creates greater ambiguity in the relationship. The two women are still not kin, but the shared child/grandchild heightens the fact that they are not strangers either. Likewise, the birth of the child further emphasizes the differentiation women feel in their relationship with their mother versus mother-in-law. Daughters are much more likely to ask their own mothers for advice and experience greater intimacy as a result of the shared maternal role.

EXCEPTIONS TO THE RULE

Slightly over one-fifth of the daughters-in-law (21 percent) in this study believed that their relationship with their mother-in-law had not changed over time or with the occurrence of significant life course events, namely their marriage and the birth of children/grandchildren. For these women, the relationship started out as close and stayed that way (but did not grow closer), or a poor relationship never got better. This reinforces the prior point that early experiences tend to determine, or at least significantly impact, the relationship over the long term.[19,20] There is little that can overcome a negative beginning, while factors that determine positive relationships tend not to change. The other 79 percent stated that there had been some change, if only they had grown slightly closer over time. By examining in-law relationships while the couple is dating and how they change as the result of marriage, the birth of children, and the passage of time, we can discern observable patterns in the creation of the daughter-in-law role or the making of a daughter-in-law.

THE INITIAL STAGE OF DEVELOPMENT: DATING

Daughters-in-law rarely saw their future in-laws while they were dating. For example, Elizabeth lived in the same town as her future in-laws while she dated. Still, she stated, "We didn't see much of them. We were more concentrated on the romantic part of our lives." Another daughter-in-law met her in-laws only once or twice during the four years that she and her future husband were dating. This likely reflects a general lack of parental involvement in a son's romantic life in postmodern society. Parents were more likely to be involved when children were marrying for financial reasons or for an economic alliance between families.[21] Love-based marriages are of less concern to parents, however. The fact that so many sons seldom united their parents and girlfriends does not speak to the disconnect between marriage and family, however, since these couples were not yet married.

Their initial contact with potential in-laws made many of the daughters-in-law nervous. For example, Ginny stated,

My introduction to the family was over fifty Italians and French Canadians! It was frightening! I could tell that I was being surveyed and studied all over. I could hear people talking about me.... I felt welcomed though.

For Elizabeth, the initial interactions were awkward because she was living with her boyfriend. She explained, "I was very nervous. [My boyfriend] was living on the second floor of his house, and he asked me to move in with him. They were on the first floor. It was very uncomfortable." Elizabeth later went on to explain though that her in-laws did not seem bothered by their living situation. Sue and Ginny had a slightly different experience. Their in-laws did not approve of the couples living together, although their mothers-in-law were very cordial to them despite that fact.

A small minority of daughters-in-law tried to establish an equal, if not dominant, status with their mother-in-law early on in the relationship. Cynthia, for example, said that right away she let her [mother-in-law] know "that I am a strong woman and that there are things that I would not tolerate [from her]...." Nicole also felt that her initial experiences with her boyfriend's mother were a power struggle. Nicole's boyfriend shared his mother's early criticisms of Nicole with her, which set the stage for an estranged relationship.

Dating was a time for future in-laws to begin adjusting to one another. For example, Janette felt that her in-laws became used to the fact that their Irish Catholic son was involved with a Jew when they were dating. She said, "I never thought that she didn't approve of me. It was an adjustment though. It was just a 'wow' for them."

THE EFFECTS OF MARRIAGE AND CHILDREN

For those daughters-in-law who felt that their relationship with their mother-in-law changed at some critical point during their history, it was usually at the time of marriage. Further, it did so by making them closer. Only a minority of the daughters-in-law (25 percent) felt that their marriage did not make a difference in their relationship with their mother-in-law.[22]

As stated earlier, most of the daughters-in-law said that they grew closer to their mother-in-law at the point of their engagement or once they were married. They also noted that the change was a swift one. Cindy shared the following observation, "The change was very pronounced and immediate. We suddenly grew closer. They were very supportive financially and emotionally. I felt very welcomed and embraced into the heart of the family." Likewise, Ellen stated,

It changed the most when we got engaged. They told me to call them "Mom" and "Dad" and that I was a part of the family now. [Their ethnic group] are very inclusive and family-oriented. They were very welcoming and personal.

Others also noted that their marriages made both generations feel more like family, although they were uncertain as to why the marriage itself made such a difference. Elizabeth explained, "There was something that changed. I really became part of the family. I felt different. Now it was complete."

The effect of marriage was not all positive though. Some of the women noted that once they were married, problems surfaced, particularly regarding with whom they would spend their holidays. Likewise, the older daughters-in-law were more likely to state that once they were married, they felt that they had "to do" for their mothers-in-law or please them. This included conforming to their in-laws' expectations for visiting.

Only one of the daughters-in-law mentioned that the wedding itself had caused problems in the relationship. Stephanie realized just how controlling her mother-in-law was when she threatened to boycott the wedding because Stephanie and Robert wanted a small, secular wedding versus a large, religious one. Stephanie believed that having to stand her ground on this matter (by calling her mother-in-law's bluff) improved the relationship in the long run though.

The birth of children or grandchildren also changed in-law relationships, but the direction of the change was not uniform. While many of the daughters-in-law said that the birth of their children made them feel closer to their in-laws, others stated that children made the relationship worse. For example, Sydney explained,

That [when the children were born] was when things got strange and bitter. When they were born, she never offered to help which I thought was odd. She helped her daughter with her granddaughters.... She wanted to take the boys to the lake one day when they were very little. I said, "no"... she was on medication. It bothered her that I wouldn't let her take them. She was resentful.... It has been that way ever since.

Another daughter-in-law felt that her relationship with her mother-in-law took a dramatic turn for the worse when her son was born because she saw what a poor grandmother (and mother) the older woman was for the first time. Monique stated that her in-laws became intrusive with advice only once their grandchildren were born. She felt that it added to the stress of the relationship because her in-laws expected her to visit more once there were children. Finally, Alexa said that in hindsight, the births of her children made a difficult relationship worse because her mother-in-law ignored her children in favor of her sister-in-law's children.

The relationships improved for the remainder of those daughters-in-law who felt that the births of their children had made a difference. Most of the daughters-in-law said that their in-laws were delighted to have (more) grandchildren. The in-laws visited more frequently to spend time with their grandchildren and to help out. They loved their grandchildren and that made them closer to their daughters-in-law. It was not clear though whether this was because the daughters-in-law themselves bore the grand-children or because they had a shared connection to the child/grandchild. Sadie though felt that being the bearer of the grandchildren increased her status with her in-laws. She explained, "They liked me even more. I was the mother of their grandchildren, their only grandchildren."

The gender of the grandchildren made a difference in bringing the in-laws together. Allison felt that her mother-in-law always wanted to have a granddaughter. The fact that Allison's first child was a girl made her and her mother-in-law much closer. In contrast, Diane said that her mother-in-law was disappointed because she wanted granddaughters and Diane had only sons. As such, the birth of grandchildren did not make the two women any closer. Kristen's mother-in-law, Dot, was particularly glad to have grandsons who would carry on the family name though. Kristen said, "That was a big thing to them. She was thrilled beyond belief. She thinks the world of my boys...and I love anyone who loves them!"

THE EFFECT OF TIME

All of the daughters-in-law who saw some change in their relationship felt that time alone had made a difference, even if it was only a very subtle change in the relationship. The women said that they became closer because they spent more time with their in-laws and/or got to know them better. One of the daughters-in-law felt that her relationship with her mother-in-law had slowly evolved into a more comfortable one over the years. Susan explained,

Yes, [we have grown closer] by having quality time together. It is just small, simple things. Like this morning, I saw that she was looking at her nails, and so I asked her if she would like me to do her nails. It only has to be some-thing small to bring you closer.

Likewise, a former daughter-in-law said,

> Yes, it [time] made us closer: the things that we did together [and] the things
> that everyone goes through. She came to my father's funeral even though we
> were divorced.

Pat felt that the passage of time had made her closer to her mother-in-law
because she lost her own mother. Over the years she came to appreciate the
gap that her mother-in-law filled more and more. Susan, who had one of
the closest relationships with her mother-in-law, felt that with time she
could read Rose's body language and know when she was not feeling well
without being told.

A few of the daughters-in-law stated that they became more assertive
with their mothers-in-law over time, which changed the relationship.
Marjorie did not get along well with her mother-in-law for many years but
eventually became her caregiver. Consider her statement:

> Eventually I did grow to care for her. I grew up and didn't feel that I had to
> answer to her. Prior to that, she was like my boss. I became my own person.
> My daughter had trouble with her eyes. I found a doctor in [our town], but
> she wanted to take us to one in Boston. I said, "Okay." They took us there.
> After a while, I realized that the doctor in [our town] was just as good, and I
> told her that I would be going there from now on. It took time for me to
> assert myself.

OBLIGATION AND SUPPORT

Learning the obligations of the daughter-in-role, and negotiating whether
and how those obligations are fulfilled, is a central aspect in the development of the relationship. What makes this process more complicated is that
those obligations, or at least some of them, tend to differ by family. As
such, mothers-in-law and daughters-in-law may have different ideas of what
is expected of themselves and one another.

Earlier researchers found that in-laws do indeed feel an obligation to and
provide support to one another. Using vignettes of different situations
under which one might experience obligation, Rossi and Rossi[23] found that
while family members do not rank their obligation to their parents-in-law
and children-in-law (also referred to as affinal kin or kin related through
marriage) as high as their own parents and children, they do rank them
higher than more distant kin such as cousins, aunts and uncles, and so on,

or nonkin. For example, the ranking of parents-in-law (6.6) is higher than that of grandparents (6.3) but not as high as that of parents (8.3) or even siblings (6.9). However, children-in-law rank higher in obligation than parents-in-law (7.1 versus 6.6), while children and parents rank similarly (8.3). This may be because one's obligations to children-in-law are so closely tied to obligations to children.

Parents (-in-law) and adult children (-in-law) provide different forms of support to one another. For example, parents are more likely to provide financial aid and services to adult children and their spouses than vice versa. In contrast, older parents want companionship, appreciation, and affection from their children. The onset of grandchildren triggers greater support between mothers-in-law and daughters-in-law. However, while mothers-in-law are more likely to *give* things, mothers are more likely to *do* things, that is, to provide services to grandchildren. This is the result of the closer relationship between mothers and daughters. In-laws, however, are not the primary sources of assistance for daughters-in-law during personal crises although parents-in-law can and do provide parental affection when a parent is not available.[24]

Provision of support to the husband's parents versus wife's parents is not equal. Instead, the wife's parents both provide and receive more assistance than the husband's parents.[25,26] While women contact and help their own parents more than their in-laws, men experience pulls in both directions. They do not help their own parents any more than their in-laws, and they talk on the phone to their parents *less* than to their in-laws. This then results in more help to the wife's parents than to the husband's parents.[27] In addition, when both sets of parents require care, children are more likely to assist the wife's parents.[28] The *presence* of one set of parents, however, does not affect relations with the other set of parents.[29] There are also class differences. While middle class children, children-in-law, and parents are more likely to provide financial help to one another, working class children and their spouses are more likely to offer services and coresidence.[30]

Authors Coleman, Ganong, and Cable[31] focused on the effect of divorce on in-law relationships and the resulting change in obligation. They found that the obligations mothers-in-law felt were actually to their grandchildren rather than to their daughters-in-law and that this held true before a divorce as well as after a divorce. It is the quality of earlier relationships and patterns of mutual support that determine whether responsibilities to in-laws continue after divorce or not.

THE OBLIGATIONS OF A DAUGHTER-IN-LAW

Becoming a daughter-in-law includes learning the obligations of the role in her husband's family and, to the extent that they exist, in the wider society. Her identity depends, in part, on what she sees as those obligations, how reasonable they seem, and how and whether she chooses to fulfill them. An analysis of the data revealed a minimum of five categories of expectations or obligations.

Daughters-in-law most commonly saw their primary obligation as being the connecting link between their husbands and children and their in-laws. This is related to women's overall kin-keeping role in the family. As daughters and sisters, they play a primary role in creating families and in fostering intergenerational ties. One would expect this role then to continue as young mothers nurture connections between their own children and extended family members, especially grandparents. Elizabeth explained it as follows,

> It is important to be a daughter-in-law, to keep that circle going.... You have a responsibility when you have children that they know both sides of the family and that both sides of the family get to see them. So you have to keep in contact.

What was perhaps more surprising was that women felt responsible for maintaining the connection between their husband and his mother as well. At a minimum, women believed that they should remind their husbands to call their mothers, invite their in-laws to dinner and for holidays, and purchase cards and gifts for them. That is, upon marriage, women became an integral part of the mother–son bond and the person who kept the daughter-in-law's new family connected to her husband's family of orientation (i.e., the family that he grew up in). One of the daughters-in-law whose in-laws were not interested in including her in their relationship with their son still believed that she was needed to facilitate the relationship. She explained,

> They made it clear when we got married that it was enough to talk just to Elliott on the phone, that they could get our news from him. I thought, "Okay." I think it is my responsibility as a spouse though to support him in that relationship and to help make it possible. I go on visits so that it is possible for him and the kids to go.

Daughters-in-law also commonly stated that they were obligated to be part of the overall extended family. However, many of them added the caveat that this should be the case for daughters-in-law only when it is not "crazy or horribly uncomfortable" to do so and only if the daughter-in-law feels welcomed into her husband's family. One of the daughters-in-law said, "Being a good daughter-in-law means being part of [the mother-in-law's] family and valuing that. It means being there with them and participating in the family." Another daughter-in-law said, "You should try to fit into that group, and they should try to accommodate you as well. Being a good daughter-in-law is just being a part of the family... being there for family matters... having a relationship with the mother-in-law and other members of the family."

In addition to being a part of the mother-in-law's family, daughters-in-law felt that they should be respectful of and not be too critical of their mothers-in-law. For example, one woman said, "You have to learn to tolerate and put up with some things. You have to embrace the things you like in the person." Similarly, another daughter-in-law offered the following advice to other daughters-in-law:

> Be open-minded in how their family might be different. Realize that this is how they do things. Pick and choose your battles if this is something you can live with or not. Don't be judgmental.

While many of the daughters-in-law pointed out that they should be respectful of their mother-in-law, a few clarified that they should be respectful of their mother-in-law's *position* as well. One of the daughters-in-law explained,

> I try to understand her place as my husband's mother. She is going to give advice, and that is not something that is going to change. To me, that is something that you have to respect to the best of your ability. Of course, she needs to respect the fact that you are his wife too. You should be as kind and warm as you can be. Be sensitive.

Respecting one's position as mother then means understanding a mother's need to continue being a mother. As part of this, one of the women felt that she should "share" her husband. She felt that it was "too harsh to say, 'I am taking your son now; he is my husband.'" What is interesting though is that she felt that she had the option of doing so.

Although not mentioned as frequently, daughters-in-law also felt obligated to include their in-laws and to make them feel welcome in their homes and families. For example, one of the daughters-in-law said, "I think [that] I should include them... invite them to things for the kids, invite them for dinner.... That is the biggest thing. Make them feel as welcome as your own family." This was something that the mothers-in-law clearly appreciated. Mothers-in-law said over and over again how thankful they were of the efforts that their daughters-in-law made to reach out to them. Likewise, they felt closer to those daughters-in-law who tried to "bridge the gap" between them. One of the daughters-in-law, who was also a mother-in-law herself, summed up the obligation with the following contribution, "The daughter-in-law should treat the mother-in-law the same as she does her own mother. You split holidays. Usually the wife's mother gets included more, but you shouldn't do that. She is still a mother." Another daughter-in-law said,

> You make it a point so that the mother-in-law feels a part of the family. The daughter-in-law wants her own family, and the mother-in-law should respect that. But still she is a mother and wants to be involved. You need to communicate that so everyone is comfortable.

Interestingly, mothers-in-law were more likely to say that they appreciated how their daughters-in-law helped their *grandchildren* to keep in touch, but they were less likely to mention what their daughters-in-law had done to facilitate their relationship with a son. To some extent, this is hidden work that the mothers-in-law do not even notice. Perhaps they assume that it is their son and not their daughter-in-law who maintains the link, not realizing that many husbands relinquish this responsibility to their wives when they marry.

Several of the daughters-in-law stated that the obligations of a daughter-in-law referred to being the wife of her (mother-in-law's) son and the mother of her (in-law's) grandchildren. That is, a daughter-in-law was obligated to be a good wife and mother, but she did not necessarily have direct obligations to the mother-in-law as well.

A few of the daughters-in-law felt that they were obligated to treat their mothers-in-law like another mother. However, this was usually in the context of dividing holidays or being open to having a loving relationship. As was stated earlier, most daughters-in-law recognized that their relationship with their mother-in-law could not duplicate their relationship with their mother. In addition, daughters-in-law felt that they should "be there" for their mothers-in-law when they needed them. This included helping during illness and times of personal crisis.

All of the daughters-in-law felt that they had some obligation to their mother-in-law. Likewise, all but one of the daughters-in-law felt as though their in-laws were family. It could be, however, that women who think of their in-laws only as *their husband's* family were less likely to volunteer for the study since they felt that they would have little to contribute to it.

Although only one of the daughters-in-law mentioned having a responsibility to help her mother-in-law when she became elderly, a small minority (8 percent) were already providing assistance either with personal care tasks or other extensive help. While some mentioned that they liked to help, others did so because they felt obligated.

All of the daughters-in-law stated that they would continue to have a relationship with their mother-in-law as long as they were married. However, several of those daughters-in-law with a poor relationship with their mother-in-law stated that they would not keep in touch with her if something were to happen to their husband. In other words, daughters-in-law do not feel obligated to a life-long connection to their mothers-in-law if they do not get along with her.

LEARNING THE OBLIGATIONS OF THE ROLE

The majority of the daughters-in-law stated that they learned the obligations of the role as they learned about their husband's family and as they made a place for themselves in the family. This did not occur right away but took place over time. Daughters-in-law also decided on what they were obliged to do based on how they wanted to be treated in turn and on what they thought was "right." For example, this included making their in-laws feel welcome in their home and splitting holidays between both sets of parents. They said that they decided on their obligations based on what they could do for the family given their position within it (such as being the connecting link to grandchildren) and on what their husbands did and did not do (such as scheduling visits and buying gifts).

A few of the daughters-in-law felt that they learned the obligations of the role from watching their own mothers and grandmothers and that they were aware of those obligations before they married. However, they also stated that they did not realize how hard it would be to fulfill those obligations, such as treating one's in-laws like one's own parents. That is, it looked easier when their mothers did it. None of the daughters-in-law said that they learned of the obligations from television, self-help books, or other forms of media. Interestingly, only one of the daughters-in-law said that her mother-in-law *told her* what was expected of her when she and her husband first became engaged. This included obligations to visit, host holiday get togethers, and provide assistance. She even decreed the appropriate level of affection that the women should have for one another. Most of the daughters-in-law though learned what was expected of their role from being a daughter-in-law and discovering their relationship to the broader family.

RESOLVING CONFLICT

In-laws must also learn to work through disagreements and discord as the relationship develops. As such, the daughters-in-law who had experienced any conflict with their mother-in-law (58 percent) developed a number of methods to resolve it. Most commonly, they either ignored the cause of the conflict or "let it go," or they confronted the problem (27 percent of the daughters-in-law who had experienced any conflict fell into each category). Those who "let the situation go" usually said that they did so out of respect for their mother-in-law or because they did not want to make the situation worse by confronting it. One daughter-in-law explained, "You ignore a lot and look the other way.... I just bite my tongue and walk away. I don't think it needs to be confronted. It takes compromising. I don't want to put gas on the fire." Another daughter-in-law explained that letting things go with her mother-in-law (which included not saying anything to her husband either) was in her best interest. More specifically, she believed that difficulty with her mother-in-law (which would result if she addressed any conflict) might harm her marriage and possibly her relationship with her son. She felt that her husband would "fall apart" if he knew that his wife did not like his mother. As a result, she explained, "I don't say anything. It is not going to help me anywhere in my life not to get along with her. I have to be able to [do so]. I don't have to love her, but I need to get along. It can be superficial." Two other daughters-in-law stated that they ignored conflict with their mother-in-law because they felt that they would not be able to "win" a battle with her. Both of these women stated that their mothers-in-law were intimidating and powerful in the family. Finally, another daughter-in-law said that she "let things go" because the source of the conflict was usually a misunderstanding.

An equal number of daughters-in-law resolved conflict using an opposing strategy; they confronted their mothers-in-law. Most of these daughters-in-law said that they were tactful in doing so. Others mentioned that they reserved confrontation for extreme situations when they did not want their mother-in-law to "butt in." That is, they picked their battles. Several daughters-in-law further explained that by confronting the situation early on, they "nipped the problem in the bud." In other words, they justified their tactic by stressing its benefits. Many also confronted their in-law despite their husband's warning not to do so. Kayla explained, "My husband says, 'Oh, don't say anything [to her]. That is just how she is.' But I have learned to speak up for myself. She may not always agree with what I say, but I say it anyway. It clears the air." Women also said that it took time to learn to confront their mothers-in-law. Only one daughter-in-law used aggression when confronting her mother-in-law. She stated, "I tell her that 'head in the sand shit' doesn't work with me. I don't want to hear her 'would'a, should'a, could'a.' When she defends her daughter [the cause of their conflict], I get right in her face and tell her, 'Let me tell you the real scoop … and don't you dare defend her.' I don't back down."

Those daughters-in-law with better relationships with their mothers-in-law said that they talked with their mothers-in-law about what was bothering them as a way of resolving conflict (16 percent). The difference between this and confrontation is that those who talked with their in-laws (versus confronting them) stressed that it was a give-and-take process with the goal of finding a mutually agreeable solution. Cynthia, who is a very forthright woman, told me, "Right away I talk about it, right then and there…. I don't start a fight or anything, but we talk it out. I hear her out and then she hears me out … and then we agree to disagree." These daughters-in-law then believed that they could come to a satisfactory outcome and usually had prior experience with doing so. One of the daughters-in-law said that she started her marriage by talking to her mother-in-law about the things that bothered her, but that she gave up on it because she felt that the older woman would not compromise. Sydney said, "I used to try to talk to her about things on the phone. Now we just don't have conversations." Monique also stopped trying to talk about conflict with her mother-in-law when she realized that it wasn't effective (i.e., it usually did not produce any change) and that usually there was nothing that she felt she had "done" to cause her mother-in-law to be upset.

Another 16 percent of the daughters-in-law had husbands who intervened in the conflict with their mothers-in-law (this is discussed in greater detail in Chapter 7). Husbands were often reluctant to intercede, although they agreed with their wives that it was their place to do so since the problem was with their mother. At least one of the daughters-in-law felt that her mother-in-law was more likely to change her behavior for her son rather than for her, the daughter-in-law. Only one woman asked her father-in-law to intervene on her behalf. She explained, "I get my father-in-law involved. He is the reasonable one, and I have always gotten along better with him. I used to ask him to talk to her [before he died]...and he did."

A minority of the daughters-in-law (7 percent) resolved their conflict with their mother-in-law by "managing the situation." This included a number of different tactics. For example, Stephanie took measures to ensure that she was at her best when interacting with her in-laws. She explained, "When I visit, I take a lot of ibuprofen beforehand. They are very loud, a lot of shouting. I also get up and go running in the morning to give me time to myself and to get the endorphins running in order to cope with the visit." Stephanie also managed her in-laws' tendency to interfere without arguing with them and without succumbing to their expectations. She explained, "I use my professional background. I say, 'Thank you for your input. I will take it under advisement.' Then I do what I want." Two other daughters-in-law avoided conflict by refusing to allow their in-laws to stay with them when they visited from out-of-town and by minimizing the number of times that they visited their in-laws as well. Stacey added, "I just count the days until they fly home. I keep concentrating on that and not the way that they are." Likewise, Sally said that she and her husband strategized over visits and set boundaries with their in-laws to minimize any conflict that could erupt but that this required compromise between the two of them as well.

Finally, another 7 percent of the daughters-in-law who had experienced conflict with their mother-in-law felt that it was never resolved. For example, one daughter-in-law said, "My mother says that I will never be able to change her [the mother-in-law], which is true.... And my husband won't say anything to her. So the problems are still there. Mostly I throw it in the back of my head. If something triggers it though, it eats me." Alexa went on to explain later that even though the conflict was still there, she took comfort in knowing that one day her children will "know how their grandmother is." Both of these daughters-in-law had an estranged relationship with their mother-in-law.

There was no discernable pattern between the cause of conflict and how daughters-in-law tried to resolve it. Instead, the way that they resolved conflict had more to do with the quality of the relationship and their own individual personality and not the cause of the conflict. In particular, daughters-in-law were more likely to "talk" about the conflict with their mothers-in-law or to ignore it if they had a better relationship with their mother-in-law.

Some of the daughters-in-law changed their method of conflict resolution over time. In particular, they went from trying to ignore the source of the conflict to either confronting their mothers-in-law or talking with them about their concerns. The change in tactic was the result of the evolution of the daughter-in-law role. As the women became more comfortable with their mothers-in-law as well as with their marriages, they developed the confidence to assert themselves. Although the relationships did not change considerably, the daughters-in-law's behavior did change from early marriage to middle life. This change appeared to be greatest for those who had married early in life or who had a difficult relationship with their mother-in-law early on. This is part of the evolution of the role or the "making of a daughter-in-law."

IN-LAW IDENTITIES

Women create an identity for themselves as daughters-in-law as part of the on-going development of their role. They come to see themselves and to project images of themselves based on their experiences and, I will argue, on a set of cultural images of daughters-in-law in Western society. Ann Swidler[32] argues that people use cultural meanings in their everyday lives to shape their expectations and behaviors. In creating an identity, people have an entire repertoire of different cultural meanings at their disposal and will use different ones, holding others in reserve or rejecting them, to orient themselves to their own experiences. This would suggest then that women have in store varied cultural meanings of being a daughter-in-law and that those meanings affect their experiences and identity construction. The remainder of this chapter will examine the identities that daughters-in-law develop for themselves, the process by which they do so, and the conditions under which women use some cultural "codes" and not others.

The women in this study adopted a number of different identities for themselves as daughters-in-law. Although for many of the women, the identities changed over time, they usually did not describe multiple identities for any one point in time. Instead, women focused on one consistent and coherent identity as a daughter-in-law.

One of the most common identities women held of themselves as daughters-in-law was that of the "connecting link" between their in-laws and their husbands and children or of the facilitators of those relationships. As such, their identity was based on what they saw as their primary obligation, or vice versa. This identity is consistent with their other identities as women in the family, for example, kin keepers, and with their roles as wives and mothers. Interestingly, in being the connecting link, women are assuming that their husbands will not sufficiently maintain ties with their family of orientation (i.e., the family that they grew up in). In addition, they are both establishing *their own* family as a separate entity from their respective families of orientation while still maintaining intergenerational linkages. This is consistent with other researchers' argument that being able to establish her own separate family is critical to a daughter-in-law's positive relationship with her mother-in-law.[33,34] For this reason and because it provides them with a role in the extended family, identifying as the connecting link is common for daughters-in-law.

Other daughters-in-law identified themselves as the "downtrodden" daughter-in-law or "martyr" in the family. They saw themselves as being treated unfairly by their in-laws or as having interfering or overbearing in-laws. They usually found these relationships to be disappointing in comparison to what they had expected (this will be discussed further later). These daughters-in-law identified heavily with popular images of daughters-in-law in the media, such as "Deborah" on *Everybody Loves Raymond*.[35] This identity was socially constructed by the media and reinforced by people's everyday comments about being a daughter-in-law.

Daughters-in-law also identified themselves as "being like a daughter." While only a few saw themselves as substituting for daughters, they were more likely to describe themselves as being *similar to* an additional daughter in the family. They understood that the mother/daughter tie was a unique one that they could not replicate but also felt that they loved and were loved like one of the children. This identity then required some sort of confirmation on the part of the mother-in-law. Indeed, the women stated that their in-laws themselves or others told them that they were like a daughter to their mother-in-law. What was less clear though was whether or not they were considered to be similar to a daughter because they were connected through a son (i.e., the equivalent relationship) or because they mimicked a mother–daughter relationship.

A minority of the daughters-in-law identified themselves as being "the peacekeeper" in the family. This required, more than anything, overlooking what they saw as their in-laws' flaws and not saying anything when their in-laws interfered or were somehow offensive. These women then were not necessarily keeping the peace between others but were doing so by not voicing their own unhappiness. Still, they identified and described themselves as peacekeeper, attaching an admirable quality to their identity.

Finally, the last identity was that of "daughter-in-law at a distance." These women rarely had contact with their in-laws and made no overtures to be closer to them. Some, but not all, had previously tried to have a better relationship. They identified themselves as family, but as uninvolved family.

CREATING AN IDENTITY

The creation of an identity actually begins prior to marriage and is based on a woman's assumptions of what a relationship with her mother-in-law will be like. Among those women who did have prior expectations, all had an image of a supportive, loving mother-in-law. Although this is not one of the predominant cultural images of mothers-in-law, women believed that their own mothers-in-law would support them. Their expected identity then was that of a cared for and integral member of an extended family.

For the majority of the daughters-in-law, this expectation did not meet their initial experiences either during dating or in the first few years of marriage. When that happened, daughters-in-law felt let down and resentful. They saw their mother-in-law as one or both of the most common cultural images: the interfering/opinionated mother-in-law or the possessive mother-in-law. They then shifted their identity to either that of a "martyr" (the long-suffering daughter-in-law) or a "daughter-in-law at a distance," that is, one with a very impersonal relationship and infrequent contact with her mother-in-law. They identified with popular television characters whose mothers-in-law were bossy or intrusive. For example, one of the women described herself as the daughter-in-law in the popular film *Monster-in-Law*.

The relationships for some of the daughters-in-law improved with time and, for some, with the birth of grandchildren. At this point in the life cycle of their marriages, their identity as a daughter-in-law developed into that of the "connecting link" between their mother-in-law and their husband and children. They identified as the one who kept the relationships close and who did things for their mother-in-law (sending gifts and cards, keeping in-laws apprised of their children's development, and arranging visits). They did not, however, identify as a friend to their mother-in-law or as someone who felt close to their mother-in-law.

For other daughters-in-law, the relationship either stayed the same or worsened. They stated that mothers-in-law were interfering/opinionated or possessive of their sons. These daughters-in-law felt that they could never do enough for their mothers-in-law (such as visit often enough or stay long enough) or that their mothers-in-law saw them as poor parents. They continued to identify as a "martyr" who was unfairly treated but who needed to continue in the relationship. They were less likely to identify as a "connecting link" to their husband and children.

Those daughters-in-law whose expectations of their mothers-in-law did meet their experiences (the third category) focused their identity on reciprocating that support and living up to their own expectations of a daughter-in-law. One of the daughters-in-law who felt that her mother-in-law was very kind and accepting from the beginning identified as part of a warm and loving bond. She reciprocated, focusing on quilting and knitting personal items for her mother-in-law and her younger sister-in-law. She did not, however, identify as a daughter or a substitute daughter. She was quite adamant that she was a daughter-in-law and not a daughter and that she was not as close to her mother-in-law as to her mother. Others felt that they were indeed "like another daughter." These women also identified as the "connecting link" between their in-laws and the rest of their family and wanted to aid their mothers-in-law in having a close relationship with their sons and grandchildren.

Women created identities that were consistent with other identities in their lives. For example, one of the women who identified as a strong Catholic used religious ideals of tolerance and respect for her mother-in-law. Another woman who was the daughter of a clergyman focused on forgiveness and looking for the good in her mother-in-law. Surprisingly, women's identities as daughter-in-law did not seem to tie in to their identities as daughters. Daughters who felt close to their mothers did not feel as though they had to be close to their mothers-in-law. However, several daughters-in-law stated that in trying to be a good wife and mother they felt it necessary to maintain a connection with their mother-in-law. This suggests that people are looking for cultural coherence by fitting their identities as daughters-in-law to their wider worldviews and their roles of wife and mother.

SOURCES OF IN-LAW IDENTITY

What sources, including cultural images, do women use in developing these identities and in creating identities for their mothers-in-law as well? All of the women at some point invoked cultural images of "the mother-in-law" in describing their mothers-in-law or in relaying an episode in their relationship. These included images of an "interfering," "possessive," "friend-like," or "loving-nurturing" mother-in-law. They also invoked one image that is not part of our cultural repertoire: that of the "hands-off mother-in-law." This mother did not provide unsolicited advice or visit without an invitation. The first two images, the "interfering" or "possessive" mother-in-law, came, in part, from the media and people's everyday comments. In contrast, the "friend-like" or "loving-nurturing" mother-in-law came from women's expectations or the ideal sentimental model of the family where all ties are mutually satisfying and based on affection. The last image, which was that of the "hands-off mother-in-law," was based on experience.

The media was also an important source of women's identities as daughters-in-law. However, it was the dearth of alternative images of daughters-in-law in the media that resulted in women's tendency to adopt the commonly portrayed stereotype of the "downtrodden" or "martyr" daughter-in-law that we see in films and sitcoms. Over and over again, women would say to me, "Just wait until I tell you about *my* mother-in-law." Then during the interview they would confess to having relationships that were just fine. Despite their positive experiences, they felt the need to conform to the common cultural image.

A second resource for women in developing an identity as a daughter-in-law included their mothers' experiences. None of the daughters-in-law mentioned the circumstances of their brothers' wives or their husband's sisters-in-law, but they certainly used their own mother's circumstances as a daughter-in-law in developing their identity. For example, their mother's own experience was often the basis of what they could expect and was used either as a confirmation of their own circumstances or as a basis of how in-laws are usually treated. One of the daughters-in-law said over and over again how terribly her mother-in-law treated her and how typical her mother-in-law was in that regard. She had few concrete examples of this poor treatment, however. She gave more examples of how her *mother* was mistreated. It became clear that her identity as a "downtrodden daughter-in-law" came not from her experience but from cultural images in the media and her own mother's experience.

A woman's identity as a daughter-in-law was also strongly tied to her experience as a daughter in her own family. Women did not compare their experience with that of their brothers' wives or their husband's sisters-in-law. Instead, they compared their experiences in the in-law's family with their experiences in their *own* family. Over and over again, women compared what their in-laws did with what their own families did: how they related to their adult children and grandchildren, how they settled conflict, and their values towards marriage. Likewise, many but not all of the women compared how their own family treated them with how their in-laws treated them. For example, one woman focused on the fact that her own mother was not critical of her parenting style while her mother-in-law was. In addition, some compared how their mothers-in-law treated their own daughters versus themselves. They were less likely to compare how they were treated versus how the other sisters-in-law were treated. One can argue then that a woman's identity as a daughter-in-law is strongly tied to how her experience matches her experience as a daughter.

A CULTURAL REPERTOIRE OF IN-LAW RELATIONSHIPS

As stated earlier, women hold in reserve a repertoire of cultural images of mothers-in-law and daughters-in-law. Many women began their relationship with their mother-in-law with positive images and expectations, holding in reserve the negative stereotypes that predominate in society or that their own mothers might have experienced. They wanted and expected to have that close relationship that we associate with parental relationships. When that initial expectation did not match their experience, they quickly jumped to the cultural stereotypes that plague mothers-in-law and daughters-in-law. This is consistent with the argument that people use cultural interpretations more when their relationships are not satisfying or they feel lost.[36] They also invoked these images when their experience as a daughter-in-law did not meet their experience as a daughter in their own families.

A few women used other interpretations to explain their relationships with their mothers-in-law. One of the women said over and over again that she and her mother-in-law did not get along because her mother-in-law was "just so old" (compared with her own mother who was a decade younger). She emphasized that her mother-in-law had impaired hearing and was old-fashioned to explain their tension. This daughter-in-law then invoked cultural images of older people to explain her own distant identity.

SUMMARY AND IMPLICATIONS

Becoming a daughter-in-law for the first time is a bewildering experience. Whether during dating or in the early years of marriage, women learn to make a place for themselves in their husband's family and to assume a new and unique set of obligations. The development of the role of daughter-in-law occurs over the long run but with discernable changes at various life course events.

Most of the daughters-in-law did indeed note changes in their relationship with their mother-in-law over time. For some, the relationship started during dating, whereas others rarely saw their future in-law during that time. Many noted that their relationship changed when they became engaged or after marriage. These daughters-in-law felt that it was then that they became members of the family. The effect of having children was mixed, however; some of the daughters-in-law stated that having a child introduced problems into their relationship or made it more ambiguous. Most commonly, daughters-in-law felt that they became closer to their in-laws over time, even if it was only a slight change.

Recognizing and learning to fulfill the obligations of being a daughter-in-law and learning to resolve conflict were two central aspects of the development of the role. Although daughters-in-law did not all identify a common set of obligations, there was still a great deal of overlap. Most commonly, daughters-in-law felt obligated to be the connecting link between their own families (i.e., their husbands and children) and their in-laws. Many of the daughters-in-law also felt that they were obligated to be part of their in-laws' family and to be respectful and not too critical of their mothers-in-law. A few mentioned that this included being respectful of their mother-in-law's position as a mother. Daughters-in-law also felt obligated to include their in-laws, and some felt that being a good daughter-in-law meant being a good wife and mother. The vast majority of the daughters-in-law believed that they learned these obligations over time and that they were based on how they would want to be treated and what they thought was "right." Daughters-in-law also determined their obligations as a result of time spent in the family and discovering what they could contribute based on their position within the family. Nearly all of the daughters-in-law felt some obligation to their in-laws.

The vast majority of the daughters-in-law learned to resolve conflict over time to the extent that it existed. Only a few had never resolved the discord between themselves and their mothers-in-law. The most common methods of conflict resolution were "letting it go" and "confrontation." As daughters-in-law gained confidence in their marriage and in their role as daughter-in-law, many also became more assertive in ending conflict. A few daughters-in-law learned to "manage the situation" by minimizing the potential for conflict.

The development of the daughter-in-law role also included the creation of an identity as such. Daughters-in-law developed a number of different identities. Most commonly it was based on their primary obligation as the "connecting link." Others identified as a "martyr" or "downtrodden daughter-in-law," the predominant cultural images in the media. Still others identified as "being like a daughter," "the peacekeeper," or a "distant daughter-in-law." Unlike our identities as mothers or daughters, there is an opportunity for far more variability in creating an in-law identity. There are few cultural images in the media, but there are also fewer universal expectations of that identity.

The creation of an in-law identity is a dynamic process with great fluidity in women's identities across the life course. Many of the daughters-in-law entered marriage with an expectation of the kind of relationship they would have with a mother-in-law. If their experiences did not meet their expectations, they became disappointed and developed an identity as a "martyr," "distant daughter-in-law," or "peacekeeper." Those daughters-in-law whose relationships improved came to see themselves as "the connecting link" between their own families and their in-laws. Those with a good relationship from the start were more likely to identify as "being like a daughter." Sources of women's identities came from popular images in the media, their own mothers' experiences as a daughter-in-law, and a comparison to their own experiences as a daughter. Their in-law identity was consistent with other identities, such as that of a religious person, for at least some of the women.

Women's identities as daughters-in-law frequently developed as a result of a comparison to their own experiences as daughters or by comparing what happened in their in-laws' families with what happened in their own families. This became the reference point much more frequently than making comparisons to the experiences of sisters-in-law. Likewise, women made comparisons to what they expected it would be like to be a daughter-in-law, but again it was an image that was not grounded in other women's experiences but in their own cultural repertoire or set of images. This is consistent with the argument that women do bring culture to bear on their experience when it does not meet their expectations and that this is more common when women feel lost,[37] bringing us back again to the ambiguity of the daughter-in-law role.

Women also used cultural resources to guide them and to help them to resolve (or try to resolve) problems. Some of the women talked about setting boundaries with their in-laws while the mothers-in-law focused more on the importance of communicating with their daughters-in-law. None of the women referred to listening to talk shows, a popular resource, to better handle their relationships with their mothers-in-law.

How then do women take these cultural meanings and make them their own? That is, how did the women name their own experiences in cultural terms? Consider the example of Linda, who has been married three times and divorced twice. At the age of fifty-one, she has had three very different identities as a daughter-in-law. Her first experience was that of a very young woman who had practically grown up before her mother-in-law's eyes. Her identity was the closest to "being like a daughter," not wanting to disappoint, and so on. By the time that her second and third mothers-in-law came along, she was already a divorced woman with one and then two children. Both of these mothers were very unhappy with Linda's involvement with their sons and believed (according to Linda) that she was using them for a meal ticket. Her third mother-in-law did not allow her to step into their family home for the first three years of their marriage. Linda used cultural images of gender inequity, stereotyping, and an overly protective mother-in-law to explain such extreme behavior. Linda also used cultural meanings surrounding her role as a single mother to make sense of her later experiences as a daughter-in-law.

Although not all of the daughters-in-law agreed on one or two obligations for their role, there was still a great deal of overlap. This suggests that it is not a totally ambiguous role, as has been suggested by others.[38] There is at least some common understanding of a daughter-in-law's place in the family and of the obligations that come with it. The ambiguity has more to do with the degrees of involvement and how best to facilitate the obligations. For example, many of the women felt obligated to be the connecting link. In some families that meant little inclusion of them; they were still outside of the parent/child/grandchild relationship but orchestrating it nonetheless. For others, being a connecting link meant being a part of the relationship between their own families and their in-laws. Thus, the ambiguity had to do with just how much they were "in" or "out" of the family, and those expectations did not always match up between the mother-in-law and daughter-in-law. Daughters-in-law who felt on the outside were more likely to have a negative relationship with their mother-in-law, however.

It is important to note that for many of the women, their identity as a daughter-in-law came in part from their role as a wife. One part of their role as wife (and mother) was to serve as the connecting link with in-laws. Some also believed that being a good daughter-in-law meant being a good wife and mother. Thus, in-law relationships are, in part, about marriage. They are predicated on marriage and can be affected by the husband's involvement in the relationship and by the mother-in-law's views of marriage and her son's marriage in particular (both to be discussed in the next chapter). Daughters-in-law in very poor relationships stated that they would not remain in contact with their mother-in-law if something were to happen to their husband. In addition, in-law relationships can also affect the quality of the marriage, although this is more likely to be the case in extreme situations (this too will be discussed in the next chapter).

What are the implications of popular culture having such a substantial effect on women's identities and experiences in the family? It seems likely that as long as popular culture, and the media in particular, perpetuates negative stereotypes about mothers-in-law and in-law relationships that daughters-in-law will continue to adopt these identities. Expecting women to be resistant to the stereotypes seems unrealistic. Women with positive or even mediocre relationships can speak out about their experiences, although they often do not because they are inconsistent with what is expected. Books like this one, however, can help women to realize the vast array of in-law experiences and the determinants of those experiences that reach far beyond anything that they or their in-laws might have done wrong. The media needs to provide alternative images of healthy relationships, although it is unlikely to do so as long as we continue to find humor at the expense of mothers-in-law everywhere.

Seven

MOTHERS AND SONS, HUSBANDS AND WIVES, AND THE MOTHER-IN-LAW'S PERSPECTIVE

I have learned that if you want to stay close to your kids after they marry, you've got to include their spouses too. Otherwise, you don't see much of your children.

—Claire (mother-in-law)

It is hard being a daughter-in-law, but it is hard being a mother-in-law too. You feel like you are always on the outside looking in, and that is a hard place for a mother to be.

—Beth (mother-in-law)

The thing that gives me the greatest pleasure is to see the love that flows between my son and daughter-in-law.

—Kim (mother-in-law)

By now, the reader is likely to ask, "What part do sons play in all of this?" and "How do *mothers-in-law* feel about their relationships with their sons and daughters-in-law?" The purpose of this chapter is to address these questions. In particular, we will examine the role of the son/husband in facilitating a relationship between his wife and mother. We will also consider the effect of the son's relationship with his mother on the in-laws' relationship and how the son's relationship with his mother changes upon marriage. I argue that the quality of the relationship between the mother-in-law and daughter-in-law is not just about what goes on between them but is affected as much by the mother and son's relationship and the daughter-in-law's perception of it.

In this chapter, we will also further examine the mother-in-law's perspective. Earlier we looked at how mothers-in-law described their relationships with their daughters-in-law and how their descriptions differed from the daughters-in-law's descriptions. In this chapter, we will discuss women's major concerns as mothers-in-law and as the mothers of married sons.

Here I will also argue that the impact of the mother-in-law and daughter-in-law relationship is far reaching. Not only does the quality of the relationship impact the interactions between the two women, but it also has consequences for the daughter-in-law and son's marriage. I will argue that in-law relationships are really about marriage and about mother and son ties.

EARLIER RESEARCH ON MOTHERS AND SONS

The relationship between a mother and her son plays an important role in the development of the in-law relationship. The effect of the mother–son bond is not straightforward, however. Adult children find themselves holding positions in two families when they marry, and thus a complicated process begins of bringing two (or even three) complex family systems together. It can go smoothly if the parent and child have been successful in the "letting go" process and if there is a healthy balance of autonomy and connectedness between the two. Yet, if the parent–child relationship is not sufficiently autonomous, the marriage may pose a threat to the mother and son relationship.[1] Thus, a daughter-in-law's relationship with her mother-in-law may depend to a great degree on the success of this earlier process of letting go. The father-in-law can be very helpful both in aiding this process and in easing any tension.[2] Peterson et al.[3] point out that older family structures (that is, those of later-life families) may not be flexible enough to accommodate the entrance of marital partners into the family system. I would argue that any family with rigid boundaries might have difficulty incorporating marital partners. Impermeable boundaries can exist within any family but may also develop as a result of divorce, death in the family, or other family disruptions.

Mothers-in-law may have legitimate fears of losing their sons upon marriage. Fingerman[4] reminds us that extended families are often based on matrilineal kinship. That is, the married couple remains closer to her family than to his family. This is certainly borne out by the research that finds that the wife's parents both provide and receive more assistance than the husband's parents.[5–7] Daughters-in-law then are often accused of drawing sons away from their families, particularly once the couple has children of their own.[8]

In an optimal situation, a mother-in-law will be able to let her son share his life with another woman and the daughter-in-law will not see his mother as a rival.[9] A mother-in-law who is too "possessive" of her son though will run into conflict with both her son and his wife. Author Lillian Rubin[10] found in her study of working class families in the 1970s that the chief struggle between daughters-in-law and their mothers-in-law was over who would be number one in the husband's/son's life. More recently, Arnstein[11] found that daughters-in-law complained about the amount of time that mothers-in-law demanded of their sons, asking them to fix things, give advice, and so on.

A mother's relationship with her son could affect her relationship with her daughter-in-law in one other way as well. For both sons and daughters, a better relationship with the adult child results in a better relationship with the in-law.[12] A mother-in-law with a good relationship with her son may spend more time with her daughter-in-law or have a greater motivation to get along with her. It may be that her affection for her son automatically transfers to his family as well.

RELATIONSHIPS BETWEEN MOTHERS AND SONS

The majority of daughters-in-law (55 percent) and all of the mothers-in-law described the sons as having positive relationships with their mothers. They described the bonds as warm and loving or affectionate and close. One daughter-in-law said, "He loves her very much. The loyalty is very strong." Another added, "He dotes on her. He is her only son. He wants to do wonderful things for her because she did so much for him." Four of the daughters-in-law though said that their husbands were *too* close to their mothers. For example, Sophie said, "He has gone through his adult life pleasing her. She manipulates him. They are close, but it is an unhealthy close. I don't know how he will function when she gets sick." Another daughter-in-law said, "He calls every week and they talk for hours. He still calls her 'Mommy.'" Kay, who was very forthright in her feelings, added, "They are too close. It bothers me. He tells her everything. It is like there is this competition. I think that he should put more of his attention on me." Some of the daughters-in-law also pointed out that their husbands loved their mothers, but that they had little in common beyond that.

A much smaller percentage of daughters-in-law (19 percent) felt that their husbands had strained or negative relationships with their mothers. For example, one of the daughters-in-law described her husband's relationship with his mother as such, "It is distant. He loves her, but he doesn't like her." Another daughter-in-law said that her husband was not close to his mother because both of his parents were always "putting him down" while he was growing up. They made him feel that he was a failure. Sydney pointed out that her husband must have been close to his mother when he was little because he was sitting in her lap in all of the pictures from that time. However, she felt that they grew apart when her father-in-law became abusive and her mother-in-law subsequently became mentally ill.

One-quarter, or 25 percent, of the daughters-in-law described their husbands as having mixed (good and bad or what is referred to as ambivalent) or "okay" relationships with their mothers. For example, Cindy said, "It is good in small doses. He feels that too much time with her is unhealthy for him though." Another daughter-in-law said, "He loves her, but he also feels responsible for her and that makes him resentful."

CHANGE AFTER MARRIAGE

The fact that a wife's parents receive more help than a husband's parents from couples[13–15] and the cultural belief that wives draw sons away from their families[16] would suggest that sons will be less close to their mothers (and other family members) following marriage. However, the majority of daughters-in-law (55 percent) felt that their husband's relationship with his mother stayed the same after they married. The mother and son neither grew distant because of his new marriage nor did they grow closer. Sophie, who wished that her husband were more independent of his mother, was unhappy that there had not been greater change. She explained,

> No, things haven't changed because I am a woos. I don't like to fight, and he can't handle separating from her. He feels bad if he has to say "no" to her, so he doesn't. She makes him feel like he always says "no," but that is not true.

Most of the daughters-in-law, however, did not mind that the relationship remained unchanged.

A substantial percentage of the daughters-in-law (32 percent) though felt that their husbands grew *closer* to their mothers following their marriages. This was either because their wives facilitated the relationship (e.g., reminding them to call and arranging get-togethers) or because they spent more time together as a family unit once the son was married. For example, one of the wives said, "He wouldn't visit if it weren't for me." Another wife pointed out that her husband had become more aware of the things that he should do for his mother since he had married.

The remaining 13 percent of the daughters-in-law felt that their husbands had become more independent of their mothers following their marriages. For example, Libby, who had an excellent relationship with her mother-in-law, shared the following:

> I suppose it must have [changed]. I am not sure if she actually said something to him, but she certainly implied to him that your wife is your family now and that is whom you are responsible to now. She never made him feel like he was ignoring her or not giving her enough attention. Never. She never gave him a hard time about us not visiting more even though we saw more of my family. The message to him was, "That is your family now and you need to do what you need to do to keep that family going." Period.

Nicole also felt that her husband's relationship had changed for the better since they were married. She believed that her mother-in-law had controlled her husband prior to his marriage. She explained the change as follows:

> It is totally different [now]. He doesn't jump when she says, "Jump." The balance of power has shifted. He is better about taking my feelings into account. He doesn't like it when she snaps at him in front of us (me and the girls). He doesn't want us treating him the way that she does.

Thus, over half of the daughters-in-law felt that their husband's relationship with his mother hadn't changed once he married. That is, they felt that he stayed as close to or as distant from his mother as he always had. This was independent of whether or not he had been living at home prior to marriage. It suggests that relationships in the family of orientation (at least the relationship between the mother and son) do not necessarily have to change when one member marries. Other daughters-in-law, however, felt that their husbands had become closer to their mothers due to their own intervention. They reminded their husbands to keep in touch with their mothers and arranged family get-togethers. Sons had less such contact when they were single. Only a small minority of the daughters-in-law felt that their marriages had made their husbands more independent of their mothers. These daughters-in-law were pleased with this change. One of the daughters-in-law was very grateful to her mother-in-law for encouraging her husband to focus on his new family and for understanding that he had his own family now.

THE ROLE OF THE SON

The mother-in-law's relationship with her son impacts her daughter-in-law's relationship with her in a myriad of ways. The most glaring of the findings was among those daughters-in-law who had a very poor relationship with their mothers-in-law. Those women with an "estranged" or "obligatory" relationship with their mothers-in-law were much more likely to say that their mothers-in-law were too attached to their sons or that they were "territorial" of their sons. Several of the women also felt that their husbands tended to put their mothers above them. Consider the following testimonials from two women, Nicole and Kay, with "obligatory" relationships with their husbands' mothers:

> She is territorial of her sons. She felt threatened when each of them married and managed to alienate all of her daughters-in-law. It is worse with my husband though because he was her favorite…. It is his first thing to defend her.

and

> He and his mother are very close and tight. If you tell him something, she will know about it. She tells everyone too. I don't like him telling her everything. He would do anything for her…. It bothers me sometimes that they are so close. Yes, it is something of a competition. I don't like to be around her too much because of it. I stay away more because he is so close to her. I know that I won't have that closeness with her.

Clearly, the relationship that a mother-in-law tries to have with her son can result in an estrangement from her daughter-in-law if the daughter-in-law feels that the mother-in-law is *too* close or if the relationship between the mother and son makes the daughter-in-law feel uncomfortable.

Even under these conditions though, daughters-in-law tried to maintain some sort of relationship with their mothers-in-law for the benefit of their husbands and children. Sophie, whose husband confided in his mother about his wife and marriage, shared the following:

> They [her husband and mother-in-law] are very close. I can't say it is a healthy close. He has gone through his adult life trying to please her. She manipulates him. Since his father died, he tells her too much personal business of ours and they discuss it. The same is true of the other brothers. There are some things that you shouldn't discuss with your mother about

your wife. I do what I have to...[having a relationship with her] for my husband and son. It is just superficial though.

Sophie also kept her feelings about her mother-in-law from her husband because she felt that he would "fall apart" if he knew that she did not like his mother.

Other wives had poor relationships with their mothers-in-law because their husbands did not intervene to help them. They wanted their husbands to take their side when there was a confrontation and to defend them (or "stick up for them") to their mothers when necessary. A few of the women mentioned wanting their husbands to agree with them when they complained about their in-laws. Consider some of the wives' comments:

> He should have sided with me. He should have told her, "This is my wife and you need to treat her that way." I wanted him to stick up for me, and he just couldn't say anything to his mother. So she continued to treat me like a piece of garbage, and I continued to stay away from her.

and

> My husband says that if it [the way that his mother ignores their children] doesn't bother him, it shouldn't bother me. I want him to say something [to her], but technically he works for his father. I don't want to bite the hand that feeds me.

When I asked the women why they thought their husband would not stick up for them, they all said that their husbands did not want to confront their mothers. One woman said that her husband was "a mama's boy." The sons' involvement in resolving conflict will be discussed in even greater detail later in this chapter.

Although none of the mothers-in-law mentioned their son's relationship with his wife as causing problems for their relationships with their son, there was some suggestion from the daughters-in-law that this occasionally did happen. Sydney told me that when she confided her feelings about her mother-in-law to her husband, he would say, "What am I supposed to do? She is my mother. Do you want me to hate her?" Clearly, husbands/sons sometimes feel caught in the middle. However, many of the daughters-in-law also felt that difficulties with their mothers-in-law revolved around the older women's overinvolvement in their sons' lives and the sons' unwillingness to do something about this.

Daughters-in-law with positive relationships with their mothers-in-law were less likely to describe their husbands' relationships with their mothers as problematic. Instead, if the mother and son were close, it resulted in the daughter-in-law and mother-in-law having a good relationship as well. They said things like, "They are close. He talks to her daily, and then he fills me in later. He says, 'Mom said...'" and "Probably because they are close, I want to be closer too." These sons were also better at setting boundaries with their mothers. One of the daughters-in-law shared, "He tries not to let her get too involved like she was before." These daughters-in-law also felt like they were a part of their husbands' relationship with his mother. Millie, for example said, "*We* are always there for her. *We* are always think-ing of her [emphasis added]. If he hadn't [had a good relationship], I might have enhanced it though because I include her and she includes me."

Many of the daughters-in-law with the better relationships with their mothers-in-law felt that their husband's relationship with his mother had no impact on their relationship with her. They felt that they would have been close to her anyway because of whom she was. A typical response was, "I would do that [reach out to her] on my own. She has that personality. It is what I would have for her either way."

The vast majority of the daughters-in-law, those with both good and bad relationships with their mothers-in-law, said that they were the ones who reminded their husbands to keep in touch with their mothers. Many of them said things like, "He would never think to call (or invite his parents over for dinner) if it wasn't for me. They are close, but I have to remind him to even call." Some of these daughters-in-law said that they actually did more for their mothers-in-law because their husbands were not attentive enough or that they were more patient or compassionate with their mothers-in-law because their husbands were less so. For example, one daughter-in-law said,

> Sometimes he can be a little abrupt with her because she can be demanding or worries too much about things. He will be abrupt whereas I try to be tol-erant. He will just come out and tell her when she is being too negative.

Other daughters-in-law pointed out that they did what they did for their mothers-in-law because of (or for) their husbands. Stephanie, for example, said, "He is the conduit (for the relationship). If he wanted to visit twice a year, we would." In other words, her relationship and how much she saw her mother-in-law was determined by her husband. Likewise, Sally explained, "I make an effort because I have a relationship [with Steve] that I want to continue. If I said, 'I never want to see your family again,' there would be problems. So I work on it." Another daughter-in-law said, "Probably because they are close, I want to be close to her too." However, only a few of the daughters-in-law said that they would not be as close to their mothers-in-law if their husbands were not close.

Based on the mother-in-law's responses, there was a consistent relationship between her attitude towards her son's marriage and her relationship with her daughter-in-law. Those mothers-in-law who saw their son's marriage as being positive for him or who were pleased by his marriage tended to have a better relationship with their daughter-in-law. Ellen's mother-in-law, Kim, said, "The thing that gives me the greatest pleasure is to see the love that flows between [my son] and Ellen. Everyone wants that for their child." Not surprisingly, Ellen and Kim shared a "tight-knit" relationship. Likewise, Connie said, "I wanted my son to settle down and have *his own* family. I wanted his wife to feel a part of *our* family too though." Finally, Kristen's mother-in-law, who was effusive about her, said, "She is the best thing that happened to our son. What is not to love about that?"

The sons' birth order had no effect on how mothers-in-law and daughters-in-law got along. Mothers with oldest sons or youngest sons got along equally well with their daughters-in-law, both from the point of view of the mothers-in-law as well as the daughters-in-law. Whether or not the son was a favorite child had mixed results. As stated earlier, Nicole felt that her relationship with her mother-in-law was worse as a result of her mother-in-law being "territorial" of her favorite child. In contrast, Libby felt that her relationship improved as a result of her husband being his mother's favorite child. She jokingly said that she was riding on her husband's coat tails. Family and friends teased that Libby was actually the favorite one though.

THE EFFECT OF IN-LAW RELATIONSHIPS ON MARRIAGE

Earlier research shows that conflict between in-laws is one of the greatest sources of marital dissolution in the first year of marriage and that it erodes marital stability, satisfaction, and commitment over time even in long-term marriages.[17,18] Such conflict seems to be greatest with parents-in-law of the same gender.[19] However, marital success does not predict the quality of a spouse's relationship with in-laws.[20] That is, there is no reciprocal effect. In the following paragraphs we will look to see whether and how daughters-in-law believe their relationship with their mother-in-law affects the quality of their marriage.

In contrast to previous research, most of the daughters-in-law said that their relationship with their mother-in-law did not affect their marriage. However, this was most often the case when the wife had a good relationship with her mother-in-law or when she and her husband were in agreement about issues concerning his mother. Rebecca explained, "No it [my relationship with her] doesn't affect it [our marriage]. We team up together where she is concerned. We are like-minded about her. We team up to meet her needs and to deal with her." One daughter-in-law pointed out though that if she did have a negative relationship with her mother-in-law [which she did not], it would probably have had an adverse effect on her marriage. One of the older daughters-in-law also pointed out that she had never *let it* affect her marriage. Although she had a very difficult relationship with her mother-in-law, she had never spoken to her husband about it. She felt that it was something that he did not need to know about and that she could handle it herself. Younger daughters-in-law were more likely to share their concerns about their mothers-in-law with their husbands.

Daughters-in-law who felt that their relationship with their mother-in-law did affect their marriage were much more likely to say that it had a negative effect than a positive one. Sydney explained that her husband was often aggravated with her because she was not more patient with her mother-in-law. Two other daughters-in-law were angry with their husbands because they "enabled" their mothers' dependence, according to the daughters-in-law. One daughter-in-law pointed out that her mother-in-law's strong dislike of her had delayed her marriage for several years. Other daughters-in-law stated that they fought with their husbands about their in-laws and that it put a strain on their marriage. Diane explained, "That was a real issue with us...I wanted him to stick up for me, and he just couldn't say anything to his mother. We would scream at each other. I threatened to have him thrown out. We lived through it though." One of the daughters-in-law said that she and her husband were always on the verge of divorce because of her in-laws.

As other researchers have found, in-law relationships can be particularly problematic during the early years of marriage.[21,22] One of the daughters-in-law explained,

> Honestly, there have been times when I have wondered if it was worth this. It is. In the past she has definitely put a huge strain on us. I would say that she was our biggest obstacle in the first few years of marriage.

Likewise, Nicole added,

> In the beginning it was really, really difficult. She and their relationship really tested our marriage. We had fights early on where we were pushed to the brink. It changed once we had kids because it took the edge off all around. He realized that he could pick his mom and side with her, but I am the one who is raising his kids with him. Plus, she has backed off some. I am wrapped up in the kids, so I ignore her.

Monique pointed out that her husband had to learn how to handle his mother over time. She intimated that their problems with her husband's mother eventually caused him to focus more on their own family, but that the problems could have resulted in divorce. She shared the following,

> In our mid-20s we did what she wanted and that was that. She was great about laying the guilt trip on him. He would always try to accommodate her, but over time he learned to do it on his own terms. If he hadn't, I know that we would have been divorced. I couldn't deal with her then; it was really torturous for a lot of years with her. But he was devoted to his own family, number one. He put our being happy first. He grew up a lot. One of the things that kept us married was the fact that he saw things the way that I did too.

Still, sons and daughters-in-law may find that even if they make it past the early years of marriage that in-laws can pose problems later on, particularly during difficult times. One of the couples was having financial problems. The daughter-in-law felt that her husband was too focused on his mother and not focused enough on finding another job and that it was harder for her to ignore her mother-in-law's frivolity when she herself was pressed for money. Both things had caused problems in her marriage.

A minority of the daughters-in-law felt that their relationships with their mothers-in-law actually improved their marriages. Kristen felt that her husband appreciated how she initiated everything with his parents. He valued the fact that she got along well with his parents and that she brought them all (including the children) together. Another daughter-in-law pointed out that her mother-in-law was able to explain her husband's "quirks" to her, thus improving her marriage. Margaret said that her mother-in-law actually stuck up for her in her marriage. She said, "Sometimes it is actually for the better. She says to my husband, 'You are a lucky man. She is so good to you.' Maybe that makes him think. Plus, she sticks up for me if we disagree or argue. It makes me happy that she feels that way about me." Two other daughters-in-law thought that their marriages were actually better because their mothers-in-law had helped them, in part because of their close relationship, when their marriages were in trouble.

THE SON'S INVOLVEMENT IN RESOLVING CONFLICT

The vast majority of the daughters-in-law who experienced some conflict with their mothers-in-law during their marriage stated that their husbands did not get involved in the conflict. Most were resentful that their husbands would not "take a stand" or "take their side" in the conflict. They believed that their husbands were the ones who could most effectively change existing circumstances (versus themselves), but that they were unwilling to confront their mothers.

Most commonly, daughters-in-law said that their husbands told them to disregard their in-laws and the conflict. For example, Cynthia stated, "He tells me to ignore her and that I have to live with it. He says, 'I've got too much going on to deal with this shit. You friggin deal with it.'" Cynthia's husband not only wished to be uninvolved, but he was not able to be sympathetic to his wife either. Kayla's husband also advised his wife to ignore his mother, but she said that she usually confronted her anyway "to clear the air." Stephanie's husband was sympathetic and willing to hear her concerns about his parents, but he told her to just ignore them and do what she wanted to do (regarding any particular situation). Other daughters-in-law also said that their husbands "didn't get involved in any conflict" or that they "didn't want to know about it." A few of the husbands told their wives to confront their mothers-in-law with what was bothering them if they had to, but they themselves did not do so. Only one of the daughters-in-law said that whether or not her husband became involved was situationally dependent and that sometimes he took her side and sometimes he defended his mother.

Many of the daughters-in-law were disappointed that their husbands did not intervene in the conflict. These were usually situations in which the wives felt that their in-laws were treating them unfairly, and they wanted their husbands to stand up for them. In describing her early years of marriage, Diane vehemently stated over and over again, "He should have sided with me. He should have told her, 'This is my wife and you need to treat her that way.'" Likewise, Nina lamented, "He didn't do anything about the conflict between us. He visited every Sunday even though she didn't speak to me. I wasn't even mentioned. I thought he was weak for doing that." Only one of the daughters-in-law said that although her husband did not take sides that he would quietly speak to his mother (who coresided with them) about his wife's concerns.

Two of the daughters-in-law said that their husbands had intervened early on when there was conflict between themselves and their mothers-in-law. Both had better relationships with their mothers-in-law. Sue's mother-in-law, June, came by to see her unexpectedly one day when Sue had the flu. June mistook Sue's behavior as an indication of drug use and said that she was going to call the Department of Social Services on behalf of the (grand)children. When Sue told her husband, Jerry, he went right over to his mother's house and said, "Don't you ever, ever threaten Sue like that again. She is a good person, and she would never, ever use drugs. She is a wonderful mother and you should never, ever say anything like that again." Sue feels that she has not had any conflict with her mother-in-law since. In-law relationships then can be improved by a husband's attention to and willingness to address what his wife sees as problematic about his (or her) relationship with his mother early on in the relationship.

Likewise, Nicole said that her husband had to "set his mother straight" early on in their relationship. Scott told his mother and sister that Nicole would be his priority from then on rather than them and that they would have to treat her better. Though their relationship was still very strained, Nicole thought that this had been necessary to get along.

Only one of the daughters-in-law stated that her husband eventually learned to confront his mother on her behalf. Monique said that Richard learned to intervene in conflict in order to stand up for his family's needs. However, she learned why he was reluctant to do so given the futility of his efforts. Another two of the daughters-in-law said that they did not need their husbands to intervene in the conflict.

THE MOTHER-IN-LAW'S PERSPECTIVE

In her book *Mother of the Groom: A Collection of Women's Voices*, Eileen Posner shares the varied perspectives of mothers-in-law. Her main point is that "no matter what age, your child is always your child"[23] and that most mothers-in-law "just want to be loved and included—not left out."[24] She argues that in some situations, a mother may "hate" her daughter-in-law as early as her son's birth knowing that she will ultimately "lose him" to this other woman. Over and over again, she and her contributors repeat the adage, "A daughter's a daughter the rest of her life, but a son is a son till he gets him a wife."[25] Although some of the mothers-in-law in her book describe warm and loving relationships with their sons' wives, her overall theme is that of the daughter-in-law as a competitor for the son.

Not all mothers-in-law see their daughters-in-law as harming their relationships with their sons, however. In fact, most of the mothers-in-law in this study reported positive bonds with their daughters-in-law. As was described in Chapter 3, the majority of the mothers-in-law (71 percent) described their relationships with their daughters-in-law as being "tight knit" or "distant but positive." Another 24 percent described the relationships as "cordial," and only 6 percent described them as "conflicted but affectionate." None of the mothers-in-law described their relationships with their daughters-in-law as being either "obligatory" or "estranged." Of the seventeen matches, twelve (71 percent) of the mothers-in-law described the relationships similarly to their daughters-in-law, but five (29 percent) did not. In situations where there was a discrepancy, mothers-in-law always described the relationships more positively. Mothers-in-law may be more positive about the relationship because they know that their daughters-in-law have already been interviewed and do not want to appear negative. However, the mother-in-law may not feel the conflict that the daughter-in-law does or may be less critical of the relationship overall. All of the mothers-in-law also described warm and loving relationships with their sons, although one of the women pointed out that her son did not call enough.

All fourteen mothers-in-law said that they thought of their daughters-in-law as family, while half said that they considered them to be friends as well. One of the mothers-in-law, Kim, pointed out that although she thought of her daughter-in-law as another daughter, she was also mindful of the fact that Ellen had her own mother. The predominant sentiment among the mothers-in-law though was that their daughter-in-law was one of their children or an extension of their children.

None of the mothers-in-law reported conflict with their daughters-in-law, although one of the women recognized that she irritated her daughter-in-law. Another mother-in-law pointed out that there was no conflict because she and her husband "minded their own business unless asked." The implication was, of course, that there might have been conflict if she had not done this. Kim felt that she and her daughter-in-law differed on child rearing, but that she respected Ellen's ways on the matter. She also pointed out that she did not share her opinions with Ellen.

All but one of the mothers-in-law kept in touch with their prior daughters-in-law (if they had any), although relationships were sometimes strained. The one mother-in-law who did not keep in touch with her son's ex-wife did not have grandchildren. Many of the women though said that they still thought of their sons' ex-wives as family and as daughters-in-law. One of the mothers-in-law said, "Once you are family, you are always family." Another said, "My first daughter-in-law practically lived in our house for years while she was growing up. She will always be my daughter-in-law."

Mothers-in-law believed that they were obligated to welcome their daughters-in-law into their families and to recognize that their sons and daughters-in-law had their own families. Kristen's mother-in-law, Dot, explained her feelings as such:

> You have to honor their family and realize that they are a family, a separate entity from you. Be there for advice, but don't give your opinion otherwise or interfere.... Being nice to your daughter-in-law is the only right thing. She is your son's wife and the mother of your grandchildren.

The need to keep their opinions to themselves and to recognize the boundaries or limits between themselves and their son's family was a common theme among the mothers-in-law.

Although they recognized the need to respect their son's place in another family, at least some of the mothers-in-law also felt that they had "lost" their sons when they married. This is consistent with the concerns expressed by mothers in Posner's book. One of the mothers-in-law said,

> I expected my sons to have their own families, and I am glad that they do.... The daughter-in-law has taken the mother-in-law's son away from her. That has to be a part of the deep relationship. I took my mother-in-law's son too.

Likewise, another mother-in-law made the following statement:

> It is hard being a daughter-in-law, but it is hard being a mother-in-law too. You feel like you are always on the outside looking in and that is a hard place for any mother to be.

Many of the daughters-in-law mentioned how grateful their mothers-in-law were when they made an effort to include them in their families or made overtures to bridge the gap between them. Given the previous comment, one can understand how such overtures would lessen a mother-in-law's feeling like an outsider, as well as make it easier for the mother-in-law to get to know her daughter-in-law. Although many of the mothers-in-law did not mention this specifically, others did express a deep appreciation for their daughters-in-law. For example, consider Dot's comment:

> Kristen is the best. Everyone loves her. I am so lucky, and I know that she loves me too. I just love her so and admire her so. If you didn't love her, there would have to be something wrong with you.

SUMMARY AND IMPLICATIONS

According to both the mothers-in-law and daughters-in-law, the vast majority of sons have good relationships with their mothers. Only 19 percent of the daughters-in-law reported negative or strained relationships between their husbands and mothers-in-law. Slightly over half of the daughters-in-law believed that their husband's relationship with his mother stayed the same after he married, whereas fully one-third believed that their husbands grew closer to their mothers, in part because of their own intervention. However, some of the daughters-in-law believed that their husband's relationship with his mother negatively affected their own relationship with her. This was more often the case when they saw their husband's relationship with his mother as being too close. Likewise, their relationship with their mother-in-law caused problems in the marriage for at least some of the women. This was particularly true during the early years of marriage. Again, this was most often precipitated by what the daughter-in-law saw as a problem in the son's relationship with his mother or his unwillingness to stick up for his wife to his mother. Among those daughters-in-law who had experienced conflict with their mother-in-law at some point in their marriages, only two had husbands who intervened in the conflict early on in the relationship, while a third husband eventually learned to intervene for the benefit of his family. Daughters-in-law were often upset and disappointed that their husbands had not "taken a stand" on their behalf.

Mothers-in-law were more likely to report positive relationships with their daughters-in-law and were less likely to report conflict on their part. Many were conscientious about not interfering and keeping their opinions to themselves. They believed that they should welcome their daughters-in-law into their families and that prior daughters-in-law were still family. It was particularly important to grandmothers that they stayed in touch with their sons' ex-wives in order to maintain contact with the grandchildren. While most mothers-in-law reported good relationships with their sons and daughters-in-law, at least some expressed a loss of their sons when they married. This was despite the fact that they fully expected their sons to have their own families. Some of the mothers-in-law also felt that they were on the outside looking in on their sons' lives and that this was a difficult position for them. Daughters-in-law believed that their mothers-in-law appreciate being included and are grateful when daughters-in-law take an initiative to bridge the gap between themselves and their mothers-in-law. This was verified by at least some of the mothers-in-law.

These findings raise several questions. First of all, should husbands involve themselves in the conflict between their wives and mothers? Many had a long history of avoiding conflict with their mothers, a method that "worked" for them. At a minimum, it is important for wives to feel that their husbands support them in their relationship with his family. It is interesting to note that the wives were less likely to be upset if their husbands agreed with them on issues regarding their mothers (so that the wives felt like they were a team) versus defending their mothers or being unwilling to listen to their wives' concerns. Although husbands and wives may not always agree, they should try to understand one another's point of view and to validate it. It is important for husbands and wives to note when in-law problems are affecting their marriage and to seek professional assistance in these circumstances.

These results also raise the question of whether the relationship between a husband and his mother (or a wife and either of her parents) should change upon his marriage and the creation of a new family. Most of the wives felt that their husband's relationship with his mother was not significantly altered by their marriage, nor did they find his relationship with his mother to be problematic. This is certainly good news for those who support both marriage and intergenerational relationships. Many families though may need to make room for the new daughter-in-law/sister-in-law and ensure that she feels welcome in the extended family. This may then require some alteration of the mother and son relationship to include her. In fact, the marriage of an adult child marks a new stage in the family's life course. As such, one can argue that some alteration is an important part of the development of relationships and that it notes a healthy adjustment. Consider, for example, Arnstein's[26] suggestion that mothers-in-law learn to include their daughters-in-law in all communications short of birthday wishes. Such an adjustment signals to the daughter-in-law that her mother-in-law recognizes her marriage and will not ignore it. However, daughters-in-law should also consider the mother-in-law's need to feel included and be part of her son's life. Many of the in-laws had successfully maneuvered these challenges. Results of these findings suggest that most mothers-in-law do not feel as though they lose their sons upon marriage. Instead, they continue to have a warm and loving relationship when they recognize their sons as being part of this new and separate entity.

Author Eileen Posner,[27] as well as many of the daughters-in-law in this sample, suggests that mothers-in-law should treat their daughters-in-law just like daughters. This is good advice if the mother-in-law and daughter-in-law get along. At least some of the mothers-in-law in this study would have found this difficult though because the daughters-in-law did not wish to be treated as such and the mothers-in-law knew this. In her book, Arnstein[28] also points out that a daughter-in-law may not want another mother. Likewise, not all mothers-in-law may necessarily love, or even like, their daughters-in-law. After all, these are women from two different backgrounds and families who are brought together by happenstance and a third person. It makes sense that it will not always be possible to treat one another as a mother or daughter. Sometimes one's husband's mother is just that, and not a mother *by law*. Thus, it is unfair to both women to assume that creating a quasi mother–daughter bond is always possible and optimal. If we understand at the outset that this is not always feasible, we relieve ourselves of unnecessary burdens and expectations. It takes, however, a recognition and understanding that in-laws are not always going to feel like a parent (or child), especially in the beginning. This does not negate the fact that many of the relationships in this study were quasi mother–daughter bonds or that this is a wonderful thing that can happen. However, many people will continue to be disappointed if we hold onto the myth that in-laws are automatically just like their biological equivalents. The importance of welcoming an in-law into the family, treating the couple like an autonomous unit, and including the in-law cannot be underestimated, however, based on the results of this study.

Eight

WHY ARE IN-LAW
RELATIONSHIPS SO HARD?

Being a daughter-in-law means having a relationship with a family that is not your own. It is hard for some women.... they have to mold into a family, which is hard to do.... You [the mother-in-law] have to honor their family and realize that they are a family, a separate entity from you.
—Dot (mother-in-law)

A colleague stopped me in the hall one morning during the early stages of this project and asked me about my new research endeavor. When I told her that I was studying relationships between mothers-in-law and daughters-in-law, she instantly replied, "That is a hard relationship."[1] While many people—neighbors, colleagues, friends, and strangers—have all commented that I picked a volatile (or "doozy" of a) subject, the women in particular have been as likely to point out how "hard" the relationship is. While they intimate that the difficulty lies more in being a daughter-in-law than a mother-in-law, older women sometimes add that it is hard to be a mother-in-law too. This chapter will examine why the relationship is so difficult and will present the advice that women offered to one another as a result of that difficulty.

What do people mean though when they say that in-law relationships are "hard?" Basically, they are referring to the fact that compared with relationships with one's own family members, it is more of a challenge to get along with and ideally to have a loving relationship with one's in-laws (the reasons for this are discussed later). It also refers to the fact that in-laws may not necessarily feel like family or have things in common on which to base a relationship. At the extreme, either in-law can resent the other person's behavior in their relationship or their relationship with the husband/son.

EARLIER RESEARCH

Given that a significant proportion of in-laws do get along, how have earlier researchers accounted for the problems that other mothers-in-law and daughters-in-law often experience? In one study, 72 percent of the daughters-in-law who did not get along with their mothers-in-law said that their mother-in-law's bossiness and intrusiveness were the main causes of the friction.[2] Being critical of the daughter-in-law was the second cause. The mothers-in-law's chief complaint was that their daughters-in-law were indifferent and thoughtless towards them. They felt that they could no longer be themselves since their daughters-in-law had become a part of the picture.

Additional researchers have looked less at interpersonal causes and instead concentrated on the nature of the relationship and other structural factors to explain the difficulties mothers-in-law and daughters-in-law some-times face. Fischer[3] focuses on the fact that daughters-in-law are strangers and kinfolk simultaneously and the implications of this for the relationship. For example, despite having family obligations, they do not share a history with their mothers-in-law and are estranged from the family culture. In addition, their relationship with their in-laws is less important to them than their husband and children's relationships. These incongruities make the relationship a difficult one.

Cotterill[4] also looks at structural factors to explain the nature of in-law relationships. She argues that the relationships are structured by the women's respective positions in the family (e.g., that of mother versus wife) and within the context of their notions of family life. These perspectives may be incom-patible, however. For example, what a mother would like for the family may diverge from what a wife would like. In addition, each woman will have an idea of how she and the other person should act as in-laws, and these per-spectives may clash. Mothers and their daughters-in-law hoped to achieve something similar to a mother–daughter bond or to be friends, but often the relationship was neither. Anger needed to be avoided since there was no emo-tional intimacy in the relationships to sustain it or to counter it. This was one way to avoid the risk of the relationship breaking down.

There are additional reasons for why the relationships are so negative. Cotterill[5] also argues that there are no real rules for an appropriate relationship or social behaviors, so the tension and conflict often become attributed to individual incompatibilities rather than to this ambiguous structuring context. Daughters-in-law, however, hold the balance of power since they are able to make more choices about kin keeping. As such, they remain more ambivalent about the relationship. I will argue later that this power imbalance also explains why mothers-in-law can be resentful. Thus, the ambiguity in the role[6]; the lack of a shared history, emotional ties, and a genetic link; and the fact that they are both kinfolk and strangers simultaneously[7] may account for negative relationships.

WHY ARE RELATIONSHIPS SO HARD?

Among my initial interests in this topic was a desire to understand why in-law relationships are "so hard" from the perspective of women. As one observer remarked, "What is the big deal about adding someone new into the family?" As we will see, in-law relationships are not just about "adding" a new family member. They are also about creating a separate and autonomous family and how to do that while also maintaining connections to the family of origin. In other words, social structural factors in the family account for much of the difficulty.

According to the results of this study, in-law relationships are difficult, in part, because of the incongruous nature of the relationship. That is, mothers-in-law and daughters-in-law are expected to treat one another like family when, in fact, they do not share the characteristics and joys of mother–daughter relationships. This is not to say that mother–daughter relationships are without their own unique challenges, but mother–daughter relationships (like many family relationships) offer one another an unconditional love and a connection because of both a shared history and blood ties that in-law relationships do not offer (especially at the beginning of the relationship). In her book *Mother of My Mother*, Edelman notes the unconditional love that daughters feel from their mothers and grandmothers.[8] Such love makes it easier to withstand the difficulties of adult relationships or the inconveniences of visiting and keeping in touch. Likewise, having a shared history and blood ties also make it more likely to get past the difficulties in a relationship and may result in having fewer overall problems. As one of the daughters-in-law stated, "I know that my mother always has my best interest at heart. I am not sure of that with my mother-in-law."

In contrast, in-laws are expected to treat one another like family without sharing any of these characteristics. Treating someone like family includes sharing one's home during extended visits for those who live far away or frequent visits for those who live nearby, sharing holidays, meeting family obligations such as providing resources or offering help, and loving one another. All of this is expected to happen despite potential individual incompatibilities (that have usually been negotiated early on in biologically based relationships) and the fact that new in-laws may still be strangers. Consider the following example of Maria:

> In the first year that we were engaged, my mother-in-law asked if my hus-
> band's younger sister could come and stay with us for a while. Not only
> would I be cooking and cleaning for this girl, but it was expected that she
> would be driving the car that my husband and I shared. I thought that this
> was too much to ask, especially when I hardly knew this girl and my
> mother-in-law should have been taking care of her. What is really annoying
> though is that she did not ask me or us, she just asked my husband as if I
> wasn't even there!

While many of the daughters-in-law got along well with their mothers-in-law, those who did not often pointed to flaws in their mothers-in-law that they could not get past. For example, women thought that their mothers-in-law were self-centered, controlling, or too old-fashioned. Yet, they might have learned to overlook these same characteristics in their own mothers or adapted to them over time. Without a shared history and unconditional love though, the differences were insurmountable for in-laws.

Is it harder though to treat an in-law like family if you are a daughter-in-law versus a mother-in-law? Certainly, daughters-in-law were more likely to note difficulty in a relationship with a mother-in-law than vice versa. Thus, it may be harder to treat someone like a second mother than like a second daughter, in part because the mother-in-law may be asking more of the daughter-in-law than vice versa. For example, the mother-in-law is looking for entrée and inclusion in the daughter-in-law's life with her husband and children. This includes inviting someone else's mother into your home and treating her like your own mother or sharing resources with her. For the mother-in-law, what she does for her daughter-in-law she also does for her son. That is, including her daughter-in-law is an extension of including her own son.

Thus, in-law relationships are difficult, in part, because they have all of the obligations and expectations of family without the benefits of family. Is this a realistic expectation? On the other hand, we have found that if in-laws are not treated like family, they will feel rejected and excluded from their husband's/son's life. At a minimum, in-laws need to be aware that their expectations or obligations of their sons are also obligations of their daughters-in-law and perhaps temper those expectations early on in the relationship. Daughters-in-law too need to understand how these differences make it more difficult to incorporate their mothers-in-law into their families in an effort to improve relationships.

A second, and equally important, reason that in-law relationships are so difficult is that a new and separate family is being created. Both the husband's and the wife's role in his family will be altered by their marriage. This requires that the family of origin have permeable boundaries so that daughters-in-law can enter the family and sons can leave it. Whether sons and daughters-in-law form a family that is outside of the boundaries of the family of origin (that is, the extended family) or that exists within it will depend upon the individual families and may require family members to learn new expectations. At a minimum though, there will be a need for boundaries around the son's new family, a place for the daughter-in-law in the overall family, and an understanding that the son's role in the overall family will change.

Making these alterations requires both a recognition that the family is changing and a willingness to accept the changes. Herein lies the difficulty. This is a development in the family life course for which parents and siblings may not be prepared. For example, one of the daughters-in-law said, "My husband said that his family never discussed the fact that they would each have their own families some day. My mother made it clear that she expected us to have our own families, our own separate families. My husband's parents never talked about it." Parents may not think about the changes that will occur when their son marries or be prepared for the fact that their son will have an independent and separate family. They may not recognize the need to maintain some distance, to incorporate their daughter-in-law into the family, or to recognize the couple. This then results in the daughter-in-law's feeling that the mother-in-law is intrusive or ignoring her son's marriage.

This second difficulty may be exacerbated by our greater emphasis on the nuclear family and marriage than in the past. Prior to the 1950s, the married couple was only one part, and not *the* part, of the family system. Ties with children and other relatives tended to be equally or even more important than ties to a spouse. Today though the couple is at the core of family life.[9,10] As such, current couples are going to place greater emphasis on their own relationship and nuclear family, thus making their autonomous status an even greater priority.

The third factor that makes in-law relationships so difficult is the ambivalent and ambiguous nature of in-law ties. Earlier researchers have noted the presence of ambivalence, that is, the coexistence of positive and negative ties, in intergenerational relationships.[11–18] Cotterill[19] also notes the ambiguity in in-law relationships, that is, the absence of rules for an appropriate relationship. However, ambivalence may take on a darker side when resentment arises. That is, the opportunity for both positive and negative sentiments tips in the balance of negative sentiments when in-laws start to harbor negative feelings towards one another. For example, some of the daughters-in-law talked about things that their mothers-in-law had said or done as far back as their courtship with their husbands. Those resentments, when not resolved, turned what had been ambivalence into estrangement.

The ambiguity in the relationship also led to problems. The lack of societal-wide expectations left women not knowing their appropriate role in the family and not knowing how to interpret (thus sometimes misinterpreting) their in-laws' actions. All of the daughters-in-law expected to be a part of their husband's families, but some felt that they were not treated as such. Their husband's families may have had different expectations of what it means to be an in-law. Certainly daughters-in-law felt welcomed into their husbands' families to varying degrees. Not fully participating in the husband's family led to hurt feelings on the part of parents-in-law as well.

In-law relationships may be harder for women than for men because of the greater importance of relationships and having one's own family for women. Women are still defined by their roles in the family to a greater degree than are men. Likewise, women are more likely to be seen as the kin keepers in the family. As such, their roles as wife and mother are an important part of their identity. Mothers-in-law in this generation, many of whom did not work, may find it particularly difficult to transition to playing a lesser part in their sons' lives. Their resentment, in fact, may be justified given a couple's tendency to spend more time with the wife's family than with the husband's family.[20] Daughters-in-law may also be more likely to feel that their mothers-in-law are stepping on their toes in their own families. The extent to which daughters-in-law have a strong identification in other realms may lessen this friction, thus accounting for the educational differences found. Friction between in-laws is often seen or defined as the result of competition for the son/husband. In reality, it has more to do with existing gender ideologies and the relative importance placed on women's identification with families and relationships.

Family differences and the difficulties of two families coming together are the fifth reason that in-law relationships are so difficult. Over and over again, daughters-in-law mentioned how different their husband's family was from their family. Likewise, mothers-in-law explained that their daughters-in-law had been raised differently than they raised their children. Typically, daughters-in-law mentioned that their husband's family was much closer (or much more independent) than that to which they were accustomed. This left daughters-in-law feeling either that their in-laws were overbearing or indifferent, both of which affected their feelings towards their in-laws. Likewise, some of the daughters-in-law who had grown up in families where in-laws were treated just like biological relatives felt very hurt if their husband's family did not do the same for them.

Some in-laws found the other family's holiday or gift-giving practices to be foreign to them. For example, one of the daughters-in-law was annoyed that her in-laws always gave their children money, rather than a gift that they had picked out, for holidays. Another daughter-in-law was angry that her in-laws watched so much television during visits, something that her family would never do. In-laws pointed out differences in childrearing practices, intergenerational assistance, holiday celebrations, and intergenerational relationships. Such differences were difficult to overlook because of the additional factors mentioned earlier.

Daughters-in-law also compared their relationships with their in-laws to their relationships with their own families. Some were disappointed by the comparison. Daughters-in-law who were not disappointed were either well integrated into their husband's family or did not juxtapose the two. The fact that daughters-in-law make such a comparison suggests that at least some women equate being an in-law with having an integral place in the extended family.

In-law relationships are also difficult because of their negative image in popular culture. With an expectation that mothers-in-law will be interfering and overly involved, it is no wonder that wives attribute any breach in their mother-in-law's behavior as evidence of a difficult relationship. Frequently, daughters-in-law would start out an interview saying how terrible *their* mother-in-law was only to confide later that they actually got along relatively well. In other words, daughters-in-law have "bought into" the popular image of in-law relationships being worse than they might otherwise be.

The generational divide too contributes to the difficulty of in-law relationships. Mary Pipher[21] argues that very real cultural differences between generations create "time zone problems" or a lack of understanding across generations. To the extent that such a divide exists, it will contribute to the difficulty of any intergenerational relationship. For example, one of the daughters-in-law felt that her mother-in-law's advanced age worsened their relationship. She explained,

> [My mother-in-law's] aging affects my relationship with her. She is just too old to deal with her, to change her. She can't hear a thing, and I worry about her driving with my kids. I just don't have anything to talk to her about because of the age difference.

While only one other daughter-in-law mentioned a specific age or cultural gap, many of the daughters-in-law found it difficult to identify things that they had in common with their mother-in-law. It was slightly more common for daughters-in-law to identify their mother-in-law as a fellow girlfriend. For example, Kristen made the following comment about her mother-in-law, Dot, "She is a goofy girl.... She is fun to be with.... She is just like one of my girlfriends." Thus, a generational divide may contribute in making in-law relationships hard for some daughters-in-law but not all daughters-in-law.

While all of these factors can and often do contribute in making in-law relationships hard, perhaps the key element is a discrepancy in how close in-laws feel that they want to be with one another, as well as an inability to integrate one another into the family. Two of the mothers-in-law, for example, said that they wished that they saw more of their sons and daughters-in-law. One of them pointed out that couples generally tend to see the wife's family more often and that this is difficult for the husband's family. She explained, "It is hard being a daughter-in-law, but it is hard being a mother-in-law too. You feel like you are always on the outside looking in, and that is a hard place for a mother to be." Their daughters-in-law did not want to spend more time together though. Thus, a discrepancy in how close the couple wanted to be to the husband's family and how much time they wanted to spend together made relationships difficult for at least some mothers-in-law. Many of the daughters-in-law too felt that one of the primary sources of tension was that their mothers-in-law wanted to see their family more or that they wanted to be involved in their lives more than the daughters-in-law felt was comfortable. Mothers-in-law want to see more of their daughters-in-law as part of seeing their sons. Daughters-in-law, however, do not have a similar need of their mothers-in-law.

In-laws also disagreed about the extent to which the son and his new nuclear family were a separate entity from his family of origin and the degree to which they should integrate one another into their families.

Mothers-in-law and daughters-in-law were often hurt if they were not included in each other's family (daughters-in-law wanting to be a part of the extended family and mothers-in-law wanting to be a part of their son's family). Consider, for example, the statement by the mother-in-law above; she felt like she was on the outside of her son's life looking in on it. It was the daughters-in-law in this study though who were more likely to say that they felt excluded from their husband's family. For example, Diane referred to her in-laws giving a birthday party for her husband and not even mentioning her own birthday that was a week later. She took this as evidence for her overall impression that she was not a welcome member of the family. Other daughters-in-law were also hurt when they were treated like an outsider in their husband's family. This was certainly not the rule, however; many of the daughters-in-law felt that they were an integral part of their in-laws' family with only minor differences between the rights and privileges that they had versus those of their husbands.

In-law relationships can be, and often are, hard for a variety of reasons. Primarily, in-laws are expected to treat one another like family when they do not share the history or unconditional love that characterize family and that make family relationships more acceptable. In addition, marriage, as defined in the postmodern family, involves the creation of a new and separate family, which is bound to create tension between in-laws. Daughters-in-law want to be able to focus on their own families, and in-law families may not have the permeable boundaries that allow sons to separate. In-laws may not successfully integrate the daughter-in-law into the extended family, nor may daughters-in-law make their husbands' parents feel a part of their lives. All of these difficulties are heightened for women because of the relative importance of family relationships in women's lives, particularly for older generations of women who may not have worked outside of the home.

Based on the fifty-three cases observed, mother-in-law and daughter-in-law relationships seem to work best under one of two circumstances. Certainly, it is ideal if a mother-in-law can treat her daughter-in-law like a daughter and the daughter-in-law is able to reach out and make her mother-in-law feel welcome in her own family. Usually these scenarios went hand-in-hand. Kristen and her mother-in-law, Dot, are a good example. Both described their relationship as excellent and raved about the other one. Dot felt that Kristen went out of her way to include her in their family and made her appreciation clear to Kristen. Likewise, Kristen felt that Dot treated her like another daughter and was touched by the many ways that Dot showed that she was thinking of her. To the extent that they felt at ease with the situation, the families saw more of one another. There were many other similar examples. For such a situation to evolve though, both women have to feel comfortable with the degree of the mother-in-law's involvement in the couple's lives and with the extent of the couple's involvement in and separation from the extended family. This was certainly not always the case. Daughters-in-law either felt that the mother-in-law was over involved in their lives or that she, the daughter-in-law, was marginalized in the extended family. Likewise, mothers-in-law felt that their daughters-in-law did not reach out to them or were uncomfortable with the son's separation from the extended family. Daughters-in-law can, and often did, adjust their expectations to the circumstances. The relationship was not what they expected, but they came to accept it. While this was not an ideal situation, it did make the relationship a more workable one.

In-law relationships also work well if both women are comfortable with not being close. Stephanie tried to get to know her mother-in-law when she and her husband were first married. She called her mother-in-law separately from her husband one time only to have her mother-in-law say that she would get their news from her son. Stephanie did not take this personally despite seeing it as an indication that her mother-in-law did not want an intimate relationship. Stephanie felt that it was fine if her mother-in-law wanted to have a more distant relationship with her, and little (if any) tension resulted from the episode. Similar to Stephanie, a small minority of the daughters-in-law felt that they were not close to their in-laws and that this was acceptable. They had not expected more, but instead saw their in-laws as their husband's family. While I did not interview all of these mothers-in-law, fewer than half of the daughters-in-law felt that their in-laws were content with this. In other words, in order to work well, both parties need to prefer some distance without feeling alienated by the other.

ADVICE

Mothers-in-law and daughters-in-law were asked to offer their advice to other women to lessen the difficulty of in-law relationships, to prevent problems from occurring, and to effectively handle those that do occur. That advice is provided in the following sections.

Advice to Daughters-in-Law

The advice that daughters-in-law offered to their peers fell into one of a number of categories. Many daughters-in-law encouraged one another to be respectful of their in-laws, include them as much as possible, and be willing to be a part of their family. This required being kind and warm, patient, and accepting of one another's faults. Consider the following advice from Sadie:

> You have to be accepting and compromise (when you may not want to do something) for the sake of family harmony and peace. Show respect. Sometimes it is about compromising. I tell my daughter that when she marries, she is marrying the whole family, not just her husband.

Likewise, Janette added:

> You should be as kind and warm as you can be. Be sensitive. People are the way that they are. Give your heart. It is important that they be able to see their grandchildren whenever they want. Be there.

Others more simply stated, "Be respectful and participate in the family" and "Welcome your in-laws and include them as much as you can. Make them feel as welcome as your own family."

This led to additional advice about the importance of the daughter-in-law maintaining relationships with her in-laws for the sake of the overall family. One of the middle-aged daughters-in-law explained,

> You keep the circle going. You keep the relationships going. You have to learn how to tolerate and put up with some things. You have to embrace the things that you like in the person.

Similarly, Monique explained,

> Be respectful of the *position* [italics added] of your husband's mother. Never forget that there is a relationship that can never be broken between your husband and his mother. But if you see the responsibility shifting from you to his mother, be wary because that can cause a lot of trouble. It is a red flag if his primary responsibility is his mother and not you, his wife. But call, visit, email, whatever.

Other daughters-in-law offered advice that was protective of a daughter-in-law's place in the family. For example, one of the women said, "Pick your battles, but don't put up with any crap." Likewise, the daughter-in-law who still had a good relationship with her mother-in-law despite being divorced said,

Be honest and open from the beginning about what your expectations are, what place she [your mother-in-law] will have in your life, and where she will fit in.... Be there if she needs you.

One daughter-in-law pointed out that following common advice is not necessarily easy though. She explained, "I used to think [you should] love your in-laws like your parents, but it is harder to do than you think." Perhaps the most sage, but simplest, advice was the following: "Don't take anything personally. Take everything with a grain of salt."

Mothers-in-law offered advice to daughters-in-law that was similar to that provided by the daughters-in-law themselves. The following is a typical piece of advice from one of the mothers-in-law to younger women: "Love your husband's family and try to get along with them. Help them out too when they need it. Socialize with them." Another mother-in-law pointed out the difficulties of getting to know one's in-laws. She explained, "It must be terrifying, marrying into a large family like mine. Everyone is sizing you up and you have to get their approval. If there is enough exposure during the courtship, some of the scary stuff will wear off. It just takes time."

Advice to Mothers-in-Law

The advice that daughters-in-law gave to mothers-in-law also fell into one of several categories. They most frequently advised a husband's mother to treat her children-in-law like her children but not to intrude in (or be too involved in) her married children's lives. They also suggested that she not be judgmental of her daughters-in-law but instead be accepting and supportive of them. Consider the following pieces of advice from Kristen and Marcia, respectively:

You need to take a back seat. Let your son and daughter [-in-law] take the lead and you follow. It is nice to offer, but don't be overbearing. (My mother-in-law makes sure that she isn't overbearing but it would be easy for her to be so). You need to be understanding and don't just defend your son.

and

Have boundaries. Realize that you have to let your children go. Their marriage comes first. Children should not have to split holiday time between their spouses and their parents. Their spouse and what they want to do should come first.

In this same vein, daughters-in-law also pointed out that it is sometimes better for a mother-in-law to "keep her opinion to herself" despite how "right" she might feel about something.

Several daughters-in-law advised mothers-in-law to recognize the separateness of their son's own family and to recognize that he has his own family once he marries. Consider the following pieces of advice from two middle-aged daughters-in-law:

> You need to respect, as hard as it might be, to see your son loves someone else besides you. Respect that and appreciate it, especially if that daughter-in-law loves, respects, and cares for [your] son. You might want to visit more as a mother-in-law, but I don't think you can put the same expectations on your son, daughter-in-law, and their family that you put on your own children.

and

> You have to see that this is their family; they might have their own values, morals, and beliefs. You want to be supportive, and open, and care, and be happy with any time that they can give [you]. It is really, really important that you respect their own lives and them as a couple. If the daughter-in-law doesn't have that respect, it gets very tense and [she will] resent having to go visit.

Going one step further with her advice about the relationship, one of the daughters-in-law also added, "[She should] love her children's spouses because [her] children love them in spite of everything else."

Thus, daughters-in-law emphasize the importance of a mother-in-law maintaining some distance and allowing for separation between herself and her son's family. At the same time though, daughters-in-law wish to be treated like a daughter and not to be judged. Interestingly, mothers-in-law offered similar advice to their peers. Consider the following advice from Dot, who had an excellent relationship with her daughter-in-law:

> You have to honor their family and realize that they are a family, a separate entity from you. Be there for advice but don't interfere. Be a good role model and grandparent.... Having a relationship with a family that is not your own is hard. Even with my own friends, I know that I would not want to be some of their daughters-in-law. Being nice to your daughter-in-law is the only right thing. She is your son's wife and the mother of your grandchildren. Something is wrong with you if you are not nice [to her].

Mothers-in-law also pointed out the importance of adult children and their families having their own lives and that this was to be expected. They were more likely than daughters-in-law though to emphasize the importance of the older generation being supportive and helpful to their children (-in-law). Consider the following contribution from Dorothy, who also had an excellent relationship with her daughter-in-law:

> Try to love and accept the spouses that your children marry. Welcome them into the family. Offer help, both financial and emotional, even if they don't ask. But if they say "no," take it gracefully. Help them out when they need it.

Finally, one of the mothers-in-law advised her peers to "cause no harm." This suggests that mothers-in-law recognize that they can do harm, both to their daughter-in-law as well to their son and daughter-in-law's marriage. That harm can come as a result of many of the behaviors referred to earlier.

SUMMARY AND IMPLICATIONS

In-law relationships indeed are hard. It is more challenging to get along with and to have a loving relationship with in-laws versus one's own biological family. In addition, in-laws may not necessarily feel like one's family. At the extreme, there can be resentment regarding relationships with one another and the couple's place in the wider family.

There are a number of reasons why relationships are so hard. By definition, in-laws are expected to treat one another like family without the benefits of unconditional love and a shared history. Visiting, sharing holidays, sharing resources, and meeting obligations are all expected, even if we do not necessarily like or feel close to an in-law. While relationships with biological relatives can also be problematic, they are at least sustained by a history of knowing one another and the reassurance of unconditional love. In-law relationships are also hard because they are precipitated by the creation of a new and separate family. This may cause resentment on the part of parents-in-law, especially if the boundaries in the family of orientation are impermeable. Such impermeability makes it harder to absorb the daughter-in-law into the family and simultaneously to allow the son to leave and create his own family. Likewise, there can be disagreement over how close the families should be and to what extent the son's nuclear family should be a part of the overall extended family or a separate entity that exists outside of the overall family.

Because the relationships are so hard, mothers-in-law and daughters-in-law were asked to offer their advice to one another. Daughters-in-law were advised to be respectful, to include their in-laws, and to be a willing part of the extended family. In order to do this, it was suggested that they overlook the other person's faults and be patient. Mothers-in-law were advised to treat their children-in-law like their children and also to recognize the separateness of their son's own family. Mothers-in-law were encouraged by both groups of women not to be too intrusive, too involved, or judgmental of their daughters-in-law or their son and daughter-in-law's family. Mothers-in-law were more likely to stress to their peers the importance of assisting children and children-in-law.

Several of the women in this study, upon reading that advice, would respond by saying, "I have done all of those things and they still don't treat me like family (or my daughter-in-law still doesn't include me)." That is, one person may feel that she is making an effort without any reciprocity. These are the daughters-in-law with the greatest resentment and the "estranged" or otherwise negative relationships. At the very least, we need to recognize that one person alone cannot make the relationship a comfortable one and support these women without judgment. It is miraculous if two women share the same perspective on their roles as in-laws and are both comfortable with the level of involvement in one another's family. Yet, we expect in-laws to love one another and to treat one another like family. Is that really realistic? New in-laws need to be reminded that building family relationships takes time and not to expect an instant change in their in-laws. We need to expect less of one another and ourselves as in-laws, especially in the early years. If your in-laws don't feel like family, it does not necessarily mean that you or they are doing anything wrong. That is, no one is at fault for such a situation. The difficulty of in-law relationships though does emphasize the need for husbands to be involved in smoothing over the rough edges or at least facilitating the process of getting to know one another or the creation of a separate family. We assume that in-laws automatically become family, but it takes time and, sometimes, effort in creating these bonds and transforming the shape and size of the extended families. Boundaries that may never have been permeable need to be made as such.

This brings to mind another important point that has not previously been addressed. The marriage(s) of one's adult child(ren) is an important life-course transition in the development of later life families. We recognize the need to support new parents when they have children or when those children go off to college or move out of the home for the first time. Having a son or daughter marry though, especially if they have already left home, has not heretofore been seen as a separate stage in the life course of the family. This is important because, as a separate stage, it requires parents and siblings to make changes to roles and reformulate relationships. A relationship with one's son (or brother) becomes a relationship with that same son (or brother) *and his wife* when he marries. He may no longer play the same roles in the family, or at least to as great an extent, because he has his own family and new roles both there and to his own in-laws. Families may need counseling as they learn to make their boundaries permeable, to both let go of sons and to welcome daughters-in-law. Without recognizing this as a separate stage though, we underplay the importance of the need for such changes and the need to find support in making them.

While many of the women in this study highlighted the necessity of respecting one's in-laws, only a few specified the importance of respecting the other person's *position* as a wife or mother. Mothers-in-law want to continue to be included in their sons' lives and still be mothers to their sons. Daughters-in-law want their marriages to be recognized and to have their own families. This requires respecting the person as well as their *role* in the overall family. It necessitates honoring the institution of marriage as well as the mother–son relationship. In a society in which divorce rates are high and respect for older generations is optional, respect for these *positions* cannot and should not be taken for granted.

In fact, I argue that in-law relationships are really about marriage and mother–son relationships. As we saw in Chapter 6, much of a woman's identity as a daughter-in-law comes from her role as a wife. For example, daughters-in-law tended to select their current husband's mother as their mother-in-law even when they had a better relationship with an earlier mother-in-law or an earlier mother-in-law was the grandparent of their children. Likewise, what causes strain in the in-law relationship often has more to do with the mother's relationship with her son than with her daughter-in-law. Yet, it is the in-law relationship that is blamed, while the marriage and mother–son relationship suffer. This suggests the need to consider in-law relationships in building and supporting marriages. The private trouble of in-laws is actually a public issue and an issue of marriage. It would also be interesting to examine the extent to which in-law problems affect support to older generations. This too will be a public matter as the baby boom generation retires. Our public policy regarding provision to the elderly assumes that families support older people. This may not be the case though if there has been long-term tension among in-laws. These matters will be discussed in greater detail in the next chapter.

Nine

CONCLUSION

Why do they say "in-law"? Valerie is my daughter. If you are going to be family, say "daughter." There is no need to say "daughter-in-law."

—Rosemary (mother-in-law)

When my husband's family is around, I am always on the outside looking in. They say that I am family, but that is not how they act. You have to be born into that family.

—Maria (daughter-in-law)

THE QUALITY OF MOTHER-IN-LAW AND DAUGHTER-IN-LAW RELATIONSHIPS

The overriding intent of this research was to determine the quality of relationships between mothers-in-law and daughters-in-law and to examine the causes of the differences in that quality. Popular culture presents a very negative portrait of mothers-in-law as interfering and domineering and of mother-in-law and daughter-in-law relationships as being fraught with problems and tensions, particularly for the daughter-in-law. Results of this research suggest though that there is a broad range of relationships with many of the relationships being very good. In fact, 38 percent of the daughters-in-law described their relationships as having high affection and little conflict. Interestingly, the majority of the relationships tended to fall at either end of the distribution. That is, over half were either "tight knit" or "estranged." This suggests that when in-laws are able to avoid significant conflict, the tendency is to develop a very close relationship rather than being indifferent to or uninvolved with one another.

Unlike the image presented in popular culture, many daughters-in-law feel close to their mothers-in-law. In particular, 40 percent said that they felt emotionally close to their mother-in-law, and 47 percent said that they felt that they could confide in her. However, they pointed out that any confidence would be about family matters versus personal matters. In other words, the connection between the women was about shared family rather than a more personal, individual bond. A few of the women said that they felt close to their mother-in-law only because they had shared so much time together. In addition, 19 percent of the daughters-in-law called their husband's mother "Mom" or some derivative of "mother." Unlike the others, these women clearly felt a primary familial bond with their mother-in-law; most of them stated that their mother-in-law was like a second mother to them. This, however, was not the norm.

While many of the women felt close to their mothers-in-law, over half experienced at least some conflict while they were married. At times, the conflict was extreme. For example, one of the women said that she fantasized about killing her mother-in-law. Another woman shook as she described her battles with her mother-in-law. The surprising news though is that nearly half of the relationships, according to the daughters-in-law, did not contain conflict. While this included the women who felt close to and had a "tight-knit" relationship with their mother-in-law, it also subsumed women who were "cordial" towards their mother-in-law. That is, they may not have felt conflict, but they also felt little or no affection towards their mother-in-law. These are included among the ambivalent relationships. They are not invested enough in their in-laws to be hurt and angry. They maintained a satisfactory, if superficial, relationship by avoiding conflict.

Many of the daughters-in-law and a far smaller percentage of the mothers-in-law described contradictory feelings. Like many parent–child relationships, in-law relationships can also be fraught with ambivalence. In-laws, however, experience even greater ambivalence as a result of both being in the family but strangers in it as well. As earlier researchers point out, they are kinfolk and strangers simultaneously.[1,2]

Thus, while many in-law relationships are quite difficult, the majority of relationships are not as poor as our popular culture suggests. Although the motivations of the media and other sources of popular culture are beyond the scope of this book, it is important to point out that those images do influence in-law relationships. It was not uncommon for a woman to joke about having a difficult mother-in-law only to later describe a very warm relationship. These women felt that they were *supposed* to have a difficult relationship; that it was expected of them. In fact, cultural representations played an important role in the development of women's identities as daughters-in-law. While a daughter-in-law's identity was most commonly based on her primary obligation as the connecting link between her in-laws and her own nuclear family, other daughters-in-law based their identity on the predominant cultural image of the "martyr" or "downtrodden daughter-in-law." Daughters-in-law interpreted any misunderstanding as evidence of malfeasance on their mother-in-law's part, which then led to tense and problematic relationships. Surprisingly, while many of the women assumed that the cultural images were accurate representations, they did not think that *they* would experience a bad relationship with their own mothers-in-law.

Given this high variability, what determines the quality of relationships between mothers-in-law and daughters-in-law? Certainly sociocultural factors play a part. Well-educated daughters-in-law and those with French or Italian backgrounds tended to have more close-knit relationships with their mothers-in-law. Well-educated daughters-in-law may be better at problem solving, and their mothers-in-law may respect them more. Daughters-in-law from French or Italian backgrounds may be more accustomed to including extended family in their lives and thus get along better with their in-laws.

In-law relationships are also affected by relationships between other family members, including the daughter-in-law's relationship with her own mother and the mother-in-law's relationship with her son. Daughters-in-law who had a poor relationship with their own mothers tended to have a better relationship with their mother-in-law. However, daughters-in-law who lost their mothers before they were young adults tended to have poorer relationships with their mother-in-law. While it was not common, some of the daughters-in-law did say that their mother-in-law was able to replace a missing or estranged mother. Surprisingly, women with no daughters tended to have a poorer relationship with their daughters-in-law. Without a daughter to role model a mother–daughter relationship, women may have had a harder time creating such a relationship and may have had unrealistic expectations of their daughter-in-law. Women with only sons may have also had greater difficulty in "letting go" of those sons. Daughters-in-law tended to have a poorer relationship with their mother-in-law if they perceived her as being too "territorial" or possessive of her son or if they did not feel accepted and welcomed into the family early on in the relationship. Early difficulties are hard to overcome later on in the relationship.

Various characteristics of postmodern family life also affect relationships between mothers-in-law and daughters-in-law. Unexpectedly, a daughter-in-law's employment status had very little effect on her relationship with her mother-in-law. Even daughters-in-law who worked but had mothers-in-law who had not worked during most of their adulthood were no less likely to get along with their mothers-in-law. There was one exception though: several of the professional women felt that their in-laws did not fully appreciate what their work meant to them. Geographic distance did have an effect though. Those daughters-in-law who lived some distance from their in-laws were more likely to have a "cordial" relationship and less likely to have an "estranged" one. Distant living in the postmodern family decreases the likelihood of extensive conflict between in-laws. When there is extensive conflict, distant living is seen as having a positive effect on the relationship. Finally, the divorce revolution has also made an impact on in-law relationships. Divorced women were more likely to have a negative relationship with their mothers-in-law, although it depended on how their mothers-in-law treated their children from their prior marriages. In contrast, daughters-in-law were more likely to have a positive relationship with their mothers-in-law if their *husbands* had been divorced.

What does this tell us? There are not many factors that affect the quality of in-law relationships. Many of the sociocultural factors such as religion made no difference, nor did women's employment matter, even when it created different life experiences for the two generations of women. Thus, in-law relationships are impervious to many of the factors that one might think of as affecting a relationship or what one has in common with another person. This then emphasizes the fact that in-law relationships are truly family relationships. Like our relationships with our biological kin, they are based on shared membership in the family rather than outside factors, such as having things in common. What does make a difference in the relationship though is feeling accepted by the other person. For daughters-in-law, feeling accepted and welcomed into the family early on had long-lasting effects on the quality of the relationship. Likewise, mothers-in-law felt closer to daughters-in-law if the younger women had tried to bridge the gap between them by making them feel welcome in their homes and by including them in their families. Relationships were also better when both women felt comfortable with the degree of the mother-in-law's involvement in the son and daughter-in-law's family and the degree to which they were autonomous from the extended family. In-law relationships were strained when daughters-in-law felt that their mothers-in-law were too close to or "possessive" of their sons. Thus, there needs to be some consensus about the degree of the couple's involvement in the extended family and the closeness of the mother–son relationship.

Characteristics of postmodern family life had mixed effects. Those characteristics with the greatest impact on the in-law relationship included the prior divorce of the son/husband, as well as the prior divorce of the daughter-in-law. Although the divorce rate has declined somewhat in the last several decades, it is still quite high. Nearly one-quarter, or 21 percent, of the daughters-in-law in this study had previously been married, and 15 percent were married to divorced men. If divorce rates remain high, what will this mean then for in-law relationships? As we saw, whether or not the mother-in-law was divorced made little difference. So, as generations age through the life cycle, their own divorces should have minimal impact on their relationships with their daughters-in-law. Mothers-in-law should be careful though of how they treat their step-grandchildren. Daughters-in-law are, of course, protective of their children from prior marriages. Ignoring one's step-grandchildren then does little for the relationship. This again reinforces the fact that in-laws really do expect to be treated like family; they also expect their children to be treated as family. Mothers-in-law tend to be appreciative of their daughters-in-law if their sons have been divorced, particularly if they were not close to their first daughters-in-law. Thus, there is the potential for high rates of divorce to have a positive impact on subsequent in-law relationships. Mothers-in-law tend to be appreciative of daughters-in-law when their sons' marriages are going well.

In-law relationships then are not as bad as popular culture suggests. Evidenced by the extent and degree of conflict that at least some of the women experienced, they can be very difficult however. Why *are* in-law relationships so difficult? Tension in in-law relationships is due to more than individual incompatibilities. The source of conflict is, in fact, structural and has to do with the often overlooked and undermined transition in the life course of later-life families. In-law relationships are about the creation of a new and separate family that requires changes in family roles and a redefinition of relationships. Family members (i.e., parents and adult siblings) may not be prepared for or aware of the need for these changes leading to strain in the relationship with the daughter-in-law and possibly the son. In addition, family boundaries need to be permeable to allow the integration of the daughter-in-law into the extended family and to allow the son to create his own separate and autonomous family. Both mother-in-law and daughter-in-law need to be comfortable with the extent of the mother-in-law's involvement with the couple and the extent to which the new nuclear family is a part of or separate from the extended family. In addition, in-laws need to recognize the significance of the son's marriage. In-law relationships are hard because family members are not always prepared for these changes. When they are not, daughters-in-law feel a greater need to isolate and protect their own nuclear family. It is precisely this need coupled with wanting to be a part of the overall in-law family that accounts for the ambivalence that so many daughters-in-law experience.[3]

Difficulty in in-law relationships also results from being expected to treat one another like family without the benefit of the unconditional love that typically exists between biological kin and a shared family history. As one of the daughters-in-law explained, treating someone like a second mother isn't as easy to do as one might assume. Family members need to be willing to renegotiate their roles and expectations of one another in order to make room for the daughter-in-law in the family and to allow the son more autonomy. Later-life families may need support in making this life-course transition when sons marry to prevent long-term conflict.

This brings up another point. Not all in-laws see one another as family. Stephanie's mother-in-law, for example, was not interested in phone conversations with Stephanie, but solely her husband Robert. However, she welcomed Stephanie into her home when she visited with Robert. Likewise, Sally saw Steve's parents as being his family but not her family. This makes sense given that in-laws do not share a history or unconditional love. Likewise, they may not continue as a family should something happen to the husband/son. An in-law relationship is often just that then, based "in law" or on a marriage contract and not based on the feelings between the parties. In other words, in-laws are not necessarily family. However, because of our "ideology of the family," which assumes that the entire extended family is a loving and cohesive unit, we assume that we should be treated like family. It makes little sense, however, to "force" a family relationship if both in-laws agree that they are not family. The problem arises when one member, mother-in-law or daughter-in-law, expects more though. That is, they expect to be treated like family. Based on the results of this study and that of Cotterill,[4] we know that conflict is heightened when one's expectations of being family are not realized. Treating one another as anything but family can create problems. This suggests the need for open communication and the expression of one's expectations in the relationship, which will be discussed in the following paragraphs.

Conflict is not uniform among family members, however; it is greatest with in-laws of the same gender.[5] Based on the literature and Web sites devoted to the topic for women versus men, one could argue that it is greatest between mothers-in-law and daughters-in-law. Why is this so? Why are the women in the family the ones to experience the greatest conflict with their in-laws, that is, their husband's mother or their son's wife? Earlier researchers and experts in women's psychology have argued that for women, family relationships are tied to their sense of well-being and quality of life.[6–9] Mothers-in-law then are more likely to feel the loss of their son's movement into his own nuclear family. Likewise, although daughters-in-law want to be close to their in-laws, they also feel the need to guard their own nuclear family and to protect their connection to their own spouse and children. That is, although mothers-in-law and daughters-in-law often wish to be close, their desire for their own nuclear family is greater.[10] For fathers-in-law and sons-in-law, their investment in (and the importance of) family connections is less central to their sense of identity. This social phenomenon is often seen as "competition" for the son. However, I argue that it is more accurate to define the ambivalence that women feel towards one another as the result of these changes in the life course of the family and that mothers-in-law (and daughters-in-law) may need support in addressing and understanding these changes.

One can also expect a mother-in-law to feel greater conflict with a daughter-in-law than a son-in-law because of the disparity in patterns of contact. Women have more visits and phone contact with their parents than do men, and men talk on the phone more with their in-laws than their parents. In addition, women help parents more than in-laws, although there is no such difference for men.[11] Thus, after marriage, the shift is in the direction of greater overall contact with the wife's side of the family. In addition, men tend to relinquish kin-keeping responsibilities to their wives upon marriage.[12–14] This then leads some credibility to the adage that when a daughter marries, you gain a son, but when a son marries, you lose a son. One can thus understand a mother-in-law's ambivalence when her son marries.

WHAT DOES IT MEAN TO BE AN IN-LAW: BEING "IN" AND "OUT" OF THE FAMILY

One of the questions that first sparked my interest in in-law relationships was how being an in-law is different from being a part of one's own biological family. The very language that we use tells us that something is different. Consider, for example, the terms *"one's own* biological family" and "mother-*in-law.*" The mothers-in-law and daughters-in-law in this study unanimously agreed that there was a difference. Still, some of the mothers-in-law tried to minimize that difference as much as they could. That is, they started out by saying that they treated their children-in-law just like their children, but then at some point during the interview, they spoke of some difference. For example, Dot never said that she felt closer to her daughter than to her daughter-in-law. She did state though that she felt *very* [her emphasis] close to her daughter and that they had a special bond because they shared the trials and tribulations of her daughter's growing up. Like Dot, several other mothers-in-law were reluctant to admit that a daughter-in-law was anything different than another daughter.

The majority of daughters-in-law stated that in-laws are family and that the obligations to in-laws are the same as those to biological kin. This included daughters-in-law who had "estranged" relationships with their mothers-in-law. However, they also described their relationships with their mothers as being closer or much closer than their relationships with their mothers-in-law. They would commonly say things like, "Well, my mother is my mother, of course." Another daughter-in-law said, "I know that my mother always has my best interest at heart. I am not sure of that with my mother-in-law." This signified that there was a special bond with their mother that they did not have with their mother-in-law. Like family, they stayed in touch with their in-laws even when relationships were difficult though. The majority felt like their husband's family was also their family, but they still felt closer to "their own" families.

Consistent with their outlook on how they should treat their in-laws, daughters-in-law felt that their in-laws should treat them like family too. For example, women were more accepting of mothers-in-law who were not close only if their mothers-in-law treated everyone in the family that way. However, tension resulted if daughters-in-law felt that their mothers-in-law treated them poorly compared with their own children. For example, daughters-in-law felt slighted if their mothers-in-law ignored their birthday but remembered the son's birthday. They also felt slighted if their mother-in-law sent cards and gifts addressed to the son only. They wanted to be treated "like" a daughter (even though they knew there would be some differences) and to be recognized as the son's wife. Such expectations are a good example of what Cotterill[15] calls the "sentimental model of the family," which states "families are [expected to be] egalitarian, complementary units founded in love and devotion between individuals." Daughters-in-law felt that they had not been accepted into the family when their in-laws failed to meet this ideal of treating them just like (biological) family members. An unrealistic ideology of the family then may cause some of the misunderstandings that we often find between in-laws.

What differences do we find between in-laws and biological kin? Simply put, in-law relationships are more precarious than bonds between biological kin. Parents and siblings love us unconditionally; it takes a significant problem to sever or even erode those ties. In-laws though understand that their relationships can more easily be estranged dependent on what they say and what they do in the family. This is consistent with Cotterill's[16] findings that in-laws avoid overt hostility because there is no emotional intimacy to counter it. Formal boundaries prevent expression of those hostilities. In-laws also know that they could unwittingly offend one another due to the lack of a shared history. In addition, even when divorce is far from their minds, women still know that their relationship with their in-laws is conditional. That is, it is dependent upon their continued marriage. It was rare for a daughter-in-law to remain a part of her ex-husband's family following divorce. They defined their current husband's mother as their in-law, often severing ties with their former mothers-in-law. Knowing that this relationship is conditional and not one that you can always count on like "your own family" lessens the strength of the bond.

In-law relationships are difficult then because there are these differences. As mothers-in-law and daughters-in-law, women are expected to treat one another like family without the benefit of that unconditional love and guarantee of a life-long relationship. Add to that the lack of a shared history and possibly different family customs, and you can image how a daughter-in-law might feel both "in" and "out" of the family. They have all the obligations of family, but they may feel that they do not always experience all of its benefits. Daughters-in-law should note that their mothers-in-law might feel the same way though: that they are expected to treat this relative stranger like a daughter without the benefit of a life-long commitment. To be "in" and "out" of the family then means to be a part of it, but not the whole part of it. In-laws should be aware though that while they may not experience all of the benefits of biological family, the obligations are not exactly the same either.

As was stated earlier, a few of the daughters-in-law explained that they did not feel that they were a part of their husband's family or that the obligations were the same. What do these exceptions tell us? These daughters-in-law were emphasizing the differences discussed previously. Without the

shared history, unconditional love, and relative security of a lifelong relationship, these women felt more "out" of the family than "in" it. They
show that the range of relationships is extensive indeed, with some women
not even feeling like family. They also show us that in-laws do not have to
be family and that that too is an option.

This brings us to another question. Is it realistic to expect in-laws to
treat one another like family? Certainly not all in-laws feel like family. Both
the mother-in-law and daughter-in-law need to be conservative in their
expectations of one another early in the relationship. However, they must
walk a fine line since it is also important for the mother-in-law to make the
daughter-in-law feel like a welcomed and accepted member of the family. It
was less crucial for the daughter-in-law to bridge the gap and reach out to
her mother-in-law early on in the relationship, but it did make a difference
later. In general, an initial expectation of being treated like family is probably unrealistic, but it is the ideal. Not all in-laws are willing to treat one
another like family though. The boundaries of some families are impermeable. Likewise, daughters-in-law may not want to be a part of their husband's family. In either case, in-laws need to keep in mind that these
instances are not personal and that they may not be able to change them.
Expecting to be treated like family is not always realistic although it does
result in greater inclusion in one another's lives. This is consistent with
Cotterill's[17] argument that investment in a family relationship is a matter
of choice.

Two of the mothers-in-law said that we should drop the term "in-law"
altogether. Rosemary asked, "Why do they say 'in-law?' Valerie [the
daughter-in-law] is my daughter. If you are going to be family, say
'daughter.' There is no need to say 'daughter-*in-law*.'" Most of the in-laws
who noted the special quality of a mother–daughter relationship would find
it uncomfortable to do this though. In fact, for those in-laws who had a difficult relationship, referring to one another as "my son's wife" or "my husband's mother" would be preferable and more genuine. One can make the
argument though for greater use of *both* familial references and indirect
references (based on the son/husband) rather than the use of the term "in-
law" given the tendency in this sample for in-laws to have relationships at
either extreme. In addition, as Rosemary pointed out, the term "family-in-
law" is really an oxymoron. Many of the daughters-in-law would have felt
far more comfortable thinking of their husband's mother as just that rather
than trying to imitate a family relationship with her. In-laws, especially
daughters-in-law, are not always going to feel like family. Rosemary's

argument that if you are going to be family, you should use a family name highlighted both the possibility of truly familial bonds though and the ambivalence that is expressed even in our own terminology.

Sadie told me at one point during our interview that she frequently reminds her daughter of the adage: "When you marry, you marry the whole family and not just your spouse." In short, Sadie is suggesting that her daughter consider her boyfriends' parents when choosing a partner. Just how true is this adage though? Although they were not specifically asked this question, I believe that nearly all of the women in this study would agree that a relationship of some kind with their husband's family is part of the package deal called "marriage." The difference was the degree to which they felt they could incorporate their husband's family given their level of comfort with one another and geographic distance. All of the women knew before marriage that their husband's family would be a part of their lives. They varied though in the extent to which they understood what this might entail and how it would at times be difficult. They also varied in how well they knew their in-laws-to-be prior to marriage and the degree to which they intended to involve their husband's family in their lives.

Given that our in-laws become a part of our lives upon marriage, the adage that you "marry your in-laws" [paraphrased] is true. The *degree* to which you marry your in-laws or include them in your life varies tremendously though. Stephanie and her mother-in-law are a good example of in-laws who rarely saw one another and who did not speak on the phone but who felt comfortable with the relationship. The daughters-in-law with "estranged" relationships were the ones though who found the relationships intolerable and, therefore, kept their distance. Thus, the expectation is that your in-laws become part of your life and your family upon marriage, but not everyone can meet this obligation. It should be noted that this study did not include couples who had divorced because of in-law problems or couples that never married because of in-law problems. To the extent that the adage is true, the fact that you "marry your in-laws" may doom some marriages. Stacey, for example, stated that her marriage was always on the brink of divorce because of problems with her in-laws.

I started this book by asking what it means to be an in-law, and I have concluded that it means to be both "in" and "out" of the family. Being a daughter-in-law means participating in your husband's family and including his parents when possible. Most of the women felt that being a daughter-in-law meant being the connecting link between their husband and children and their in-laws. Daughters-in-law are not full-fledged members of the family though. They are careful of what they say and do, knowing that their own place in the family is precarious. Being both "in" and "out" of the family has some benefits. At least some of the obligations, such as caregiving, are more optional than they are to one's biological kin. However, being both "in" and "out" of the family also increases the ambivalence that the women experience. Resentment and conflict also arise for daughters-in-law when they feel as though they are more "out" of the family than "in" it.

IMPLICATIONS FOR FAMILY RELATIONSHIPS

More often than not, the son/husband was not involved in resolving the conflict that arose between his mother and wife, nor did women talk about their husbands consciously building relationships between them and their mothers-in-law. The relationship was left to the two women despite the fact that it was the result of both being connected to this third person. Although the husbands/sons were not interviewed, their wives told me that they did not want to get involved. This was particularly true if the problem between the two women was one that either did not bother or concern the husband. However, the relationship between the mother-in-law and daughter-in-law has far ranging implications. It can affect any and all relationships between four and sometimes five generations. Consider for example a four-generation family with young children, their parents (including the daughter-in-law), grandparents (including the mother-in-law), and great grandparents. A close relationship between the daughter-in-law and mother-in-law will increase the amount of time that the children spend with cousins, aunts and uncles, grandparents, and great grandparents. Likewise, the quality of in-law relationships can affect marriage and the bonds between adult children and their parents. A minority, but still a significant number, of daughters-in-law spoke of problems early on in their marriages due to difficulties with their mothers-in-law. I would argue then that the husband/son has an obligation to try to resolve conflict between his wife and mother and to be part of the process of building a healthy relationship between them. Husbands and wives need to be in agreement on how to proceed with in-law concerns so as to avoid marital problems. Husbands also need to be willing to communicate with their mothers about thorny issues. As important, the parents may need support as they make the transition to having married children with their own separate and autonomous families.

What is it that mothers-in-law and daughters-in-law really want of one another? Are their desires incompatible or is it reasonable to expect them to get along? Mothers-in-law wanted their daughter-in-law to respect their position as their son's mother. This involved being included in their son's and daughter-in-law's lives rather than being an outsider looking in on their son's life. None of the mothers-in-law mentioned wanting time alone with their sons or wanting their daughter-in-law to maintain more distance. If anything, mothers-in-law were particularly pleased when daughters-in-law made an effort to connect with and involve them.

Daughters-in-law wanted their mothers-in-law to recognize their position as the son's wife and to allow them the space to be a separate and autonomous family. This included hoping that the mother-in-law would offer minimal advice or intrusion and respect the boundaries between the two families. They hoped to be treated like a member of the family and to be accepted. These desires, at least in theory, seem perfectly compatible. Mothers-in-law can be a part of their son and daughter-in-law's family without intruding. However, they need to be respectful of their son's new family. Likewise, the daughter-in-law can include her husband's parents in her family without losing her family's independence and autonomy. Having a healthy relationship requires *both* women to be respectful of the other person's position. It requires being aware of the other person's needs and being willing to compromise. The most common source of problems seemed to be when one of the in-laws felt that the other was either not including her or was not respectful of her position, which then led her to keep her in-law at arm's length. In other words, it became a vicious cycle.

In-law relationships then are precarious, or susceptible to fragmentation and estrangement, because of three things. In-laws are dependent upon one another to respect their positions and to include one another. This does not always happen. Second, the relationships are characterized by ambivalence. Like parents and adult children, they have mixed feelings towards one another. Unlike biological kin though, they are at least partly outside of one another's families, and they share neither a joint history nor a guarantee of a life-long relationship. Finally, in-law relationships are ambiguous, meaning that there is no agreed upon expectation for behavior. Instead, those expectations vary from family to family, and members may feel that their in-law is not behaving in accordance with her role. They often feel that the other person has not accepted them because of misunderstandings that result from this ambiguity. All three of these factors increase the possibility that women will pull away from one another.

In order to strengthen the bond between in-laws and therefore strengthen extended families, in-laws need to be willing to articulate their expectations and to come to some sort of agreement, perhaps with the help of the son/husband. This is particularly important during a time in which marriage and the family are separating and families are undergoing enormous changes.

This then brings us to the topic of the "in-law bargain." Whether done consciously or not, in-laws strike a bargain in their early interactions that continues throughout the life course. In-laws who get along with one another make decisions early on to do just that. This includes, primarily, being respectful of one another's place in the son/husband's life and including one another in their respective families. This is often done by avoiding conflict and resolving it when it does arise and, sometimes, by maintaining formal boundaries. It requires overlooking one another's faults and, as I have argued, open communication about the relationship. However, when one person fails to live up to the expectations, whether it is not including their in-law, not accepting her into their family, or not respecting her position in the family, it causes the other in-law to forgo their end of the "deal" or "bargain." This sets off the vicious cycle described earlier. In-laws may still feel the ambivalence inherent in the relationship and they may end up with something other than a "tight-knit" relationship even when they do try to communicate effectively and respect the other person's position. Either way, they need to be aware of the choices that they may unconsciously be making and the messages that they are unknowingly sending to their in-laws.

Many of the in-laws in this study would remind me though that they have tried to compromise and to be sensitive to the other person's needs. The other person, however, is not holding up her end of the bargain. What do these in-laws do? Many of these women had the "estranged" or "obligatory" relationships. There was little that they could do but to accept the relationship for what it was. I believe that some of these relationships could have been improved though with family education and early intervention. The relationships started poorly because of misunderstandings that were really due to the nature of the relationship or the changes that families undergo when an adult child marries. Parents-in-law, not aware of the daughter-in-law's need to start her own family, hung on too tightly and were defined as possessive. Community-based education and early counseling (discussed later in this chapter) could have helped many of these families.

THEORETICAL IMPLICATIONS

The daughter-in-law role and the creation of her identity within the family are socially constructed. Yet, there is no agreed upon set of obligations and expectations for daughters-in-law the way that there is for other family roles, such as that of a mother or daughter. While some of the expectations of a parent are clear cut enough to constitute laws, we cannot imagine laws based on how we are to act as in-laws. While we saw that there was some overlap in women's statements about how mothers-in-law and daughters-in-law are expected to behave, the role and the creation of an identity clearly vary from family to family.

To some extent then, the daughter-in-law is "made" in each family. While she enters her husband's family with some expectation of what it will be like to be a daughter-in-law, the role is constructed as a result of the synthesis of the expectations of the husband's family, the mother's relationship with her son, the daughter-in-law's relationship with her own mother, and other factors. As such, the role is constituted by interactions among family, expectations based on popular perceptions, and diverse family cultures. This results in the variation from family to family. Certainly there is no one role or relationship, which then creates a great deal of ambiguity in how one is expected to behave and weakens the relationship by causing misunderstandings.

The making of a daughter-in-law occurs over time. Although the interaction between mother-in-law and daughter-in-law early on in the relationship sets the stage for how well the two women get along later, relationships tend to become closer with time alone. Change also results when the couple marries; at least some of the women felt that they became a part of the family either when they were engaged or married. Unexpectedly, the arrival of a child/grandchild did not necessarily make in-laws feel closer to one another. Having a child introduced problems into the relationship or increased ambiguity for at least some of the respondents. The way that women see themselves as daughters-in-law, that is, their identity, is the synthesis of their (socially constructed) role and their interpretation of their experiences as a daughter-in-law.

As stated earlier, the daughter-in-law's role is constituted as a result of the interplay between the two women and the husband/son. The mother-in-law's role is also interactionally constituted and will involve the son to an even greater degree. The fact that women often felt closer to one mother-in-law over another or one daughter-in-law over another offers evidence of the importance of this interplay. The interplay also results in the roles being indeterminate, thus some of the women were best friends or like a mother/daughter to one another.

The language that mothers-in-law and daughters-in-law used illustrates how people attach meaning to the relationship. Rosemary made clear her feelings towards her daughter-in-law when she suggested that we drop "in-law" from the terms that we use for one another. Rosemary saw her relationship with Valerie as being closer in fact than her relationship with her own daughter. To Rosemary, a daughter-in-law was family and not an in-law. Likewise, a minority of daughters-in-law called their mother-in-law by the name "Mom" or a similar derivative of "mother." They too attached a particular meaning to the relationship by the name that they used. In contrast, women who referred to their in-law as their "husband's mother" or "Mrs. ———" cast a very different meaning.

Interpretive work is an important component of managing family systems. Women try to make sense of their everyday realities, in this case their experiences as a daughter-in-law, through their interpretation of their mother-in-law's behavior. This interpretation then gets woven into their identity as a daughter-in-law. For example, a daughter-in-law may interpret her mother-in-law's behavior as "stepping on her toes" as a wife and take on the common identity of the "downtrodden" daughter-in-law. This then becomes her construction of reality in the family. Daughters-in-law also use these interpretations to "manage" their roles as a coping strategy in the overall family.

The results of this research have important implications for life-course analysis. The results suggest that the marriage of a son (or daughter) is a crucial stage of the life course in later-life families. We have paid attention to "nest leaving" as an important period. Having a child marry also has significant implications for the family though. It requires that the family be ready to integrate a new member and that it be ready to allow the son and his wife to create a separate and autonomous family. This necessitates that the family's boundaries be permeable and that the parents, siblings, and perhaps grandparents be ready to redefine relationships. As we saw, these two things did not occur in all families, which then led to conflict. This suggests the importance of providing support to many families as they undergo this transition. While it would not be wise for daughters-in-law to suggest the need for such support, extended family, professionals, and family friends should be cognizant of the potential need. Family scholars and gerontologists are also advised to recognize this as an important and distinct phase of the (later-life) family life cycle that affects intergenerational relationships, marriage, and extended family relationships.

THE PUBLIC NATURE OF PRIVATE FAMILY MATTERS

Most family matters, with the exception of the protection of children and the creation and dissolution of a marriage, are defined as private. This includes the bond between in-laws. Few people would dare to intrude on someone else's relationship with their in-law, such as offering advice. This work suggests, however, the public nature of this very private family matter.

As we have seen, relationships between in-laws do have implications for marriage and divorce. For example, one of the daughters-in-law stated that problems with her in-laws resulted in the couple postponing their marriage for several years. Another daughter-in-law stated that she and her husband were constantly on the verge of divorce because of her in-laws. More commonly though, daughters-in-law stated that difficulties with their in-laws created problems in their marriage early on but that the couple resolved the problems. What we cannot tell from this study though is the number of people who never married or who divorced because of in-law problems. These results are consistent with earlier research that shows that conflict between in-laws is one of the greatest sources of marital dissolution in the first year of marriage and that conflict erodes marital stability, satisfaction, and commitment over time even in long-term marriages.[18,19]

This is important particularly at a time when divorce rates are high and society is concerned both about the future of marriage and the well-being of children from divorced families. I argue that to the extent that the state defines and regulates marriage, it should also support those same marriages. In the 1990s, the federal government took measures to do just that. In 1996, it enacted the Personal Responsibility and Work Opportunities Reform Act (PRWORA) to reform welfare legislation and to promote marriage among unmarried welfare recipients. In February 2006, the president also signed the Deficit Reduction Act of 2005 (DRA) that, among other things, allocated $150 million per year for five years to promote healthy marriages and responsible fatherhood for all Americans.[20] Whether one agrees that this is an appropriate role for the government or whether the PRWORA is an effective way to promote marriage, the point is that resources are now available to improve marriages. I argue that by using the resources to promote healthy in-law relationships, we can also help to improve marriages.

In their recent book *Alone Together: How Marriage in America Is Changing*, authors Paul Amato et al.[21] argue that resources allocated by the DRA be used to offer marital education and mentoring programs to help couples develop better communication and conflict resolution skills. Couples previously had only private counseling to turn to. Resources are now available to make assistance accessible to a much broader range of couples. To the extent that in-law problems affect marriages and are a reflection of marriage and mother–son relationships, I argue that those marital education and mentoring programs, as well as other initiatives, also address the in-law relationship. For example, wives would like their husbands to be more involved in negotiating their relationship with their mother-in-law. It is also beneficial if the husband and wife are in agreement as to how to handle in-law problems. For these and other reasons that we have seen, healthy marriages and healthy in-law relationships can benefit one another.

The parents of adult children also need to be educated before problems between in-laws develop. More specifically, churches, synagogues, and other community-based institutions need to offer community workshops and presentations to help families to better understand the changes that they are undergoing prior to a child's marriage, as well as provide counseling for families that are already experiencing in-law problems. Turner, Young, and Black[22] argue that we need to educate family members about the developmental differences between generations,[23] about how to understand and present their own concerns in the relationship and sources of misunderstanding, and how to clarify their own perceptions and listen effectively. I agree with all three of these recommendations. Premarital counselors and family life educators, such as those who work with extension services, need to include relationships with in-laws as part of their counseling. For those who are already experiencing difficulties, mediators and family therapists need to discuss interactions with in-laws in effectively treating the entire family. We as members of the community can also support one another. Friends and family need to talk honestly about in-law difficulties rather than hide them as private concerns. In-law relationships are not only a public issue; they are also an issue of marriage. To that extent, husbands in particular need to play a greater role in negotiating the relationship between their wives and mothers and in signifying the validity of their new and separate autonomous family. Resources are now available to support these initiatives.

Communication between in-laws needs to include people's expectations of one another and a clear articulation of one's concerns. This would allow individuals to rectify misunderstandings and enter again into the "in-law bargain" with a clean slate. Because blunt expressions could worsen the situation, however, counselors and others trained to facilitate dialogue should be involved in this process. Professionals are also needed because we have no common language to discuss in-law-specific concerns and because there is no shared history to buffer the discomfort of difficult dialogue. Likewise, family life education, provided at the community level, would aid individuals in recognizing the influence of outside forces and better understanding the other person's behavior.

To the extent that in-law relationships are a public matter, the state and other social institutions need to support them. More specifically, the state should extend the same rights and privileges that it offers to children to children-in-law. For example, the Family and Medical Leave Act of 1993 provides up to 12 weeks of unpaid leave for parental responsibilities. This same opportunity should extend to parental-in-law responsibilities. Among the five daughters-in-law between the ages of 56 and 65, all except for one had provided care for their parent-in-law on a regular basis.[24] These daughters-in-law should be given the same benefits as daughters. Likewise, many workers have the option of purchasing long-term care insurance for their parents. This option should be extended to children-in-law so that more of the elderly can be covered if families so choose. The point though is to provide children-in-law with the same benefits as children.

Relationships between mothers-in-law and daughters-in-law also have important implications for intergenerational relationships. It is the daughter-in-law who fulfills the kinship management role for both sides of the family.[25–27] She is described as the bridge between the generations[28,29] and the one who creates family bonds and maintains ties to and the traditions of both sides of the family.[30–33] Her involvement then is essential to the continuity of intergenerational family relationships.[34–37] Although all of the daughters-in-law in this study maintained some contact with their in-laws, problems between mothers-in-law and daughters-in-law still weaken ties between paternal grandparents and their grandchildren and possibly parents and sons. This is certainly the case when visiting is curtailed. In fact, in-law relationships affect four and sometimes five generations and all of the relationships between the parties. What we don't know is the extent to which in-law problems may affect support for the elderly in later life and the so-called "generational stake" or expectation of support from one generation to another. This will have important implications for the state, which depends on and assumes family support for the elderly. It is particularly important given the aging of the population and the looming entry of the baby boomers into retirement. To the extent that the public depends on private support of the elderly, we need to investigate the implications of in-law conflict on later life support for the elderly and insure its continuation. Again, practitioners who work with families can do much to improve inter-generational relations by improving in-law ties.

FAMILIES DURING A TIME OF CHANGE AND TURMOIL

What do our results tell us about family during a time of significant change and turmoil? We hear over and over again in the news that families are falling apart. Scholars indicate a similar trend, although with less alarm. More recently, scholars have argued that marriage and the family are grow-ing apart. In their book *Promises I Can Keep*, Edin and Kefalas[38] show how low income urban women consciously separate marriage from child-bearing. The findings in this study, however, offer mixed support for the idea that marriage and family are growing apart. Daughters-in-law felt a strong obligation to be in touch with their mothers-in-law, particularly for the sake of their husbands and children and to maintain connections across the generations, even when they did not get along with their in-laws. Their identification as a daughter-in-law and the things that they did for their mother-in-law were the result of their role as wife and their connection to their husband. To that extent, marriage and family are highly connected. On the other hand, older daughters-in-law tended to express greater con-cern for their mothers-in-law than younger daughters-in-law. While this may be the result of the greater length of time that older mothers-in-law and daughters-in-law have known one another, it could also be the result of a generational difference. This may lead to later generations of daughters-in-law providing less support to their mothers-in-law in the future.

Results suggest the importance of family relationships even during a time of significant change and turmoil in families. All of the daughters-in-law maintained some contact with their in-laws along with their husbands and children. All got together with their in-laws at least once a year even in estranged relationships and even when they lived long distance. Most, how-ever, saw one another much more regularly. More importantly, mothers-in-law and daughters-in-law *cultivated* those relationships. Mothers-in-law were particularly pleased when daughters-in-law reached out to them and diminished the distance between them. Daughters-in-law too were grateful when their mothers-in-law included them in the family. Being part of their husband's family and having their marriage recognized by their in-laws was important to daughters-in-law. Overall, family was important to daughters-in-law.

Daughters-in-law cultivated relationships with their mothers-in-law even when they did not get along in part to meet their marital and parental obligations. They felt that it was their place to maintain connections between their husbands and children and their in-laws. However, the vast majority of the daughters-in-law also felt a direct obligation to their mothers-in-law. They felt obliged to make her feel welcomed in their homes, to be respectful and not too critical, and to be a part of their mother-in-law's family. This was for the sake of their mother-in-law as well as their husband. Some had even provided care to their mothers-in-law. All of this is to suggest that family continues to be significant, even under difficult circumstances, despite our assumptions that the family is falling apart.

The last century saw enormous changes in women's labor force participation, gender role expectations, and expectations of marriage. How though have these changes affected in-law relationships? Women's employment seemed to have little effect on in-law relationships. Employed women were no more or less likely to get along with their in-laws even when their mothers-in-law had not worked outside of the home. This suggests that having a common lifestyle is not important to maintaining in-law relationships. Instead, other factors matter more. However, more educated women did report better relationships with their mothers-in-law. A higher education provides women with better problem-solving skills and it likely increases a mother-in-law's respect for her daughter-in-law. More highly educated couples may also have better marriages that can improve in-law relationships.

Changing gender role expectations has meant greater involvement of husbands in the home and in childrearing and greater participation of wives in the labor force even when children are young. It has also meant a more shared division of power and perhaps decision making in the family.[39,40] Although this was not specifically tested, it is quite likely that greater equality has resulted in women feeling more confident in meeting their own needs in the extended family or standing their ground if they wish to see less of their in-laws. Most of the daughters-in-law said that they avoided conflict with their in-laws whenever the possibility of it arose. This helps to protect the relationship. However, younger daughters-in-law were more likely to express their concerns about their in-laws to their husbands than were older daughters-in-law. As one of the oldest daughters-in-law stated, "He [my husband] didn't need to know about that [conflict with my mother-in-law]." The youngest daughters-in-law though, those 35 years of age and younger, were most likely to voice their concerns both to their mothers-in-law and to their husbands. This may improve relationships in the long run if the in-laws are able to work out their differences. The oldest daughters-in-law believed that it was better to keep their opinions to them-selves and to "grin and bear" the problems that they had with their mothers-in-law. While this may have lessened overt conflict at the time, it also led to deep resentment on the part of the daughters-in-law.

Expectations within marriage have also changed over time. Husbands and wives assume that their marriages will be places of emotional fulfill-ment. In contrast, they predominately provided for economic need by building alliances between families and secured a place to raise children in the past.[41] If today's married couples are primarily looking for personal ful-fillment though, one would assume that wives would be less accepting of problems with their in-laws. Indeed, younger women were more likely to address in-law problems and to expect their husbands' involvement in doing so. That is, they expected their husbands to help them to make their marriage an overall positive experience. In the long run though, women accept in-law relationships as part of the package deal called marriage and do their best to meet their obligations.

Overall, this book has demonstrated the importance of family relation-ships even at a time in which the family is undergoing significant changes. While those changes are also affecting in-law relationships, the relationships remain strong and a source of personal fulfillment for many women. Thirty-eight percent of daughters-in-law described in-law relationships as having high affection and little conflict. Even when daughters-in-law do not necessarily get along with their mothers-in-law, they remain committed to maintaining those relationships for the benefit of family. Women remain committed to their marriages and their families at a time in which they are also undergoing significant changes in work, gender role expectations, and the nature of marriage.

This book has also demonstrated the very public nature of what has only been seen as a private family matter. In-law relationships are about mar-riage, and they are also about intergenerational ties. To the extent that the state supports and regulates both marriage and meeting the needs of the elderly population, it should recognize and help support families as they attempt to address in-law difficulties and meet in-law needs. For too long, women have felt alone in their problems with their in-laws and shared the common belief that in-law problems are both to be expected and the result of individual inadequacies. This book shows that indeed in-law relationships can be hard, but the problems are the result of social structural forces, such as the changing life course of later-life families and the creation of a new family upon marriage. In-law relationships are also hard because we expect virtual strangers to treat one another like family without the benefit of a shared history and the unconditional love that characterizes most biological relationships. Perhaps we need to expect less of our in-laws, particularly in the early years of marriage, and acknowledge the need to foster healthy in-law relationships, as well as healthy marriages. Women need to be cognizant of the "bargain" that they make with their in-laws and learn to communicate effectively to avoid a vicious cycle of conflict. Family relationships are important, particularly for women, and we need to help one another to make them better. This is even more critical at a time in which the family is assumed to be failing. Let me end then with a quote from one of the mothers-in-law, "Yes, it is hard being a daughter-in-law. But it is hard being a mother-in-law too. You feel like you are always on the outside looking in, and that is a hard place for a mother to be."

APPENDIX I: METHODOLOGY

RECRUITING RESEARCH SUBJECTS

Finding research subjects for this study was, at first, a difficult task. I did not want to conduct a random telephone survey or send out random questionnaires because of the private nature of the subject. I was skeptical about getting honest or thoughtful responses if women felt that something so personal and private was being explored in an impersonal manner. I was also concerned that I would not get a full picture of the relationship (as seen by either woman) from the short answers characteristic of surveys. As a result, I started out by asking for volunteers for an in-depth interview from local women's groups and through word of mouth, thus using a snowball sampling technique. This, however, was a slow process, and I had only eighteen subjects by the end of two summers. The third summer I was fortunate to have faculty development funds at my disposal to pay research subjects. I put an ad in the local newspaper and again posted flyers at the local supermarkets and convenience stores.[1] This time, however, I offered to pay subjects $25.00 for the interview. I started getting calls immediately, and they continued over the next two (and more) weeks. I completed fifty-three interviews. Of these, thirty respondents were paid and recruited from the newspaper ad or flyers, six were recruited from local women's groups, and seventeen were found by word of mouth or a snowball sampling technique.

Daughters-in-law had to fulfill several criteria to be included in the survey. They had to be currently married for two or more years[2] and have a mother-in-law who was still living. I did, however, include three women whose mothers-in-law were living in a nursing home and two whose mothers-in-law had died within the last three months. I included them because I wanted to get older daughters-in-law as well as younger daughters-in-law in the sample. I made the judgment that such a short period of separation would not color the relationship substantially.[3] I inadvertently interviewed two women whose mothers-in-law had been deceased for longer than that. However, because they were such rich data, I decided to keep them in addition to the 50 interviews that I went on to complete. I also interviewed one woman who was no longer married but who had kept in touch with her mother-in-law. I was particularly interested in her because of her decision to remain in contact. Thus, these three anomalous cases were added to the baseline fifty cases. As such, I ended up with fifty-three cases in total.

My main objective in this study was to understand the nature of in-law relationships. I believed that I could best do this by interviewing both daughters-in-law and their mothers-in-law. I made the decision to recruit mothers-in-law through their daughters-in-law. At the end of each interview, I asked the daughters-in-law if they would allow me to interview their mothers-in-law. If they said "yes," I requested that they ask their mother-in-law to call me and gave them my business card. I decided to recruit mothers-in-law this way rather than requesting only mother-in-law and daughter-in-law dyads. I did this because I thought that I would miss a significant subpopulation of daughters-in-law if I took only those whose mothers-in-law were willing to participate and who wanted to ask their mothers-in-law to do this with them (i.e., a joint activity and one that could potentially create a rift between them). Overall, I was more interested in the nature of the relationship from the perspective of the daughter-in-law though than that of her mother-in-law (although I did try to interview the mother-in-law whenever possible). Furthermore, I did not contact the mothers-in-law myself because I did not want to intrude on their privacy. Of the thirty daughters-in-law who originally said that they would be willing to ask their mothers-in-law, I heard from 40 percent (or twelve) of their mothers-in-law. I then contacted the daughters-in-law a second time and repeated my request. This increased the number of mothers-in-law to fourteen (47 percent). Three daughters-in-law recommended a fellow sister-in-law to be interviewed, which I followed-up on in all three cases. This then means that I actually have seventeen mother-in-law and daughter-in-law pairs.

Women who did not want their mothers-in-law to be interviewed gave me a number of reasons for their decision. The most common reason given was that the women did not want their mother-in-law to know that they themselves had been interviewed and/or they did not want their mother-in-law to know that they had "issues" with her. Similarly, others said that they did not want to cause family problems. This group of women was most likely to have mediocre relationships with their mothers-in-law. Less common, but still mentioned several times, was the excuse that the women did not want to ask their mothers-in-law because they were "horrible" and they did not want to have to call them or be indebted to them. These women were most likely to have poor relationships. Another daughter-in-law did not think that her mother-in-law would be analytical enough to answer the questions. Interestingly, those women with very good and poor relationships were most likely to ask their mothers-in-law to be interviewed.

This data is not meant to be a portrayal of *the* in-law relationship. Like any family relationship, each person has his or her own perspective. This book primarily addresses the perspective of the daughter-in-law using additional data from the mother-in-law to supplement the daughter-in-law's view and to provide a more complete picture.

I deliberately sought women with certain characteristics. In particular, I looked for women who were divorced, nonwhites, and those of diverse incomes, ages, and places of residence. This allowed me to increase heterogeneity in the sample as much as possible. This does not mean that I have established a representative sample. I do, however, have sufficient variation to look at overall patterns. The religious, ethnic, and class variables are indicative of the Massachusetts population.

Sample Bias

Recruiting subjects in this way may have resulted in some bias. I may not have women whose experiences are so painful that they do not wish to share them. I also may have lost those women who do not want their in-laws to identify their responses (despite assuring anonymity and confidentiality). However, I believe that recruiting this way rather than through random digit-dialing or mail surveys has increased the quality of the data because I have included only those who are willing to talk about their experiences. The range of experiences also reassures me that I have included those who have had significantly troubled relationships.

THE INTERVIEWS

I told the daughters-in-law that I would interview them at whatever place was most convenient for them: their homes, my office, or at a public place. Most of the women chose to be interviewed in their homes. I also met women at a local public garden, my office, area restaurants and coffee shops, and a mall. I completed all of the interviewing and transcribing myself. In most cases, other adults and children were not present at the interviews due to the sensitive nature of the questions. One of the daughters-in-law did, however, request that she and her mother-in-law be interviewed together. The women were very good friends, verified by the way that they finished one another's sentences and asked one another "What is it I am trying to say?" I granted their request but asked each separately at a later time if she had anything else to add to the interview or wished to amend. They did not. Interviews lasted anywhere from one to two hours and were usually tape-recorded.

Five of the mother-in-law interviews were conducted by telephone because of the distance. This meant that I could not probe when I noted certain facial expressions, although I was mindful of pauses and probed the reasons for the pauses. Mothers-in-law were paid for their interviews if the daughters-in-law had been paid (assuming that there might be a similar expectation). The mother-in-law interviews lasted approximately one hour.

The interviews were typically quite pleasant. Although the women were told that they could decline to answer any question, no one did. I felt welcomed and comfortable in their homes, for which I was most appreciative. Women seemed relaxed in answering my questions. I never had the impression that I was not hearing the whole story, at least from the point of view of the subject. Nor did women seem like they were evading questions. They were candid and honest, most likely because they had volunteered. Emotions did, however, run high at times. Several daughters-in-law became very teary eyed, and I discreetly gave them time to compose themselves. Others became quite angry. At the end of those interviews, I turned the conversation to other topics and was able to calm them before leaving their homes. All in all, getting to know the women and their mothers-in-law and sharing their stories was one of the highlights of my professional career. I feel very fortunate and privileged to have had this experience.

CHARACTERISTICS OF THE SAMPLE

Descriptions of the daughter-in-law and mother-in-law samples are included in Tables A.1 and A.2. Three-quarters of the daughters-in-law were between the ages of thirty-six and fifty-five, which is consistent with the fact that 72 percent had been married for up to twenty years. A little less than one-third had a high school diploma or GED, while another one-third

TABLE A.1 Description of the Daughters-in-Law (*N*=53)

Characteristic	%
Age, y	
≤35	15
36–45	26
46–55	49
56–65	9
66+	0
Number of years married	
2–10	32
11–20	40
21–30	21
31+	8
Education	
Some high school	6
High school diploma or GED	30
Associate's or college degree	34
Master's degree or PhD	30
Religion	
Protestant	32
Catholic	57
Jewish	8
Other	
Mormon	2
Atheist	2
Class	
Upper-middle	28
Middle	43
Lower-middle/working	26
Poor	2
Race	
White, non-Latino	92
Latino	2
African American	6
Primarily worked outside of the home	
Yes	72
No	28
Ever divorced	
Yes	28
No	72
Distance from their mother-in-law	
<1 hour	70
1–3 hours	13
>3 hours (may require a flight)	17

TABLE A.2 Description of the Mothers-in-Law (*N*=14)

Characteristic	%
Age, y	
60–70	43
71–80	43
81–90	7
91–100	7
Religion	
Protestant	36
Catholic	36
Jewish	21
Other	
Ethical Culturist	7
Class	
Upper middle	50
Middle	29
Working	14
Poor	7
Race	
White, non-Hispanic	100
Worked outside of the home while younger	
Yes	57
No	43
Marital status	
Married	50
Widowed	43
Divorced	7

had an associate's or college degree. The fact that 30 percent had an advanced degree reflects the fact that many of the subjects were recruited through a newspaper ad. Over half of the subjects were Catholic, reflecting the dominant religion of the area. Nearly half were middle class, and the majority was white. This allows one to understand and describe typical patterns surrounding in-law relationships but does not allow one to make comparisons between racial groups. The majority (70 percent) lived less than one hour from their mother-in-law.

Over three-quarters of the mothers-in-law were between the ages of sixty and eighty, and over one-third was Catholic. A higher percentage of the mothers-in-law than the daughters-in-law were upper middle class (50 percent versus 28 percent). This may reflect both an historical difference in economies, as well as the fact that upper middle class mothers-in-law may have been more willing to be interviewed than middle or working class older women. More of the mothers-in-law were also housewives when they were younger (43 percent versus 28 percent). Finally, 43 percent of the mothers-in-law were widowed.

DATA ANALYSIS

Content analysis was used to examine the data. After reading all of the responses for a particular question, themes were identified. Cases were divided according to the presence or absence of that theme or placed into multiple categories derived from the theme. Often, this was a multileveled process resulting in finer distinctions across cases. This is a common methodology used with qualitative data. It is referred to as a "grounded" methodology because the categories and analysis derive from the data themselves, or from the respondents' own words.

For example, to analyze the quality of the relationship, I read through the interviews several times looking for common themes or terms that were used by the daughters-in-law. I discovered that the daughters-in-law often spoke about the presence and degree of conflict that they experienced, as well as whether or not they felt any affection for their mothers-in-law and on what it was based. I noted that they also referred to how often they saw their mothers-in-law both as a cause and result of the affection and conflict. Those who did not see their mother-in-law frequently often did not feel as close to her. It was therefore a separate, but connected, dimension of the quality of the relationship. I then divided the cases into high and low levels of affection, conflict, and frequency of interaction, creating six categories for the quality of the relationship. This created a fuller and more in depth understanding of the quality of the relationship.

APPENDIX 2: SYNOPSIS OF SOURCES OF CONFLICT

1. "My mother-in-law disapproved that [we] moved in together before we were married." [single occurrence]

2. "My mother-in-law always sees the glass half-empty and is controlling." [for short periods]

3a. "It is mostly differences of opinion."

3b. "My mother-in-law is negative and talks about people."

4. "She is negative about all marriages... due to her own divorce."

5. "My mother-in-law is territorial of her son. She does not accept that her children have their own families."

6a. "It is little things... like leaving the dishes in the sink." [coresident in-laws]

6b. "She says my house is like living in a museum.... It is too clean."

6c. "She is too dependent on us; my husband waits on her hand and foot."

6d. "We are both fighting for my husband's attention."

7. "There is no open conflict, but there is always underlying tension. I am the black sheep [of the family]. I had no education.... We married when we were young. I was pregnant."

8. "Only before we got married. The conflict was about the wedding. They wanted a big, religious service.... We were married outside by the Justice of the Peace. They threatened to boycott the wedding, so I threatened not to invite them."

9. "They tried to control our lives, like in what directions my husband's career and my career should go." [only in beginning of marriage]

10. "She used to invite my husband's ex-wife to Christmas dinner." [early on only]

11. "It is my mother-in-law's personality. Everything is rigidly scheduled."

12. "There were a lot of problems all along. She takes everything the wrong way.... She takes it personally that [my husband] is close to my family. She told my sister-in-law that I discourage him from calling."

13. "I come from a so very connected family. [My in-laws] are cold and distant, that Irish Catholic way while my family is very, very close."

14. "She was always upset that we didn't visit more. We would split the holidays, like most families. She wanted us there all day though."

15. "It is about privacy [coresident in-laws]. [My mother-in-law] does things for [my husband] that I feel I should be doing to take care of him."

MOTHER-IN-LAW: "There is no real conflict. We work things out."

16. "[She] has a hard time letting go and losing control of her sons."

17. "She is just cold."

MOTHER-IN-LAW: "I think my daughter-in-law is insecure."

18. "I am used to doing things my own way and not being told what to do. She is so strong willed and opinionated." [coresident in-laws]

19a. "She is mean to my children. One of my sons is overweight, and she is verbally abusive to him."

19b. "Things normal people wouldn't have the balls to do, she does. It is constant, constant. She'll say, 'Oh, you bought that tablecloth. God, that is ugly.' I will be planning ways that I can kill her and get away with it, and then she buys me some shoes that I want. It is a head fuck.... Money is tight, and she will rub it in that the mortgage hasn't been paid in two months or the phone bill hasn't been paid."

20. "It has been constant from the beginning. They did not want their son to marry me. Their issues were: I was divorced and I was not Catholic."

21. "She is very intrusive in other people's lives."

MOTHER-IN-LAW: "There was no conflict on my part. I know that I did things to annoy her though."

22. "She calls my younger son 'Kyle' not 'Caleb' and me either 'Donna' or 'Martha,' not 'Maureen.' She sends gifts and boxes of clothes to my husband and my older son but not me or my younger son who looks like me. They are both her grandsons.... I told her once that I would send the boys' school pictures, and she said not to bother to send one of my younger son because she did not need it.... She wants nothing to do with our younger son."

23a. "She is very impersonal. She just sends us cards with money at holidays, never gifts."

23b. "She insinuates that I am a bad housekeeper every chance that she gets, but my house is cleaner than hers! One time that we asked her to feed the cat while we were away, she totally recleaned my house."

24. "She does nothing with my kids. For my son's birthday, she gave him a card with money. But rather than stopping by with it, she gave it to her husband to give to my husband [they work in a family business]. She is very close to my sister-in-law's children though. She buys their clothes, takes them out for dinner.... It is as if she feels [my husband] should not have had a second family."

25. "The conflict is over space and disruption of our routine when she visits." [daughter-in-law works at home]

26. "It is class bias. I was the black sheep. I was nothing because I had no education."

27a. "We have firm boundaries with her, which she tries to ignore if she does not like them."

27b. "She tries to live through her kids."

27c. "Her style is so different from my parents."

MOTHER-IN-LAW: "I can't think of any conflict."

28. "It was bad to begin with. They would leave me out of family photos...tell me that only they were family. Then they tried to take my baby from the hospital while I was recovering and my husband was at work." [crying; cannot talk about it any further]

29. "They are not close to anyone. No one in the family is close. They just sit around and play Nintendo when they visit. They even eat in front of the TV.... They don't pay any attention to our kids when they visit.... *Plus*, they are cheapskates."

30. "My husband works for the family business. They have threatened not to support him unless he leaves me.... They tried to buy me off with a check." [irate]

Author's note: The responses of one mother-in-law and daughter-in-law pair are not reported because of a request for confidentiality.

APPENDIX 3: THE PRACTICE
OF INTERVIEWING

I sat on the respondent's deck in the early hours of the morning. "Carla" shook with rage as she told me of her plight with her in-laws, occasionally spitting around her words as her anger peaked. A German shepherd and a bullmastiff watched me closely, blocking my only exit from the deck. I struggled to make sense of what Carla was telling me as she jumped from topic to topic, while never forgetting that I was being watched. Carla's ferret, which had until then been perched on her shoulder, suddenly jumped from her shoulder, scurried down her leg, and leapt onto my lap. Seemingly unaware of what had just happened, Carla continued to curse her mother-in-law, who slept on the second floor of the house. I spoke softly, intending that Carla might follow suit and her mother-in-law would be spared her invectives. Throughout it all, I thought to myself, "We never covered how to handle *this* in graduate school."

Interviewing family members about highly sensitive matters in the (sometimes) chaotic environment of their own homes is a skill. It does not require any particular talent, but it does require practice, dedication to the task, and an endless amount of tact. Yet, sharing people's lives and hearing their stories has also been one of the highlights of my career. Below is a discussion of just some of the challenges that I have encountered.

The thing that struck me the most in interviewing respondents was their sheer humanness. For example, I found that people often do not even see their own characteristics. One of the respondents emphasized throughout the interview that her mother-in-law was a "control freak." Yet, it was this same woman who had scheduled and then rescheduled our appointment several times, had insisted that we meet in an independent location of her choice so that I would not know where she lived, and who restated my questions during the interview to better suit her. Another daughter-in-law criticized her mother-in-law for her negative demeanor while she herself never smiled or showed any affect in person or on the phone. I learned that while we often do not see our own "faults," we notice them in others.

Valerie and Rosemary offered a different type of humanness. I also came to refer to them as "Click" and "Clack." When I arrived at Valerie's home, Rosemary, her mother-in-law, was present. My understanding was that I was to interview Rosemary after my interview with Valerie, in her home across the street. I mentioned this to the two women, but they insisted on being interviewed together. It quickly became apparent that they were the best of friends and that these were two women who enjoyed a good time. They teased one another good-naturedly throughout the interview, laughing and having fun with every question. They finished one another's sentences so frequently that I had to struggle to parcel the interview into two parts. At one point, Rosemary turned to Valerie and said, "What is it I am trying to say?" Needing to be sure though that neither woman had anything to say that she would not want the other to hear, I asked them separately at a later point if there was anything else that they wanted to add or amend to the interview. As I had by then expected, neither did.

The most challenging aspect of interviewing people though is trying to understand what they are telling you. This occurs at two stages: during the interview itself and then while transcribing the tapes. Most of us are not articulate enough to say precisely what we mean without any sort of probing on the part of the other person. Still, I was surprised by the number of times that I had to ask respondents to clarify what they meant. Often the older women would speak in clichés that I would then have to ask them to explain (e.g., "[Our relationship] is what it is."). Respondents would also jump from time period to time period or from topic to topic, which required constant clarification on my part. What was most problematic though were inconsistencies or vague statements that I discovered while transcribing the tapes. In these instances, I would call the respondent on the telephone and ask for clarification. Sometimes this was helpful, but not always. If I were unsure of a statement, I would treat it as missing data.

I started every interview with idle conversation to help the respondent and myself to relax and to get to know one another. In one of my initial interviews, I realized though that I had to pick my topics carefully. Sue had escorted me into her cozy kitchen for our interview. I sat down at the table and proceeded to take out my tape recorder and questionnaire from my brief case when I noticed a beautiful and unusual canister on Sue's kitchen table. Sue broke down crying though when I remarked at how beautiful it was. My attempt to make her feel comfortable had had the opposite effect. She then told me that the "canister" was an urn with the family dog's remains. Since the kitchen was his favorite place, the family had not been able to take the urn anywhere else. After that, I was more cautious in people's homes and assumed nothing.

Perhaps the most ubiquitous challenge though was handling people's high emotions. As noted in the example of Carla previously, a few of the daughters-in-law were extremely angry. Carla cursed extensively throughout the interview. At least she was able to vent her anger though. It was Alexa who I was most concerned about. She became visibly upset while telling me of her frustrations with her mother-in-law. I felt a professional obligation to leave without causing any harm. Like I had done for other respondents, I gave Alexa a phone number that she could call for counseling, but I also stayed longer than was necessary after the interview to help her to calm down. We talked mainly about her sons and their educations. It was only when I had assured myself that Alexa had transitioned back to her pre-interviewed demeanor that I left. Still, I checked on her later on the pretext of a follow-up question.

Interviewing people about family raises other sensitive issues as well. Respondents were asked to compare their relationship with their mother-in-law to that of their mother. This was particularly difficult for people who had lost their mother as they tried to envision what their relationship with her might be like now. I found that the best thing that I could do was to pause to give the women time to acknowledge their grief. I trusted my instincts and placed my hand upon theirs when it seemed appropriate, but I was careful to respect the boundaries. Never did I try to hurry the women through their grief.

Throughout the interviews I was treated to the kindness of strangers. While I went out of my way to make them feel comfortable, they too went out of their way to make me feel welcome in their homes. One young woman insisted on treating me to a soft drink at the local ice cream parlor. Mothers-in-law, all older than myself, reciprocated the respect that I gave to them. All of the respondents were generous with their time and willing to help. I wanted to get to know some of the mothers-in-law better; I wished that some of the daughters-in-law were my friends. I came to care for all.

Interviewing requires that the interviewer control the physical environment. You need to assure privacy for your respondents, a quiet environment where they can think and not be distracted, and plenty of time for the interview. Most of the respondents wanted to be interviewed in their homes, which added some challenges. The vast majority of the women ensured these three things for themselves. Still, I would occasionally enter a home where other family members wandered in and out of the room or were too close to assure privacy. In other situations I was concerned that excessive noise (e.g., piano playing, outside road work) would interfere with the taping. In the latter situation, I coped by using two tape recorders at different points in the room and stopping to taking copious notes. The former situations though required tact and diplomacy. As mentioned earlier, I suggested that Valerie and Rosemary be interviewed separately. Likewise, a few children played nearby as their mother spoke of their grandmother (these were usually positive relationships though). In the end, I chose to leave it to the respondent but only after I had made it clear that I could come back at a later date. No one took me up on this offer.

Interviewing requires maturity and tact. With these two things in hand, one can manage any interviewing situation that they encounter. I would be careful though about using undergraduate researchers to interview people about highly sensitive family matters. It is my belief that respondents feel most comfortable talking to others like them, in this case, other married or middle-aged women. As such, not all students would be effective in eliciting the trust of their respondents. Most importantly though, an interviewer needs to want to get to know her subjects better and, if possible, to care about the things that matter most to them. In this situation, that was the subject of family.

NOTES

CHAPTER 1: INTRODUCTION

1. Lynda Basye, e-mail message to author, September 5, 2006.

2. Lucy Rose Fischer, *Linked Lives: Adult Daughters and Their Mothers* (New York: Harper and Row, 1986).

3. Pamela Cotterill, *Friendly Relations? Mothers and Their Daughters-in-Law* (London: Taylor and Francis, 1994).

4. Joyce Emmons Nuner and Lillian Chenoweth, "A Qualitative Study of Mother-in-Law and Daughter-in-Law Relationships" (paper presented at the annual meetings of the National Council on Family Relations, Phoenix, AZ, November 2005).

5. Helene S. Arnstein, *Between Mothers-in-Law and Daughters-in-Law: Achieving a Successful and Caring Relationship* (New York: Dodd, Mead, 1987).

6. Elaine M. Brody, *Women in the Middle: Their Parent-Care Years* (New York: Springer, 1990).

7. Fischer, *Linked Lives.*

8. Arnstein, *Between Mothers-in-Law and Daughters-in-Law.*

9. J. Silverstein, "The Problem with In-Laws," *Journal of Family Therapy* 14 (1990): 399–412.

10. Arnstein, *Between Mothers-in-Law and Daughters-in-Law.*

11. Fischer, *Linked Lives.*

12. Cotterill, *Friendly Relations?*

13. Fischer, *Linked Lives.*

14. Cotterill, *Friendly Relations?*

15. Linda J. Waite and Maggie Gallagher, *The Case for Marriage: Why Married People Are Happier, Healthier, and Better Off Financially* (New York: Doubleday, 2000).

16. Judith S. Wallerstein, Julia M. Lewis, and Sandra Blakeslee, *The Unexpected Legacy of Divorce: A 25-Year Landmark Study* (New York: Hyperion, 2000).

17. Nicholas Wolfinger, *Understanding the Divorce Cycle: The Children of Divorce in Their Own Marriages* (New York: Cambridge University Press, 2005).

18. Anne-Marie Ambert, "Relationships with Former In-Laws after Divorce: A Research Note," *Journal of Marriage and the Family* 50 (1988): 679–86.

19. Ann Goetting, "Patterns of Support Among In-Laws in the United States," *Journal of Family Issues* 11 (1990): 67–90.

20. Colleen Leahy Johnson, "In-Law Relationships in the American Kinship System: The Impact of Divorce and Remarriage," *American Ethnologist* 16 (1989): 87–99.

CHAPTER 2: MOTHERS-IN-LAW AND DAUGHTERS-IN-LAW IN POPULAR CULTURE

1. Kathy Mitchell and Marcy Sugar, "Dear Annie," *Worcester Telegram and Gazette*, August 1, 2005–May 31, 2006.

2. Ibid., September 19, 2005, E2.

3. Terri Apter, http://www.motherinlawstories.com, Accessed October 13, 2005.

4. Ibid.

5. http://www.monsterinlaw.com/funnieststories/index.php?browse=1&story_id=152, Accessed October 24, 2005.

6. http://www.cartoonstock.com/directory/d/daughters-in-law.asp, Accessed June 7, 2006.

7. Turlough O'Carolan, "Daughters-in-Laws Are Our Grandchildren's Mothers," http://www.poemsforfree.com/daught.html, Accessed May 25, 2006.

8. Ruth 1:8, 1:16.

9. Internet Movie Database (IMDb), http://imdb.com, Accessed May 31, 2006.

10. *Monster-in-Law*, directed by Robert Luketic, written by Anya Kochoff, New Line Cinema, 2005.

11. *Everybody Loves Raymond*, Creator Philip Rosenthal, CBS, 1996–2005.

12. *The Mothers-in-Law*, directed by Dezi Arnaz and Elliott Lewis (originally aired 1967–1969), http://www.bbc.co.uk/comedy/guide/articles/m/mothersinlawthe_1299002160.shtml, Accessed October 24, 2005.

13. *The Waltons*, "The Homecoming," directed by Fiedler Cook, Executive Producer Lee Rich, Producer Robert Jacks, Written by Earl Hammer, Fox Video, 1971, dinner scene.

14. Dr. Phil, "Meddling Future Mothers-in-Law," http://www.drphil.com/shows/show/579, Accessed October 24, 2005.

15. Suzanne Cole, "The End of a Marriage," *Newsweek*, Vol. 131, no. 25, June 22, 1998, 20.

16. Susan Dworkin, "My Mother-in-Law and Me," *Ladies Home Journal* 115, no. 4 (April 1988): 62–66.

17. Annie Chapman, *The Mother-in-Law Dance: Can Two Women Love the Same Man and Still Get Along?* (Eugene, OR: Harvest House Publishers, 2004).

18. Susan Shapiro Barash, *Mothers-in-Law and Daughters-in-Law: Love, Hate, Rivalry, and Reconciliation* (Far Hills, NJ: New Horizon Press, 2001).

19. Camille Russo, *How to Be the Perfect Mother-in-Law* (Riverside, NJ: Andrews McMeel Publishing, 1998).

20. Mary Tatum, *Just Call Me Mom: Practical Steps to Becoming a Better Mother-in-Law* (Camp Hill, PA: Christian Publications, 1994).

21. Eileen Posner, *Mother of the Groom: A Collection of Women's Voices* (Lahore, Pakistan: Distinctive Publications Corporation, 1996).

22. Sue Verra, *What Every Mother-in-Law Wishes Her Daughter-in-Law Knew But Was Afraid to Tell Her* (Lima, OH: Fairway Press, 1996).

23. Liz Bluper and Renee Plastique, *Mothers-in-Law Do Everything Wrong: M.I.L.D.E.W.* (Riverside, NJ: Andrews McMeel Publishing, 2004).

24. Eden Unger Bowditch and Aviva Samet, *The Daughter-in-Law's Survival Guide: Everything You Need to Know About Relating to Your Mother-in-Law* (Oakland, CA: New Harbinger Publications, 2002).

25. Helene S. Arnstein, *Between Mothers-in-Law and Daughters-in-Law: Achieving a Successful and Caring Relationship* (New York: Dodd, Mead, 1987).

26. "Marvelous Mothers-in-Law," *Today's Christian Woman*, November/December 1998, http://www.christianitytoday.com/tcw/8w6/8w6118.html, Accessed October 24, 2005.

27. Pamela Cotterill, *Friendly Relations? Mothers and Their Daughters-in-Law* (London: Taylor and Francis, 1994).

CHAPTER 3: THE QUALITY OF MOTHER-IN-LAW AND DAUGHTER-IN-LAW RELATIONSHIPS

1. Helene S. Arnstein, *Between Mothers-in-Law and Daughters-in-Law: Achieving a Successful and Caring Relationship* (New York: Dodd, Mead, 1987).

2. Elaine M. Brody, *Women in the Middle: Their Parent-Care Years* (New York: Springer, 1990).

3. Lucy Rose Fischer, *Linked Lives: Adult Daughters and Their Mothers* (New York: Harper and Row, 1986).

4. Joyce Emmons Nuner and Lillian Chenoweth, "A Qualitative Study of Mother-in-Law and Daughter-in-Law Relationships" (paper presented at the annual meetings of the National Council on Family Relations, Phoenix, AZ, November 2005).

5. Fischer, *Linked Lives.*

6. Pamela Cotterill, *Friendly Relations? Mothers and Their Daughters-in-Law* (London: Taylor and Francis, 1994).

7. Arnstein, *Between Mothers-in-Law and Daughters-in-Law.*

8. M. Jean Turner, Carolyn R. Young, and Kelly I. Black, "Daughters-in-Law and Mothers-in-Law Seeking Their Place Within the Family: A Qualitative Study of Differing Viewpoints," *Family Relations* 55 (2006): 588–600.

9. Cotterill, *Friendly Relations?*

10. Ingrid Arnet Connidis, *Family Ties and Aging* (Thousand Oaks, CA: Sage Publications, 2001), 126.

11. Conflict refers to *present* conflict. Daughters-in-law may be categorized as having low conflict even if they experienced conflict in the past.

12. Arnstein, *Between Mothers-in-Law and Daughters-in-Law.*

13. Fischer, *Linked Lives.*

14. Nuner and Chenoweth, "A Qualitative Study."

15. Fischer, *Linked Lives.*

16. Ibid.

17. Roseann Giarusso, Du Feng, Merril Silverstein, and Vern L. Bengtson, "Grandparent-Adult Child Affection and Consensus: Cross Generational and Cross Ethnic Comparison," *Journal of Family Issues* 22 (2001): 456–77.

18. Alice S. Rossi and Peter H. Rossi, *Of Human Bonding: Parent-Child Relations Across the Life Course* (New York: Walter de Gruyter, 1990).

19. A. Shapiro, "Revisiting the Gender Gap: Exploring the Relationships of Parent/Adult Child Dyads," *International Journal of Aging and Human Development* 58 (2004): 127–46.

20. Debra Umberson, "Relationships Between Adult Children and Their Parents: Psychological Consequences for Both Generations," *Journal of Marriage and the Family* 54 (1992): 664–74.

21. Nuner and Chenoweth, "A Qualitative Study."

22. Jaber F. Gubrium and James A. Holstein, "Phenomenology, Ethnomethodology, and Family Discourse," in *Sourcebook of Family Theories and Methods: A Contextual Approach* (New York: Springer, 1993), 651–72.

23. Fischer, *Linked Lives.*

24. Arnstein, *Between Mothers-in-Law and Daughters-in-Law.*

25. Andrea E. Willson, Kim M. Shuey, and Glen H. Elder Jr., "Ambivalence in the Relationship of Adult Children to Aging Parents and In-Laws," *Journal of Marriage and the Family* 65 (2003): 1055–72.

26. Fischer, *Linked Lives.*

27. Karen L. Fingerman, *Aging Mothers and Their Adult Daughters: Mixed Emotions, Enduring Bonds* (Amherst, NY: Prometheus Books, 2003).

28. Fischer, *Linked Lives.*

29. Cotterill, *Friendly Relations?*

30. Gubrium and Holstein, *Sourcebook of Family Theories and Methods.*

31. Ingrid Arnet Connidis and Julie Ann McMullin, "Sociological Ambivalence and Family Ties: A Critical Perspective," *Journal of Marriage and the Family* 64 (2002): 558–67.

32. Kurt Luescher and Karl Pillemer, "Intergenerational Ambivalence: A New Approach to the Study of Parent-Child Relations in Later Life," *Journal of Marriage and the Family* 60 (1998): 413–25.

33. Ibid.

34. Karen Fingerman, Elizabeth L. Hay, and Kira S. Birditt, "The Best of Ties, the Worst of Ties: Close, Problematic, and Ambivalent Social Relationships," *Journal of Marriage and the Family* 66 (2004): 792–808.

35. Karl Pillemer and J. Jill Suitor, "Explaining Mother's Ambivalence Toward Their Adult Children," *Journal of Marriage and the Family* 64 (2002): 602–13.

36. For example, 29% of mothers agreed or strongly agreed that they "often get on each others' nerves" but nevertheless "feel very close."

37. Glenna Spitze and Mary P. Gallant, "'The Bitter with the Sweet': Older Adult Strategies for Handling Ambivalence in Relations with Their Adult Children," *Research on Aging* 26 (2004): 387–412.

38. Kim M. Shuey, Andrea E. Willson, and Glen H. Elder Jr., "Ambivalence in the Relationship Between Aging Mothers and Their Adult Children: A Dyadic Analysis" (paper presented at the annual meeting of the American Sociological Association, Atlanta, August 17, 2003).

39. Ibid.

40. Rossi and Rossi, *Of Human Bonding.*

41. Cotterill, *Friendly Relations?*

42. Pauline Boss, *Family Stress Management: A Contextual Approach* (Thousand Oaks, CA: Sage Publications, 2002).

43. Pillemer and Suitor, "Explaining Mother's Ambivalence."

44. The other three had deceased in-laws during their first marriages.

CHAPTER 4: DETERMINING THE QUALITY OF THE RELATIONSHIPS

1. Joyce Emmons Nuner and Lillian Chenoweth, "A Qualitative Study of Mother-in-Law and Daughter-in-Law Relationships" (paper presented at the annual meetings of the National Council on Family Relations, Phoenix, AZ, November 2005).

2. Pamela Cotterill, *Friendly Relations? Mothers and Their Daughters-in-Law* (London: Taylor and Francis, 1994).

3. Nuner and Chenoweth, "A Qualitative Study."

4. M. Jean Turner, Carolyn R. Young, and Kelly I. Black, "Daughters-in-Law and Mothers-in-Law Seeking Their Place Within the Family: A Qualitative Study of Differing Viewpoints," *Family Relations* 55 (2006): 588–600.

5. Cotterill, *Friendly Relations?*

6. Turner, Young, and Black, "Daughters-in-Law and Mothers-in-Law."

7. Nuner and Chenoweth, "A Qualitative Study."

8. EPIC, MCR Poll, "Relationships with Mothers-in-Law Improve with Age," *Jet* 90 (1996): 12.

9. Britta H. Limary, "The Mother-in-Law/Daughter-in-Law Dyad: Narratives of Relational Development Among In-Laws," In *Dissertation Abstracts International, A: The Humanities and Social Sciences* 63 (August 7, 2002).

10. Ramona Marotz-Baden and Deane Cowan, "Mothers-in-Law and Daughters-in-Law: The Effects of Proximity on Conflict and Stress," *Family Relations* 36 (1987): 385–90.

11. Positive relationships included those that were "tight knit" and "distant but positive." "Cordial" and "conflicted but affectionate" relationships were excluded from the analysis.

12. Poorer relationships included those that were "estranged" and "obligatory." "Cordial" and "conflicted but affectionate" relationships were excluded from the analysis.

13. Cotterill, *Friendly Relations?*

14. Turner, Young, and Black, "Daughters-in-Law and Mothers-in-Law."

15. This included one woman whose mother had been mentally ill since she was a child.

16. Hope Edelman, *Motherless Daughters* (Reading, MA: Addison-Wesley, 1994).

17. Lynn Davidman found in her study of motherless daughters that daughters tend to idealize their deceased mothers. Lynn Davidman, *Motherloss* (Berkeley: University of California Press, 2000).

18. Edelman, *Motherless Daughters.*

19. Ibid.

CHAPTER 5: THE EFFECTS OF POSTMODERN FAMILY LIFE ON IN-LAW RELATIONSHIPS

1. Rose M. Kreider and Jason M. Fields, "Number, Timing, and Duration of Marriages and Divorces: 1996," *U.S. Census Bureau Current Population Reports* (February, 2002): 18.

2. Pamela Cotterill, *Friendly Relations? Mothers and Their Daughters-in-Law* (London: Taylor and Francis, 1994).

3. Anne-Marie Ambert, "Relationships with Former In-Laws after Divorce: A Research Note," *Journal of Marriage and the Family* 50 (1988): 679–86.

4. Ann Goetting, "Patterns of Support Among In-Laws in the United States," *Journal of Family Issues* 11 (1990): 67–90.

5. Colleen Leahy Johnson, "In-Law Relationships in the American Kinship System: The Impact of Divorce and Remarriage," *American Ethnologist* 16 (1989): 87–99.

6. Ibid.

7. Ambert, "Relationships with Former In-Laws after Divorce."

8. Goetting, "Patterns of Support."

9. Ambert, "Relationships with Former In-Laws after Divorce."

10. Goetting, "Patterns of Support."

11. Alan Booth and Paul R. Amato, "Parental Marital Quality, Parental Divorce, and Relations with Parents," *Journal of Marriage and the Family* 56 (1994): 21–34.

12. Peter Uhlenberg, "The Role of Divorce in Men's Relations with Their Adult Children after Midlife," *Journal of Marriage and the Family* 52 (1993): 677–88.

13. Pamela S. Webster and A. Regula Herzog, "Effects of Parental Divorce and Memories of Family Problems on Relationships Between Adult Children and Their Parents," *Journal of Gerontology: Social Sciences* 50B (1995): S24–S34.

14. Carol L. Wright and Joseph W. Maxwell, "Social Support During Adjustment To Later-Life Divorce: How Adult Children Help Their Parents," *Journal of Divorce and Remarriage* 15 (1991): 21–48.

15. Uhlenberg, "The Role of Divorce in Men's Relations."

16. Gayle Kaufman and Peter Uhlenberg, "Effects of Life Course Transitions on the Quality of Relationships Between Adult Children and Their Parents," *Journal of Marriage and the Family* 60 (1998): 924–38.

17. Booth and Amato, "Parental Marital Quality, Parental Divorce."

18. Charles D. Hoffman and Debra K. Ledford, "Adult Children of Divorce: Relationships with Their Mothers and Fathers Prior to, Following Parental Separation and Currently," *Journal of Divorce and Remarriage* 24 (1995): 41–57.

19. Arlie Russell Hochschild, *The Time Bind* (New York: Metropolitan Books, 1997), 6–7.

20. Ge Lin and Peter A. Rogerson, "Elderly Parents and the Geographic Availability of Their Adult Children," *Research on Aging* 17 (1995): 303–31.

21. Jacob Climo, *Distant Parents* (New Brunswick, NJ: Rutgers University Press, 1992).

22. Lin and Rogerson, "Elderly Parents."

23. Alice S. Rossi and Peter H. Rossi, *Of Human Bonding: Parent-Child Relations Across the Life Course* (New York: Walter de Gruyter, 1990).

24. Linda J. Waite and Scott C. Harrison, "Keeping in Touch: How Women in Mid-Life Allocate Social Contacts Among Kith and Kin," *Social Forces* 70 (1992): 637–55.

25. David J. DeWit, Andrew V. Wister, and Thomas K. Burch, "Physical Distance and Social Contact Between Elders and Their Adult Children," *Research on Aging* 10 (1988): 56–80.

26. Brian Gratton and Carole Haber, "In Search of 'Intimacy at a Distance': Family History from the Perspective of Elderly Women," *Journal of Aging Studies* 7 (1993): 183–94.

27. Douglas Wolf, "Household Patterns of Older Women," *Research on Aging* 12 (1990): 463–86.

28. Climo, *Distant Parents.*

29. The typical child visits twice a year. One-third visit once a year and only 10 percent visit less than once a year. At the other end of the distribution, one-third visits three times a year or more. Average visits last for four days but range from one day to six weeks. See note 21 above.

30. Joshua R. Goldstein, "The Leveling of Divorce in the United States," *Demography* 36 (1999): 409–14.

31. National Center for Health Statistics, http://www.cdc.gov/nchs/data/nvsr54/nvsr54_20.pdf, Accessed March 1, 2007.

32. Kreider and Fields, "Number, Timing, and Duration."

33. National Center for Health Statistics, *Health, United States, 2002* with *Chartbook on Trends in the Health of Americans,* http://www.cdc.gov/nchs/hus.htm, Accessed February 28, 2007.

34. Mary Lyndon Shanley, "Should We Abolish Marriage?" (lecture, Clark University, Worcester, MA, February 16, 2006).

CHAPTER 6: THE MAKING OF A DAUGHTER-IN-LAW

1. Zygmunt Bauman, *Liquid Modernity* (Malden, MA: Blackwell, 2000).

2. Zygmunt Bauman, *Liquid Love* (Malden, MA: Blackwell, 2003).

3. Man-hua Chen, "The Relationship of Mothers and Daughters-in-Law in Urban Chinese Families," *Dissertation Abstracts International, A: The Humanities and the Social Sciences* 60 (1999): 3542.

4. Myung-Hye Kim, "Changing Relationships Between Daughters-in-Law and Mothers-in-Law in Urban South Korea," *Anthropological Quarterly* 69 (1996): 179–93.

5. Helene S. Arnstein, *Between Mothers-in-Law and Daughters-in-Law: Achieving a Successful and Caring Relationship* (New York: Dodd, Mead, 1987).

6. Ibid.

7. Pamela Cotterill, *Friendly Relations? Mothers and Their Daughters-in-Law* (London: Taylor and Francis, 1994).

8. Joyce Emmons Nuner and Lillian Chenoweth, "A Qualitative Study of Mother-in-Law and Daughter-in-Law Relationships" (paper presented at the annual meetings of the National Council on Family Relations, Phoenix, AZ, November 2005).

9. Ibid.

10. Arnstein, *Between Mothers-in-Law and Daughters-in-Law.*

11. Ibid.

12. Jacqueline Jackson and Linda Berg-Cross, "Extending the Extended Family: The Mother-in-Law and Daughter-in-Law Relationship of Black Women," *Family Relations* 37 (1988): 293–97.

13. Lucy Rose Fischer, "Mothers and Mothers-in-Law," *Journal of Marriage and the Family* 45 (1983): 187–92.

14. EPIC, MCR Poll, "Relationships with Mothers-in-Law Improve with Age," *Jet* 90 (1996): 12.

15. Emmons Nuner and Chenoweth, "A Qualitative Study."

16. EPIC, MCR Poll.

17. Emmons Nuner and Chenoweth, "A Qualitative Study."

18. Fischer, "Mothers and Mothers-in-Law."

19. Arnstein, *Between Mothers-in-Law and Daughters-in-Law.*

20. Emmons Nuner and Chenoweth, "A Qualitative Study."

21. Stephanie Coontz, *Marriage, a History: How Love Conquered Marriage* (New York: Penguin Group, 2005).

22. This included those who felt that the relationship had not changed at all over time or as the result of any specific event.

23. Alice S. Rossi and Peter H. Rossi, *Of Human Bonding: Parent-Child Relations Across the Life Course* (New York: Walter de Gruyter, 1990).

24. Ann Goetting, "Patterns of Support Among In-Laws in the United States," *Journal of Family Issues* 11 (1990): 67–90.

25. Ibid.

26. Kim Shuey and Melissa Hardy, "Assistance to Aging Parents and Parents-in-Law: Does Lineage Affect Family Allocation Decisions?" *Journal of Marriage and the Family* 65 (2003): 418–31.

27. Eunju Lee, Glenna Spitze, and John R. Logan, "Social Support to Parents-in-Law: The Interplay of Gender and Kin Hierarchies," *Journal of Marriage and the Family* 65 (2003): 396–403.

28. Shuey and Hardy, "Assistance to Aging Parents."

29. Lee, Spitze, and Logan, "Social Support to Parents-in-Law."

30. Goetting, "Patterns of Support."

31. Marilyn Coleman, Larry Ganong, and Susan Cable, "Beliefs About Women's Intergenerational Family Obligations to Provide Support before and after Divorce and Remarriage," *Journal of Marriage and the Family* 59 (1997): 165–76.

32. Ann Swidler, *Talk of Love: How Culture Matters* (Chicago: University of Chicago Press, 2001).

33. Arnstein, *Between Mothers-in-Law and Daughters-in-Law.*

34. Eileen Posner, *Mother of the Groom: A Collection of Women's Voices* (Lahore, Pakistan: Distinctive Publications Corporation, 1996).

35. *Everybody Loves Raymond*, Creator Philip Rosenthal, CBS, 1996–2005.

36. Swidler, *Talk of Love.*

37. Ibid.

38. Cotterill, *Friendly Relations?*

CHAPTER 7: MOTHERS AND SONS, HUSBANDS AND WIVES, AND THE MOTHER-IN-LAW'S PERSPECTIVE

1. Gary Peterson, Debra Madden-Derdich, and Stacie A. Leonard, "Parent–Child Relations Across the Life Course: Autonomy Within the Context of Connectedness," in *Families Across Time: A Life Course Perspective* (Los Angeles: Roxbury Publishing, 2000), 187–203.

2. Helene S. Arnstein, *Between Mothers-in-Law and Daughters-in-Law: Achieving a Successful and Caring Relationship* (New York: Dodd, Mead, 1987).

3. Peterson, Madden-Derdich, and Leonard, "Parent–Child Relations."

4. Karen L. Fingerman, *Aging Mothers and Their Adult Daughters: A Study of Mixed Emotions* (New York: Springer, 2001).

5. Ann Goetting, "Patterns of Support Among In-Laws in the United States," *Journal of Family Issues* 11 (1990): 67–90.

6. Eunju Lee, Glenna Spitze, and John R. Logan, "Social Support to Parents-in-Law: The Interplay of Gender and Kin Hierarchies," *Journal of Marriage and the Family* 65 (2003): 396–403.

7. Kim Shuey and Melissa Hardy, "Assistance to Aging Parents and Parents-in-Law: Does Lineage Affect Family Allocation Decisions?" *Journal of Marriage and the Family* 65 (2003): 418–31.

8. C. N. Nydegger, "Asymmetrical Kin and the Problematic Son-in-Law," in *Lifespan Developmental Psychology: Intergenerational Relationships* (Hillsdale, NJ: Lawrence Erlbaum Associates, 1986), 99–123.

9. Arnstein, *Between Mothers-in-Law and Daughters-in-Law.*

10. Lillian B. Rubin, *Worlds of Pain: Life in the Working Class Family* (New York: Basic Books, 1992).

11. Arnstein, *Between Mothers-in-Law and Daughters-in-Law.*

12. Karen L. Fingerman, "The Role of Offspring and In-Laws in Grandparents' Ties to Their Grandchildren," *Journal of Family Issues* 25, no. 8 (2004): 1026–49.

13. Goetting, "Patterns of Support."

14. Lee, Spitze, and Logan, "Social Support to Parents-in-Law."

15. Shuey and Hardy, "Assistance to Aging Parents."

16. Nydegger, "Asymmetrical Kin."

17. Chalandra Bryant, Rand Conger, and Jennifer Meehan, "The Influence of In-Laws on Change in Marital Success," *Journal of Marriage and the Family* 63 (2001): 614–26.

18. Goetting, "Patterns of Support."

19. J. Silverstein, "The Problem with In-Laws," *Journal of Family Therapy* 14 (1990): 399–412.

20. Bryant, Conger, and Meehan, "The Influence of In-Laws."

21. Goetting, "Patterns of Support."

22. Bryant, Conger, and Meehan, "The Influence of In-Laws."

23. Eileen Posner, *Mother of the Groom: A Collection of Women's Voices* (Lahore, Pakistan: Distinctive Publications Corporation, 1996), 1.

24. Ibid., 4.

25. Ibid., 15.

26. Arnstein, *Between Mothers-in-Law and Daughters-in-Law.*

27. Posner, *Mother of the Groom.*

28. Arnstein, *Between Mothers-in-Law and Daughters-in-Law.*

CHAPTER 8: WHY ARE IN-LAW RELATIONSHIPS SO HARD?

1. Tenenbaum, informal conversation with the author, August 30, 2005.

2. Helene S. Arnstein, *Between Mothers-in-Law and Daughters-in-Law: Achieving a Successful and Caring Relationship* (New York: Dodd, Mead, 1987).

3. Lucy Rose Fischer, *Linked Lives: Adult Daughters and Their Mothers* (New York: Harper and Row, 1986).

4. Pamela Cotterill, *Friendly Relations? Mothers and Their Daughters-in-Law* (London: Taylor and Francis, 1994).

5. Ibid.

6. Ibid.

7. Fischer, *Linked Lives.*

8. Hope Edelman, *Mother of My Mother* (New York: Dell Publishing, 1999).

9. Stephanie Coontz, *The Way We Really Are: Coming to Terms with America's Changing Families* (New York: Basic Books, 1997).

10. Anthony Giddens, "The Global Revolution in Family and Personal Life," in *Family in Transition*, 13th ed. (Boston: Allyn and Bacon, 2005), 26–31.

11. Ingrid Arnet Connidis, *Family Ties and Aging* (Thousand Oaks, CA: Sage Publications, 2001).

12. Ingrid Arnet Connidis and Julie Ann McMullin, "Sociological Ambivalence and Family Ties: A Critical Perspective," *Journal of Marriage and the Family* 64 (2002): 558–67.

13. Karen Fingerman, Elizabeth L. Hay, and Kira S. Birditt, "The Best of Ties, the Worst of Ties: Close, Problematic, and Ambivalent Social Relationships," *Journal of Marriage and the Family* 66 (2004): 792–808.

14. Kurt Luescher and Karl Pillemer, "Intergenerational Ambivalence: A New Approach to the Study of Parent-Child Relations in Later Life," *Journal of Marriage and the Family* 60 (1998): 413–25.

15. Ruth Katz et al., "Theorizing Intergenerational Family Relations Solidarity, Conflict, and Ambivalence in Cross-National Contexts," in *Sourcebook of Family Theory and Research* (Thousand Oaks, CA: Sage Publications, 2005), 393–407.

16. Karl Pillemer and J. Jill Suitor, "Explaining Mother's Ambivalence Toward Their Adult Children," *Journal of Marriage and the Family* 64 (2002): 602–13.

17. Glenna Spitze and Mary P. Gallant, "'The Bitter with the Sweet': Older Adult Strategies for Handling Ambivalence in Relations with Their Adult Children," *Research on Aging* 26 (2004): 387–412.

18. Andrea E. Willson, Kim M. Shuey, and Glen H. Elder Jr., "Ambivalence in the Relationship of Adult Children to Aging Parents and In-Laws," *Journal of Marriage and the Family* 65 (2003): 1055–72.

19. Cotterill, *Friendly Relations?*

20. Willson, Shuey, and Elder Jr., "Ambivalence in the Relationship of Adult Children."

21. Mary Pipher, *Another Country: Navigating the Emotional Terrain of Our Elders* (New York: Riverhead Books, 1999).

CHAPTER 9: CONCLUSION

1. Pamela Cotterill, *Friendly Relations? Mothers and Their Daughters-in-Law* (London: Taylor and Francis, 1994).

2. Lucy Rose Fischer, *Linked Lives: Adult Daughters and Their Mothers* (New York: Harper and Row, 1986).

3. Andrea E. Willson, Kim M. Shuey, and Glen H. Elder Jr., "Ambivalence in the Relationship of Adult Children to Aging Parents and In-Laws," *Journal of Marriage and the Family* 65 (2003): 1055–72.

4. Cotterill, *Friendly Relations?*

5. J. Silverstein, "The Problem with In-Laws," *Journal of Family Therapy* 14 (1990): 399–412.

6. Carol Gilligan, *In a Different Voice: Psychological Theory and Women's Development* (Cambridge, MA: Harvard University Press, 1982).

7. Karen L. Fingerman, *Aging Mothers and Their Adult Daughters: Mixed Emotions, Enduring Bonds* (Amherst, NY: Prometheus Books, 2003).

8. Karen A. Roberto, Katherine R. Allen, and Rosemary Blieszner, "Older Women, Their Children, and Grandchildren: A Feminist Perspective on Family Relationships," *Journal of Women and Aging* 11 (1999): 67–84.

9. Willson, Shuey, and Elder Jr., "Ambivalence in the Relationship of Adult Children."

10. Lucy Rose Fischer, "Mothers and Mothers-in-Law," *Journal of Marriage and the Family* 45 (1983): 187–92.

11. Eunju Lee, Glenna Spitze, and John R. Logan, "Social Support to Parents-in-Law: The Interplay of Gender and Kin Hierarchies," *Journal of Marriage and the Family* 65 (2003): 396–403.

12. Chalandra Bryant, Rand Conger, and Jennifer Meehan, "The Influence of In-Laws on Change in Marital Success," *Journal of Marriage and the Family* 63 (2001): 614–26.

13. Cotterill, *Friendly Relations?*

14. Willson, Shuey, and Elder Jr., "Ambivalence in the Relationship of Adult Children."

15. Cotterill, *Friendly Relations?*

16. Ibid.

17. Ibid.

18. Bryant, Conger, and Meehan, "The Influence of In-Laws."

19. Ann Goetting, "Patterns of Support Among In-Laws in the United States," *Journal of Family Issues* 11 (1990): 67–90.

20. Paul Amato et al., *Alone Together: How Marriage in America Is Changing* (Cambridge, MA: Harvard University Press, 2007).

21. Ibid.

22. M. Jean Turner, Carolyn R. Young, and Kelly I. Black, "Daughters-in-Law and Mothers-in-Law Seeking Their Place Within the Family: A Qualitative Study of Differing Viewpoints," *Family Relations* 55 (2006): 588–600.

23. This would include the fact that the mother-in-law is witnessing the dissolution of her own nuclear family as her children marry while the daughter-in-law is working to build her nuclear family.

24. One of these daughters-in-law did the laundry for her mother-in-law weekly because she was unable to do it herself. The other three provided physical care.

25. Bryant, Conger, and Meehan, "The Influence of In-Laws."

26. Cotterill, *Friendly Relations?*

27. Willson, Shuey, and Elder Jr., "Ambivalence in the Relationship of Adult Children."

28. Fischer, "Mothers and Mothers-in-Law."

29. Willson, Shuey, and Elder Jr., "Ambivalence in the Relationship of Adult Children."

30. Bryant, Conger, and Meehan, "The Influence of In-Laws."

31. Cotterill, *Friendly Relations?*

32. Fischer, "Mothers and Mothers-in-Law."

33. Willson, Shuey, and Elder Jr., "Ambivalence in the Relationship of Adult Children."

34. Cotterill, *Friendly Relations?*

35. Fischer, "Mothers and Mothers-in-Law."

36. Fischer, *Linked Lives.*

37. Willson, Shuey, and Elder Jr., "Ambivalence in the Relationship of Adult Children."

38. Kathryn Edin and Maria Kefalas, *Promises I Can Keep: Why Poor Women Put Motherhood Before Marriage* (Berkeley: University of California Press, 2005).

39. Frances K. Goldscheider and Linda J. Waite, *New Families, No Families: The Transformation of the American Home* (Berkeley: University of California Press, 1991).

40. Arlie Russell Hochschild, *The Second Shift* (New York: Avon Books, 1989).

41. Stephanie Coontz, *Marriage, a History: How Love Conquered Marriage* (New York: Penguin Group, 2005).

APPENDIX 1

1. Subjects were assured that the interviews were both anonymous and confidential when I called them.

2. One of the daughters-in-law was not legally married but had a lifelong commitment to her partner, with whom she had lived for seventeen years and with whom she shared a child. Both she and her mother-in-law considered one another to be in-laws.

3. In fact, neither daughter-in-law "sugar-coated" their portrayals of their mothers-in-law because of their deaths. They were both quite candid about the relationships. If anything, the deaths freed them to be more honest in exploring the relationship.

BIBLIOGRAPHY

Amato, Paul R., Alan Booth, David R. Johnson, and Stacy J. Rogers. *Alone Together: How Marriage in America Is Changing*. Cambridge, MA: Harvard University Press, 2007.

Ambert, Anne-Marie. "Relationships with Former In-Laws after Divorce: A Research Note." *Journal of Marriage and the Family* 50 (1988): 679–86.

Apter, Terri. Mother-in-Law Stories. http://www.motherinlawstories.com (accessed October 13, 2005).

Arnstein, Helene S. *Between Mothers-in-Law and Daughters-in-Law: Achieving a Successful and Caring Relationship*. New York: Dodd, Mead, 1987.

Barash, Susan Shapiro. *Mothers-in-Law and Daughters-in-Law: Love, Hate, Rivalry, and Reconciliation*. Far Hills, NJ: New Horizon Press, 2001.

Bauman, Zygmunt. *Liquid Love*. Malden, MA: Blackwell, 2003.

———. *Liquid Modernity*. Malden, MA: Blackwell, 2000.

Bengtson, Vern L., Roseann Giarrusso, J. Beth Mabry, and Merril Silverstein. "Solidarity, Conflict, and Ambivalence: Complementary or Competing Perspectives on Intergenerational Relationships?" *Journal of Marriage and the Family* 64 (2002): 568–76.

Bluper, Liz, and Renee Plastique. *Mothers-in-Law Do Everything Wrong: M.I.L.D.E.W.* Riverside, NJ: Andrews McMeel Publishing, 2004.

Booth, Alan, and Paul R. Amato. "Parental Marital Quality, Parental Divorce, and Relations with Parents." *Journal of Marriage and the Family* 56 (1994): 21–34.

Boss, Pauline. *Family Stress Management: A Contextual Approach*. Thousand Oaks, CA: Sage Publications, 2002.

Bowditch, Eden Unger, and Aviva Samet. *The Daughter-in-Law's Survival Guide: Everything You Need to Know About Relating to Your Mother-in-Law.* Oakland, CA: New Harbinger Publications, 2002.

Brody, Elaine M. *Women in the Middle: Their Parent-Care Years.* New York: Springer, 1990.

Bryant, Chalandra, Rand Conger, and Jennifer Meehan. "The Influence of In-Laws on Change in Marital Success." *Journal of Marriage and the Family* 63 (2001): 614–26.

Chapman, Annie. *The Mother-in-Law Dance: Can Two Women Love the Same Man and Still Get Along?* Eugene, OR: Harvest House Publishers, 2004.

Chen, Man-hua. "The Relationships of Mothers and Daughters-in-Law in Urban Chinese Families." *Dissertation Abstracts International, A: The Humanities and the Social Sciences* 60 (1999): 3542.

Climo, Jacob. *Distant Parents.* New Brunswick, NJ: Rutgers University Press, 1992.

Cole, Suzanne. "The End of a Marriage." *Newsweek* Vol. 131, June 22, 1998, 20.

Coleman, Marilyn, Larry Ganong, and Susan Cable. "Beliefs about Women's Intergenerational Family Obligations to Provide Support before and after Divorce and Remarriage." *Journal of Marriage and the Family* 59 (1997): 165–76.

Connidis, Ingrid Arnet. *Family Ties and Aging.* Thousand Oaks, CA: Sage Publications, 2001.

Connidis, Ingrid Arnet, and Julie Ann McMullin. "Sociological Ambivalence and Family Ties: A Critical Perspective." *Journal of Marriage and the Family* 64 (2002): 558–67.

Coontz, Stephanie. *Marriage, a History: How Love Conquered Marriage.* New York: Penguin Group, 2005.

———. *The Way We Really Are: Coming to Terms with America's Changing Families.* New York: Basic Books, 1997.

Cotterill, Pamela. *Friendly Relations? Mothers and Their Daughters-in-Law.* London: Taylor and Francis, 1994.

CSL CartoonStock. http://www.cartoonstock.com/directory/d/daughters-in-law.asp (accessed June 7, 2006).

Davidman, Lynn. *Motherloss.* Berkeley: University of California Press, 2000.

DeWit, David J., Andrew V. Wister, and Thomas K. Burch. "Physical Distance and Social Contact Between Elders and Their Adult Children." *Research on Aging* 10 (1988): 56–80.

Dr. Phil. "Meddling Future Mothers-in-Law." http://www.drphil.com/shows/show/579 (accessed October 24, 2005).

Dworkin, Susan. "My Mother-in-Law and Me." *Ladies Home Journal* 115, no. 4 (April 1998): 62–66.

Edelman, Hope. *Motherless Daughters: The Legacy of Loss.* Reading, MA: Addison-Wesley, 1994.

———. *Mother of My Mother.* New York: Dell Publishing, 1999.

Edin, Kathryn, and Maria Kefalas. *Promises I Can Keep: Why Poor Women Put Motherhood Before Marriage.* Berkeley: University of California Press, 2005.

EPIC, MCR Poll. "Relationships with Mothers-in-Law Improve with Age." *Jet* 90, (1996): 12.

Eyer, Joseph. "Capitalism, Health, and Illness." In *Issues in the Political Economy of Health Care*, edited by J. B. McKinlay, 23–58. New York: Tavistock Books, 1984.

Fingerman, Karen L. *Aging Mothers and Their Adult Daughters: Mixed Emotions, Enduring Bonds.* Amherst, NY: Prometheus Books, 2003.

———. *Aging Mothers and Their Adult Daughters: A Study of Mixed Emotions.* New York: Springer, 2001.

———. "The Role of Offspring and In-Laws in Grandparents' Ties to Their Granchildren." *Journal of Family Issues* 25 (2004): 1026–49.

Fingerman, Karen, Elizabeth L. Hay, and Kira S. Birditt. "The Best of Ties, the Worst of Ties: Close, Problematic, and Ambivalent Social Relationships." *Journal of Marriage and the Family* 66 (2004): 792–808.

Fischer, Lucy Rose. *Linked Lives: Adult Daughters and Their Mothers.* New York: Harper and Row, 1986.

———. "Mothers and Mothers-in-Law." *Journal of Marriage and the Family* 45 (1983): 187–92.

Freund, Peter E. S., Meredith B. McGuire, and Linda S. Podhurst. *Health, Illness, and the Social Body: A Critical Sociology.* Upper Saddle River, NJ: Prentice Hall, 2003.

Giarusso, Roseann, Du Feng, Merril Silverstein, and Vern L. Bengtson. "Grandparent-Adult Child Affection and Consensus: Cross-Generational and Cross-Ethnic Comparison." *Journal of Family Issues* 22 (2001): 456–77.

Giddens, Anthony. "The Global Revolution in Family and Personal Life." In *Family in Transition*, 13th ed., edited by Arlene S. Skolnick and Jerome H. Skolnick, 26–31. Boston: Allyn and Bacon, 2005.

Gilligan, Carol. *In a Different Voice: Psychological Theory and Women's Development.* Cambridge, MA: Harvard University Press, 1982.

Globerman, Judith. "Motivations to Care: Daughters- and Sons-in-Law Caring for Relatives with Alzheimer's Disease." *Family Relations* 45 (1996): 37–45.

Goetting, Ann. "Patterns of Support Among In-Laws in the United States." *Journal of Family Issues* 11 (1990): 67–90.

Goldscheider, Frances K., and Linda J. Waite. *New Families, No Families: The Transformation of the American Home.* Berkeley: University of California Press, 1991.

Goldstein, Joshua R. "The Leveling of Divorce in the United States." *Demography* 36 (1999): 409–14.

Gratton, Brian, and Carole Haber. "In Search of 'Intimacy at a Distance': Family History from the Perspective of Elderly Women." *Journal of Aging Studies* 7 (1993): 183–94.

Guberman, Nancy. "Daughters-in-Law as Caregivers: How and Why Do They Come to Care?" *Journal of Women and Aging* 11 (1999): 85–102.

Gubrium, Jaber F., and James A. Holstein. "Phenomenology, Ethnomethodology, and Family Discourse." In *Sourcebook of Family Theories and Methods: A Contextual Approach*, edited by Pauline G. Boss, William J. Doherty, Ralph LaRossa, Walter R. Schumm, and Suzanne K. Steinmetz, 651–72. New York: Springer, 1993.

Hochschild, Arlie Russell. *The Second Shift*. New York: Avon Books, 1989.

———. *The Time Bind*. New York: Metropolitan Books, 1997.

Hoffman, Charles D., and Debra K. Ledford. "Adult Children of Divorce: Relationships with Their Mothers and Fathers Prior to, Following Parental Separation and Currently." *Journal of Divorce and Remarriage* 24 (1995): 41–57.

Jackson, Jacqueline, and Linda Berg-Cross. "Extending the Extended Family: The Mother-in-Law and Daughter-in-Law Relationship of Black Women." *Family Relations* 37 (1988): 293–97.

Johnson, Colleen Leahy. "In-Law Relationships in the American Kinship System: The Impact of Divorce and Remarriage." *American Ethnologist* 16 (1989): 87–99.

Katz, Ruth, Ariela Lowenstein, Judith Phillips, and Svein Olav Daatland. "Theorizing Intergenerational Family Relations Solidarity, Conflict, and Ambivalence in Cross-National Contexts." In *Sourcebook of Family Theory and Research*, edited by Vern L. Bengtson, Alan C. Acock, Katherine R. Allen, Peggye Dilworth-Anderson, and David M. Klein, 393–407. Thousand Oaks, CA: Sage Publications, 2005.

Kaufman, Gayle, and Peter Uhlenberg. "Effects of Life Course Transitions on the Quality of Relationships between Adult Children and Their Parents." *Journal of Marriage and the Family* 60 (1998): 924–38.

Kim, Myung-Hye. "Changing Relationships Between Daughters-in-Law and Mothers-in-Law in Urban South Korea." *Anthropological Quarterly* 69 (1996): 179–93.

Kirschner, Steve, and John Huehnergarth. *No Good Mothers-in-Law*. New York: Pocket Books, 1985.

Kreider, Rose M., and Jason M. Fields. "Number, Timing, and Duration of Marriages and Divorces: 1996." *U.S. Census Bureau Current Population Reports* (February 2002): 18.

Lee, Eunju, Glenna Spitze, and John R. Logan. "Social Support to Parents-in-Law: The Interplay of Gender and Kin Hierarchies." *Journal of Marriage and the Family* 65 (2003): 396–403.

Limary, Britta H. "The Mother-in-Law/Daughter-in-Law Dyad: Narratives of Relational Development Among In-Laws." *Dissertation Abstracts International, A: The Humanities and Social Sciences* 63, no.2 (August 7, 2002).

Lin, Ge, and Peter A. Rogerson. "Elderly Parents and the Geographic Availability of Their Adult Children." *Research on Aging* 17 (1995): 303–31.

Luescher, Kurt, and Karl Pillemer. "Intergenerational Ambivalence: A New Approach to the Study of Parent-Child Relations in Later Life." *Journal of Marriage and the Family* 60 (1998): 413–25.

Marotz-Baden, Ramona, and Deane Cowan. "Mothers-in-Law and Daughters-in-Law: The Effects of Proximity on Conflict and Stress." *Family Relations* 36 (1987): 385–90.

Marotz-Baden, Ramona, and Claudia Mattheis. "Daughters-in-Law and Stress in Two-Generation Farm Families." *Family Relations* 43 (1994): 132–37.

"Marvelous Mothers-in-Law." *Today's Christian Woman*, November–December 1998. http://www.christianitytoday.com/tcw/8w6/8w6118.html (accessed October 24, 2005).

McCubbin, Hamilton I., Elizabeth A. Thompson, Annie I. Thompson, and Jo A. Futrell. *The Dynamics of Resilient Families*. Thousand Oaks, CA: Sage Publications, 1999.

Merrill, Deborah. "Daughters-in-Law as Caregivers to the Elderly: Defining the In-Law Relationship." *Research on Aging* 15 (1993): 70–91.

Mitchell, Kathy, and Marcy Sugar. "Dear Annie." *Worcester Telegram and Gazette.* August 1, 2005–May 31, 2006.

National Center for Health Statistics. *Health, United States, 2002* with *Chartbook on Trends in the Health of Americans*. http://www.cdc.gov/nchs/hus.htm (accessed February 28, 2007).

Nuner, Joyce Emmons, and Lillian Chenoweth. "A Qualitative Study of Mother-in-Law and Daughter-in-Law Relationships." Paper presented at the annual meetings of the National Council on Family Relations, Phoenix, AZ, November 2005.

Nydegger, C. N. "Asymmetrical Kin and the Problematic Son-in-Law." In *Lifespan Developmental Psychology: Intergenerational Relationships,* edited by N. Datan, A. L. Greene, and H. W. Reese, 99–123. Hillsdale, NJ: Lawrence Erlbaum Associates, 1986.

O'Carolan, Turlough. "Daughters-in-Law Are Our Grandchildren's Mothers." http://www.poemsforfree.com/daught.html (accessed May 25, 2006).

Peters-Davis, Norah, Miriam Moss, and Rachel Pruchno. "Children-in-Law in Caregiving Families." *Gerontologist* 39, no. 1 (1999): 66–75.

Peterson, Gary, Debra Madden-Derdich, and Stacie A. Leonard. "Parent-Child Relations Across the Life Course: Autonomy Within the Context of Connectedness." In *Families Across Time: A Life Course Perspective*, edited by Sharon J. Price, Patrick C. McKenry, and Megan J. Murphy, 187–203. Los Angeles: Roxbury Publishing, 2000.

Pillemer, Karl, and J. Jill Suitor. "Explaining Mother's Ambivalence Toward Their Adult Children." *Journal of Marriage and the Family* 64 (2002): 602–13.

Pipher, Mary. *Another Country: Navigating the Emotional Terrain of Our Elders.* New York: Riverhead Books, 1999.

Posner, Eileen. *Mother of the Groom: A Collection of Women's Voices.* Lahore, Pakistan: Distinctive Publications Corporation, 1996.

Roberto, Karen A., Katherine R. Allen, and Rosemary Blieszner. "Older Women, Their Children, and Grandchildren: A Feminist Perspective on Family Relationships." *Journal of Women and Aging* 11 (1999): 67–84.

Rossi, Alice S., and Peter H. Rossi. *Of Human Bonding: Parent-Child Relations Across the Life Course.* New York: Walter de Gruyter, 1990.

Rubin, Lillian B. *Worlds of Pain: Life in the Working Class Family.* New York: Basic Books, 1992.

Russo, Camille. *How to Be the Perfect Mother-in-Law.* Riverside, NJ: Andrews McMeel Publishing, 1998.

Shanley, Mary Lyndon. "Should We Abolish Marriage?" Lecture at Clark University, Worcester, MA, February 16, 2006.

Shapiro, A. "Revisiting the Gender Gap: Exploring the Relationships of Parent/Adult Child Dyads." *International Journal of Aging and Human Development* 58 (2004): 127–46.

Shuey, Kim, and Melissa Hardy. "Assistance to Aging Parents and Parents-in-Law: Does Lineage Affect Family Allocation Decisions?" *Journal of Marriage and the Family* 65 (2003): 418–31.

Shuey, Kim M., Andrea E. Willson, and Glen H. Elder Jr. "Ambivalence in the Relationship Between Aging Mothers and Their Adult Children: A Dyadic Analysis." Paper presented at the annual meeting of the American Sociological Association, Atlanta, August 17, 2003.

Silverstein, J. "The Problem with In-Laws." *Journal of Family Therapy* 14 (1990): 399–412.

Silverstein, Merril, and Vern L. Bengtson. "Intergenerational Solidarity and the Structure of Adult Child-Parent Relationships in American Families." *American Journal of Sociology* 103 (1997): 429–60.

Spitze, Glenna, and Mary P. Gallant. "'The Bitter with the Sweet': Older Adult Strategies for Handling Ambivalence in Relations with Their Adult Children." *Research on Aging* 26 (2004): 387–412.

Swidler, Ann. *Talk of Love: How Culture Matters.* Chicago: University of Chicago Press, 2001.

Tatum, Mary. *Just Call Me Mom: Practical Steps to Becoming a Better Mother-in-Law.* Camp Hill, PA: Christian Publications (Wingspread Publishers, Zur Limited), 1994.

Turner, M. Jean, Carolyn R. Young, and Kelly I. Black. "Daughters-in-Law and Mothers-in-Law Seeking Their Place Within the Family: A Qualitative Study of Differing Viewpoints." *Family Relations* 55 (2006): 588–600.

Uhlenberg, Peter. "The Role of Divorce in Men's Relations with Their Adult Children after Midlife." *Journal of Marriage and the Family* 52 (1993): 677–88.

Umberson, Debra. "Relationships Between Adult Children and Their Parents: Psychological Consequences for Both Generations." *Journal of Marriage and the Family* 54 (1992): 664–74.

Verra, Sue. *What Every Mother-in-Law Wishes Her Daughter-in-Law Knew but Was Afraid to Tell Her*. Lima, OH: Fairway Press, 1996.

Waite, Linda J., and Maggie Gallagher. *The Case for Marriage: Why Married People Are Happier, Healthier, and Better Off Financially*. New York: Doubleday, 2000.

Waite, Linda J., and Scott C. Harrison. "Keeping in Touch: How Women in Mid-life Allocate Social Contacts Among Kith and Kin." *Social Forces* 70 (1992): 637–55.

Wallerstein, Judith S., Julia M. Lewis, and Sandra Blakeslee. *The Unexpected Legacy of Divorce: A 25-Year Landmark Study*. New York: Hyperion, 2000.

Webster, Pamela S., and A. Regula Herzog. "Effects of Parental Divorce and Memories of Family Problems on Relationships Between Adult Children and Their Parents." *Journal of Gerontology: Social Sciences* 50B (1995): S24–S34.

Weiner, Herbert. *Perturbing the Organism: The Biology of Stressful Experience*. Chicago: University of Chicago Press, 1992.

Willson, Andrea E., Kim M. Shuey, and Glen H. Elder Jr. "Ambivalence in the Relationship of Adult Children to Aging Parents and In-Laws." *Journal of Marriage and the Family* 65 (2003): 1055–72.

Wolf, Douglas. "Household Patterns of Older Women." *Research on Aging* 12 (1990): 463–86.

Wolfinger, Nicholas. *Understanding the Divorce Cycle: The Children of Divorce in Their Own Marriages*. New York: Cambridge University Press, 2005.

Wright, Carol L., and Joseph W. Maxwell. "Social Support During Adjustment to Later-Life Divorce: How Adult Children Help Their Parents." *Journal of Divorce and Remarriage* 15 (1991): 21–48.

Wright, H. Norman. *The Other Woman in Your Marriage: Understanding a Mother's Impact on Her Son and How It Affects His Marriage*. Ventura, CA: Gospel Light Publications, 1994.

INDEX

About the Author

DEBORAH M. MERRILL is an associate professor of sociology at Clark University. Her areas of specialization are families, aging, medicine, and research methodology. Her previous book with Greenwood Publishing Group is *Caring for Elderly Parents: Juggling Work, Family, and Caregiving in Middle and Working Class Families* (Auburn House, 1997).